EMPOWERED!

A Guide to Leadership in the Liberated Organisation
Rob Brown and
Margaret Brown

NICHOLAS BREALEY
PUBLISHING
LONDON

This book is dedicated to
Victoria, Declan, Jack, Richard, Michael and Peter:
our future

First published in Great Britain by
Nicholas Brealey Publishing Limited in 1994
21 Bloomsbury Way
London WC1A 2TH

© 1994 by Rob Brown and Margaret Brown
The rights of Rob Brown and Margaret Brown to be identified as
the authors of this work have been asserted in accordance with
Copyright, Designs and Patents Act 1988.

ISBN 1-85788-022-6

British Library Cataloguing in Publication Data
A catalogue record for this book is available from the British
Library.

Typeset by Servis Filmsetting Ltd, England

Printed and bound in Finland by Werner Söderström Oy

Contents

Acknowledgements

We would like to thank:

- Penny Clark for her patience, and for her role in supportively but incisively testing many of the ideas in this book;
- The staff and management committee of Airspace Charity whose dedication and commitment demonstrated that empowerment does work in practice;
- Tony Allen and Cheryl Coppell whose example and guidance were invaluable in coming to understand and change the workings of power within a traditional bureaucracy;
- The staff (and especially Paul Hoggett) at the School for Advanced Urban Studies in Bristol University for encouraging the development of our thinking in this field;
- Ann Brown and Peter Brown for their technical knowledge and help freely given;
- Sir Max Brown, for sharing with us his wide industrial and commercial knowledge over many years;
- Elizabeth Sidney, an ever-inspiring innovative colleague and friend;
- Joy Maitland, ex-Director of fundraising and publicity LEPRA, for the cooperation and support she gave so freely;
- Andrew Forrest, Director of Human Resources, the Industrial Society for reading our manuscript and adding material from his own long experience;
- The library and information services of the Institute of Personnel and Development for their progressive approach, their willing help and

support and the unlimited resource of books and journals produced through their database;

- Frank Burgum, who practises the ideal of excellence we have described, for typing our manuscript and producing our diagrams;
- Our copy-editor, Sally Lansdell Yeung, for her professional knowledge, advice and kindness;
- Our publisher, Nick Brealey, for offering many helpful suggestions and nurturing the evolution of the book.

Preface

This is a workbook about empowering leadership for everyone. And we mean everyone. Empowerment is a shift in philosophy which questions all the old relationships and assumptions. It affects the way work is done as well as how people relate to each other. Whatever their current position, everyone has something to gain from empowerment.

Indeed, empowerment is a fundamental challenge to the ways people currently organise at work. It means that everyone is a leader sometimes, and that traditional 'leaders' do not always exercise that role. It is not an easy option, representing, as it does, a discontinuous break from the past, so in this book we describe some of the pitfalls you may encounter, as well as the satisfaction and success you will experience as you become more empowered. There are workshops at every stage, as an encouragement to help you think about the material we discuss and act on your decisions.

Empowerment challenges the way we organise

A growing body of evidence is suggesting that unless the approach we describe in this book is adopted by manufacturing and service industries, together with other institutions in the public and private sectors, they will cease to be successful in the increasingly competitive and rapidly changing world of tomorrow. We therefore describe the philosophy, knowledge and strategies which underpin empowerment and outline with numerous examples and case studies the practical leadership styles and actions this new approach involves.

Future success depends on empowerment

This book offers a practical programme for empowering leadership which:

A practical programme

- Enables each individual to reach and use his or her own full potential.
- Liberates the way organisations operate so that individuals and teams are empowered to participate in and own decisions. In turn this gains their commitment to contribute their best to goals which they and their organisation share.

The programme follows a logical sequence. Understanding is crucial to empowerment: without it people cannot take charge of themselves and their own development. Part I therefore explains what we mean by empowerment, and why it is so vital today.

Part II considers how to liberate an organisation for empowerment by redistributing control and encouraging continuous learning. A five-point model for organisational transformation is introduced, together with practical programmes for its implementation.

Part III turns to empowering leadership and explains the main aspects of how to empower people and yourself.

Part IV describes the people, technical and business skills of empowering leadership, and some of the many different ways of training people to become proficient.

The concluding chapter tries to put empowerment into perspective, outlining understandable reasons why some people may not want to be empowered, followed by positive advice and a checklist on how to make empowerment more enjoyable.

If you want to get the best out of the workshops in the book, it may be helpful to work alongside someone else. Sharing experiences and thoughts produces new insights and ideas. Some work you may prefer to do alone, but consider collaborating on other workshops with a partner or a small group, which could be colleagues from work or friends from a social organisation.

In particular, if you are in employment, strengthen your knowledge by drawing on the experience of people known to you who are currently unemployed or in training. Equally, we hope the book will be useful to you if you are unemployed. By drawing on their own past experience and that of others, everyone can prepare for a fast-changing employment future.

Part I
What is
empowerment?

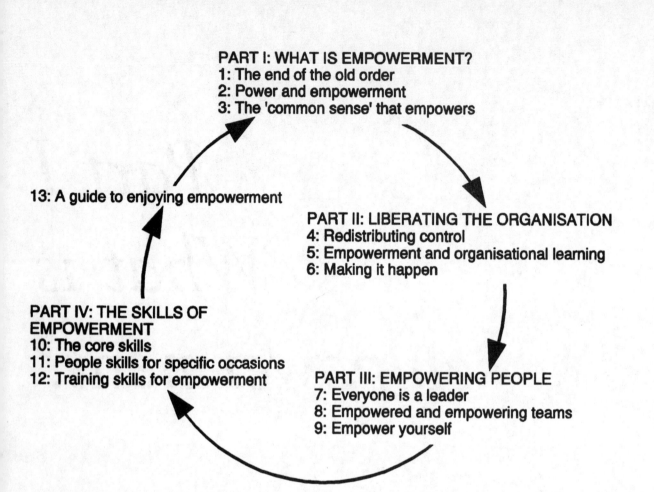

PART I: WHAT IS EMPOWERMENT?
1: The end of the old order
2: Power and empowerment
3: The 'common sense' that empowers

13: A guide to enjoying empowerment

PART II: LIBERATING THE ORGANISATION
4: Redistributing control
5: Empowerment and organisational learning
6: Making it happen

PART IV: THE SKILLS OF
EMPOWERMENT
10: The core skills
11: People skills for specific occasions
12: Training skills for empowerment

PART III: EMPOWERING PEOPLE
7: Everyone is a leader
8: Empowered and empowering teams
9: Empower yourself

The End of the Old Order 1

This book is about how to empower everyone, from the front-line worker to the chief executive. We believe that this is the only way of releasing the full potential of every individual within an organisation – and that only those organisations which liberate themselves by empowering their members will survive into the twenty-first century. The reason for this is simple. The old certainties about how to organise have passed their sell-by date. Bureaucratic management and 'control by command' no longer work in today's more demanding conditions.

> We are going to win and the industrial West is going to lose out; there's not much you can do about it because the reasons for your failure are within yourselves.
> *Konosuke Matsushita – Founder of Matsushita Electric Ltd, one of Japan's largest companies (quoted in Pascale, 1991)*

But why should you believe this? There have been many such predictions of doom in the past and people seem to go on muddling through. Indeed for most of the twentieth century there has been something of a gulf between management theory and management practice. Managers trying to survive in the real world often label the theorists as impractical do-gooders. And it is true that almost all the major writers and thinkers on management – Barnard, Chandler, Deming, Handy, Herzberg, Kanter, McGregor, Maslow, Schumacher and so on – have, in their different ways, exhorted employers to be more sympathetic to their workers.

Sometimes the appeal was for ethical reasons – it was said to be morally better to make jobs more interesting (as the quality of life movement asserted). But more often a variety of evidence, starting with the famous Hawthorne experiments of the 1920s (described in Chapter 8), was used to demonstrate that improving working conditions would result in greater productivity.

The dehumanising of the workplace

The trouble was that the managers on the ground clearly did not believe these theorists. Private sector or public, capitalist West or communist East, the twentieth century has seen the triumph of the conveyor belt and its dehumanisation of the workplace. Most slaves had more autonomy over how and what they were expected to produce (and at what pace) than workers on the stereotypical assembly line.

Of course there have been experiments into alternatives – the introduction of team working at Volvo and the experiment with worker ownership at John Lewis to name but two. But ironically these beacons of good practice only serve to highlight the gloom in which they float. It seems it did not pay to take a more rounded view. In the commercial world competitive advantage appeared to come from bigger and better plant, from increasing use of mass production techniques and from keeping labour costs low, not from innovations in work practices. And public sector organisations have shown little inclination to do anything but borrow these principles and apply them second hand.

So what is the point of yet another book talking about such concepts as 'empowering the worker' and predicting the death of 'management by command'? Why should practising managers, sweating to meet ever shortening deadlines, listen to this advice when they have ignored that of our illustrious predecessors?

The new demands of coping with change

One answer is provided by the history of the London Stock Exchange's FT-SE 100 index. Of the 100 companies listed when the index commenced in 1984, 43 no longer appeared only 10 years later. Coping with change is the name of the current game, and the traditional advantages enjoyed by players able to exploit economies of scale, or call upon massive reserves of capital, apparently no longer guarantee success.

In response some people point out that there has always been competition. It is now more global and intense and therefore it is even more important to keep the customer satisfied. But the fact that Ford has moved so far away from the philosophy of its founder that it has replaced the option of one model ('any colour so long as it's black') with over half a million separate customer choices does not prove that a totally new approach is needed. Isn't it merely more of the same?

That's just the point – *it isn't more of the same.* Seeking to derive competitive advantage from producing goods and services which are more in tune with what the customer requires, has led a number of companies into a new world where the traditional organisational rules simply do not apply. These companies have found that if you make a total commitment to quality, innovation and value (as you must if you are genuinely trying to get close to the customer) then you make demands of an entirely new order on your staff.

These demands can only be met by a workforce which is empowered to respond. Empowerment is about releasing the full potential of every individual to contribute to the common enterprise. It is a quantum leap in thinking about how to organise.

An empowered workforce to respond to empowered customers

> Your firms are built on the Taylor model. Even worse so are your heads. With your bosses doing the thinking while the workers wield the screw-drivers, you're convinced deep down that this is the right way to run a business. For you the essence of management is getting the ideas out of the heads of the bosses and into the hands of labor.
>
> *Konosuke Matsushita (in Pascale, 1991)*

The sudden collapse of an old economic order followed by frantic experimentation with new ideas and ways of doing things is a recurring pattern. In fact, ever since the Industrial Revolution this has been the characteristic cycle of economic development. Periods of comparative stability are suddenly punctured by revolutionary turmoil, which in turn is followed by more gradual and evolutionary adaptation.

Each phase sees the coming together of a number of seminal technological innovations with the development of the social changes necessary to allow their full exploitation. Minting the two halves of the coin at the same time is a hit or miss affair, driven more by the failure of existing arrangements and by luck than by any historical inevitability. For example:

Technical innovations lead to social changes

- As a social invention the factory had been around for a long time, but it was only with the technological development of the steam engine that it became the dominant site of production. Steam power was expensive and immobile. Economics decreed that people should leave their homes and gather round the engine, rather than the other way round. It was the confluence of the two elements, social and technological, which was necessary to unleash the productive power offered by steam and so launch the industrial revolution.

- Similarly the twentieth century has been characterised by the technology of the telephone, the electric light and the internal combustion engine. Making these products in the volumes demanded meant exploiting for the first time the full potential of mass production techniques (which these technological advances had made possible), in particular the conveyor belt and the assembly line. Organising and controlling organisations large enough to exploit the advantages of mass production and instant but expensive long-distance communication led to the development of a new social invention: the corporate bureaucracy.

The complex twentieth-century stew of products, production methods and forms of social organisation has been called Fordism, taking its name from the industrialist who pioneered some of its key aspects.

Each phase, whether of stability or turmoil, develops a self-consistent 'paradigm' (or set of basic assumptions), which becomes so ingrained as the way the world should be viewed that it is not even talked about, let alone questioned. Just as the divine right of kings was rarely challenged in the fifteenth century, so twentieth-century managers of the Fordist period have always assumed the 'divine right' of bureaucracy with its hierarchical lines of command and its strict division of labour. The most influential, if not eloquent, advocate of these principles in the period when they were still being codified was Frederick Taylor. His ideas and their importance are described in the case study below.

A CASE STUDY IN CONTROL: SCIENTIFIC MANAGEMENT

The shadow of Frederick Taylor looms large over the whole of the twentieth century. He created a system of control which he termed 'functional management'. Through this system, all the elements needed to control the work process were organised so that the individual worker was left with no discretion. There was no need for managers to *trust* workers; the system kept them in line. First published in 1911, Taylor's *Principles of Scientific Management* have formed the basis of this view of the world ever since.

Taylor did not invent management, but he was certainly one of the first to study 'work' as a subject in itself. To a dispassionate desire to maximise production he brought his experience as a labourer in a US steel mill, combined with a personal obsession with order.

---

continued

The methods of 'functional management' were simple. A science of work should be devised to allow for the proper subdivision of each activity into the many separate and discrete tasks necessary for its successful completion. Once this was done the job of management became that of allocating each task (along with an accurate timing for how long it should take) to particular workers, all according to a rational plan for the most effective coordination of the work process.

In effect, the last link between the brain and the hand was severed. Mental labour was the sole preserve of the manager, with the labourer charged only with a limited choreograph of physical actions. Thereafter the productivity of each worker could be individually measured and pay varied accordingly. Scientific selection of workers for the particular abilities necessitated by each task was the final guarantee of optimum performance.

As we described earlier, organisations are driven by the coincidence and harmonisation of social and technological developments. The instant popularity of Taylor's views was not because they represented a huge intellectual breakthrough, rather it was because the minute subdivision of tasks that he proposed was precisely the technique required to tap the enormous productive capacity of the new mechanical production lines. When Henry Ford's revolutionary Model T started rolling off the line at Highland Park in 1913 it signalled more than the triumph of the internal combustion engine; it also marked the death knell of craft production techniques and the victory of scientific management.

The world of business is still coming to terms with this legacy. Although the naked emphasis on control advocated by Taylor may look like a caricature of modern practice, caricatures are recognisable because they exaggerate what is already there. There have been many management gurus since the days of Frederick Taylor, some more benign than others, but none has really disputed Taylor's basic assumptions. The evolution of the theory and practice of management since 1911 may have served to ameliorate some of the more clinical of his prescriptions, but the deep-rooted emphasis on control remains. It is the challenge of empowerment to create alternative organisations based on willing commitment.

The Taylor system [. . .] like all capitalist progress, is a combination of subtle brutality of bourgeois exploitation

continued

> and a number of its greatest scientific achievements in
> the field of analysing mechanical motions during work . . .
> The Soviet Republic must at all costs adopt all that is
> valuable in the achievements of science and technology in
> this field.
>
> *Lenin*

However, the Fordist assumptions are beginning to break down as we move into a new era of experimentation, ushered in by the availability of cheap global communications and the processing power of the computer. We are moving, so the social scientists tell us, into the strange new world of post-Fordism.

In the next section we explore some of the forces which are destroying the old order and driving the creation of the post-Fordist framework. We believe this new framework will be based on empowering both people and organisations, because this is the social approach and attitude which will most usefully exploit the full productive capacity of the new technology.

THE NEW WORLD OF EMPOWERMENT

We are just starting to understand some of the awesome possibilities opened up by computer and electronic communication. In the language of the Starship Enterprise, they have the effect of collapsing time and space. To illustrate this Scott Morton uses the example of changing speed and costs of transmitting a page of text between New York and Chicago (about 850 miles) as the technology has changed from horse to railway to telegraph to today's 'integrated data communication' (technology which combines in one process the conversion, storage, processing and communication of information – all very separate elements in the traditional paper-based information process). He found that:

- the time taken in hours reduced from 252 in the 1840s before the advent of the railways, to 0.083 in the 1850s using telegraph, to 0.0019 in the 1980s.
- the speed in miles per hour increased from 3.37 for a letter in the 1840s, to 10,240 using telegraph, to 447,000 with data communication technology.
- the miles/hour/US$ ratio leapt from 13.5 in the 1840s, through 1,370 in the 1850s, to 1.4 million in the 1980s.

If the effects of inflation are taken into account, the contrast in the last ratio is even more dramatic: the figure for miles/hour/US$ in the 1980s increases to 4.2 billion.

It is the qualitative change in the unit costs which is particularly significant in this example. With the advent of the telegraph, high-speed communication became a reality (thus making possible the large, geographically dispersed corporation of the last hundred years) although its use was at first greatly limited by the capacity and cost of the technology.

Even more dramatic is the changing cost/capacity ratio in the pure processing of information. In 1980 it cost $4,500,000 to buy a computer with the processing power of 4.5 MIPS (million instructions per second); or the equivalent of the annual salary bill for about 200 semi-skilled workers. The same processing power cost $100,000 in 1990, the equivalent of six of the same semi-skilled workers. Projections for the year 2000 suggest that by then the cost of that capacity will have fallen to a mere $10,000, or 0.125 of a semi-skilled worker.

We can now communicate instantly with almost anywhere in the world (anywhere, at least, that has a phone, a fax or a satellite receiver) for a cost which is negligible compared to the past. Moreover millions of complex calculations can be accomplished in the time that it used to take to make a single ledger entry.

In themselves these developments are not causing a revolution. Information technology (IT), like any technology, does not determine human arrangements, but it does create the conditions which human ingenuity can exploit. It is an enabler, not a driver.

And developments in IT are certainly enabling big changes. They do not just mean we can do the same things more quickly – far from it. These developments have the potential to strike at the very logic of how work is organised, in two ways:

- First, they are opening up the possibility of flexible forms of production more reminiscent of the 'batch' production methods of craft industry than the industrial age. Automation of mechanical production, and the introduction of computer-aided design techniques, mean that the single uniform product that monotonously rolled off the end of the conveyor belt has been replaced by a multitude of variants and by a vastly quicker product cycle.

    Flexible production

- Secondly, IT is having a huge impact on the 'coordinating' and 'controlling' techniques within and between organisations, which used to be the undisputed domain of the manager. One way of thinking about this is in terms of the organisation's capacity for 'learning'. Learning means knowing where you are and how you got there, which involves both memory and knowledge about performance. The computer database represents a step-jump in the

    Non-hierarchic coordination and control

capacity of the organisational memory, while at the same time it is now cost effective to gather and process information on performance as and where it happens, bypassing the management layers. Control by command, and therefore traditional line management, has been rendered obsolete. Instead of obtaining results by ensuring conformity to a rule book and surveillance of work processes, performance can now be monitored directly.

This is one of the key differences between the traditional corporation and the empowering organisation. The former relies on layers of management, each tier deriving its existence from the need to control the one below. By contrast, the empowering organisation puts its whole emphasis on performance. It maximises the resources devoted to the front line where value is created. Any additional management structure is there because it *actively* supports the front line in creating value. The centre no longer has a need for hierarchy merely to find out how things are going or to offer direction; it communicates with its front line direct.

CHANGES IN SOCIAL ATTITUDES

It is easy to forget that the introduction of full suffrage only occurred in the UK in 1924, and then only for people over 21. In other words, the invention of the telegraph, the wireless and the telephone came long before the evolution of modern British parliamentary democracy. Indeed, this chronology may be significant. Whether cause or consequence, the industrial age has tended to be accompanied by a relative growth in political emancipation and democracy.

In more recent times the decreasing cost of making transactions has been one of the main contributors to the triumph of the market over state planning as the tool for distributing resources. It is ironic that the communist dream was to empower the individual through the abolition of the inequalities of the market. However, in the twentieth century at least, capitalism has made itself the more durable economic system because direct communication between producer and buyer within a (properly regulated) market has proved a cheaper mode of exchange, and one that gives better feedback on customer requirements. These same markets have also given the consumer a historically new sense of empowerment, one based on choice and competition.

Social emancipation

As a consequence, people are no longer prepared to put up with the humiliating conditions that used to be an integral part of earning a living. The disharmony between the freedom that most people feel in their private lives and the constraints of the majority of work situations is likely to increase unless work is reorganised. In a hundred years' time it will seem an absurd anachronism that at the time when adults could have a say in national decisions on the social and macroeconomic level, the prevailing form of organisation, the hierarchic bureaucracy, was based on removing as much individual autonomy as was humanly possible.

The primacy of the customer

Thus technology and social changes are pushing the industrial world to take another giant step. For organisational theorists these developments come together into a single new phenomenon – the primacy of the customer.

Whether in the private or public sector, the new imperative is 'getting closer to the customer' by:

● exhaustive market research to understand individual preferences
● anticipating trends and new requirements
● customising products with many different variations so that customers can choose the precise specifications
● producing goods at a quality and a price that is better than your competitors

As the cost of transactions falls, so markets become more accessible and global and competition becomes more intense. Corporations which rest on their laurels are sitting in mansions built on sand: even the once all-powerful IBM recently reported huge losses.

It is no longer adequate to structure organisations around the principle of mass production (whether it is the manufacturing conveyor belt, the office paperchase or the inflexible processing of people by the public services). The genie of flexible production and customised quality products is out of the bottle, and the 'customer' has thrown away the cork.

GOALS OF A MODERN LIBERATED ORGANISATION

Organising around this new principle demands a whole new logic. The table below compares the goals which are intrinsic to a traditional corporation to those of a 'liberated organisation'.

ORGANISATIONAL GOALS

Traditional bureaucracy		Liberated organisation
low cost	→	no waste
control of inputs	→	monitoring of output
standardisation	→	flexibility
predictability	→	innovation
obedience	→	commitment
create demand	→	react to demand
detect defects	→	no defects
occasional improvement	→	continuous improvement

The goals of the liberated organisation are a lot tougher than those set by a traditional bureaucracy. In particular they:
- welcome differences
- positively force change and uncertainty
- demand speedy decision making from anyone, not just from the high-flying executive, in situations where there are no precedents

In the liberated organisation enterprise and commitment are as necessary on the front line as they are in the executive suite. This is why modern organisations need empowerment.

[Empowerment] is the quality which makes the difference between doing a job adequately (as it might be done if it were delegated), and doing it intelligently, creatively and with the commitment which goes together with accountability – a difference often referred to as 'discretionary effort'. This discretionary effort is the key to gaining competitive edge. In other words, empowerment is the key to business survival.

Clare Hogg

To respond to the unexpected, to see and seize new opportunities, every member of staff must have:
- the knowledge and understanding to evaluate the position
- the self-confidence to trust their own judgement
- the authority and skills to act effectively
- the ability to work in teams

These are the qualities nurtured by empowerment. As we shall see in the next chapter, the corollary is organisations that can involve everyone in decision making.

WORKSHOP: CONTROL IN ORGANISATIONS

Pick two organisations you know well. Try and choose one which is traditional in approach and another which has started to go down the path of liberation. Compare the two control systems. The following questions may stimulate some thoughts, but it is not an exhaustive list.
- Who is involved in planning for the future?
- Who is involved in decision making?
- Who recruits new staff?

continued

- To whom would you take a complaint if you wanted to be sure of action?
- Who decides on what everyone gets paid?
- What dictates the sort of clothing that the members of each organisation wear?

MANAGING TO MAKE A DIFFERENCE

The discussion so far has avoided a vital question. If everyone in the organisation of the future is empowered, can some people be more empowered than others? In other words, what is the role of the manager of the future? For a start, it is unlikely that they will be called managers at all; indeed, the whole concept of 'management' needs to be reinvented. The managers of the future will be accountable to the teams they work with, and they will succeed through influence rather than command. They will need to acquire new knowledge and more sophisticated skills and so will be in place by virtue of the respect of their peers. Their role will be to lead and support, not to control.

But leadership will still exist. Even within liberated organisations of all types there will be a need for empowering leaders and coordinators who are the guardians of the new order. For empowerment is not something that can be done once and then forgotten. It is a continual process of combating debilitating attitudes and offering encouragement and support. Nor, as we shall see in Chapter 2, is it a 'zero sum' exercise where empowering one person necessarily means weakening another. Empowerment is the opposite of a dull equality around the lowest common denominator.

Instead, empowerment means that everyone can take action to enhance his or her worth, either in personal or in organisational terms.

THE KEY MESSAGE OF EMPOWERMENT

We are beyond your mindset. Business, we know, is now so complex and difficult, the survival of firms so hazardous in an environment increasingly unpredictable, competitive and fraught with danger, that their continued existence depends on the day-to-day mobilization of *every ounce of intelligence*.

Konosuke Matsushita (in Pascale, 1991)

Everyone can affect an organisation

This is one of the key messages of this book. Organisations are not huge, timeless objects carved by the implacable forces of nature into their current inevitable state. They are human constructs, and everything about them is open to questioning and reconstruction.

You can affect the way the system works in countless ways; by, for example:

- questioning goals
- influencing the culture
- reviewing systems and procedures
- strengthening targets
- analysing reporting patterns or cycles of meetings
- demanding training

The list is almost endless. We are not rabbits frozen in the headlights of the future, but empowered individuals who can make a difference!

Power and *2*
empowerment

Empowerment is:

- A work team going into seclusion for three months to design a new generation of computer without a single visit from head office.
- A worker stopping production at the cost of thousands of pounds a minute because he or she has observed a defect.
- People with a common cause organising themselves into a self-help group in order to combat the problem.
- Having not just the right but the duty to appraise your boss.
- Having a vote on the future strategy of your workplace.
- Being judged on your individual qualities, not according to some racial, sexual or educational stereotype.
- Having all the training and information necessary for a job or task.

These are examples of empowerment that most people would recognise. Empowerment means every member of a society or organisation being able to take control of their own destiny and realising their potential to the full. It involves giving more power to those who currently have little control over what they do and little ability to influence the decisions being made around them.

Empowerment means having more power

But to redistribute power we must first know what power is. Common sense suggests that this should not be too big a problem. After all, everyone intuitively understands when someone has, or does not have, a lot of power.

Yet on closer examination power turns out to be a tricky customer to pin down. Trying to get behind the façade and unpick its constituent elements is like trying to grab a handful of fog. It is plainly visible all around us but when we open our fist it is empty.

WORKSHOP: POWER IN ORGANISATIONS

- Consider the following list in relation to your workplace or a social organisation that you know well. How do all these factors affect the power relations present in the organisation?
  - wealth
  - status
  - personality
  - organisational culture and/or morality
  - knowledge
  - information
  - formal decision-making structures
  - rules and punishment
  - peer group pressure
  - gender
  - ethnic origin
- Consider your own experience of organisations and add any other aspects of power that you can think of.

This workshop on power demonstrates the wide range of very different forces and influences that constitute what is called power. It is hard to distil some common element, some pure essence of power which is present in them all. Yet this is the simplistic goal of some modern-day management alchemists.

Power cannot be sliced and redistributed

The problem is that, like the alchemists' elixir of life, a pure essence of power does not exist. In fact, the search is not just futile, it is fundamentally flawed. Power is not a resource that can be discovered and then given out on the basis of some means test of how much someone has in the bank. To look only at the possession of such things as money, or guns, or the means of production, or formal status or even professional knowledge is only to scratch the surface.

Indeed, the discussion on the 'disempowering history of power' below shows that because such traditional conceptualisations of power are so one-dimensional they have actively contributed to its unequal distribution. This is why it is so important to arrive at a workable and understandable definition of power which is adequate to the task of its redistribution.

Power is better understood as a mass of interacting forces and systems rather than as a resource or a 'thing in itself'. Some of these forces and systems are physical, some are social and some are intellectual constructions. Most major institutionalised power systems, such as a large religious order or a national government, combine all three aspects.

Power is also better understood from its consequences for human behaviour than its abstract causes. In the main these power systems have force only because we give them credence. Guns only have force if it is believed that they will be used; money only has value if it is generally accepted that little pieces of paper bearing the picture of the head of state can be exchanged for goods and services.

The history of power is elusive. The debate over power makes one of its first appearances with Aristotle nearly 2500 years ago, but there have only been infrequent sightings since, for example Macchiavelli's famous attempts to describe how to rule in Renaissance Italy. Thus it is only very recently that people have begun to discuss the nature of power in a wider sociological and less philosophical sense. Max Weber started it with his famous categorisation of power as:

THE DISEMPOWERING HISTORY
OF POWER

- traditional: (power derived from precedent and history – that of the church, for example)
- coercive: (power derived from the use of, or threatened use of force)
- charismatic: (power derived from the appeal of a strong and influential leader)
- formal: (power derived from the use of rational rules, procedures and status)

Others have trodden gingerly in Weber's considerable footsteps. At various times, power has been said to have 'hidden faces' of internalised beliefs, to be the result of economic subjugation, or to be the consequence of 'dependency'. Others have described the current age as a 'disciplinary society', every action being potentially under surveillance. If you want to explore this interesting, if sometimes arcane, academic debate in greater depth, some of the seminal texts are given in the Recommended Reading for Part I.

The failure to describe power convincingly has meant that people who produce theories about how organisations work have been allowed to get away either with not discussing the subject at all, or with gross simplifications.

The conception of power within traditional organisational theory and practice is almost comically rudimentary. It is broadly that of the average movie western. Power makes its entrance either cast as the sheriff's badge pinned to the reluctant hero's breast, or more usually emerging from the barrel of a gun.

Simplistic view of power in organisational theory

This is the essence of Dahl's famous definition of power as 'the ability of actor A to force actor B to act against his will'. It is the 'zero sum' assumption at its most crude – the view that to empower someone you must first take power from someone else because the total sum of power always remains constant – and its limitations are pernicious. It suggests that power can only be understood in the form of an overt coercive force such as that derived from hierarchical status (or from the use of weapons). It is also win/lose thinking at its most naked. Only one person can win a shoot-out, or wear the sheriff's badge. There can be no possibility of a general programme of empowerment.

A comfortable theory for bureaucracy

This kind of thinking suited the traditional bureaucracy very well. It legitimises the formal hierarchy. Moreover, it creates the comfortable idea that conflict can only occur between two protagonists who possess more or less equal power and who disagree. In an unequal situation the exercise of power is trivially easy and cannot give rise to argument. By definition, in a hierarchy such circumstances are minimised and on the rare occasion when disagreement between colleagues of a similar position does occur, there will always be a boss to knock heads together.

This view of 'power' disempowers

However, this description of power and conflict is fundamentally disempowering. It rules out any systematic attempt to empower before you can even start, for a number of reasons:

1. If power only exists in the formal structure, then the scope for empowering the individual is restricted to flattening that structure – effectively just the negative act of taking away someone else's power. This is both too narrow and, in itself, a recipe for disaster. History is not full of examples of the strong voluntarily giving up their power to the weak.

2. A narrow conception of power leaves out the possibility of empowering people on a huge range of fronts, from extra training to more 'holistic' working practices. Yet these and many other areas increase the general 'sum' of power.

3. The problem with traditional thinking goes even deeper. It believes conflict to be inherently bad, a sign that the proper, rational, hierarchic processes are not working properly. But, as we have seen, within this world view conflict can only occur between people both of whom possess power. It follows that it would be a fundamental error to level the distribution of power within an organisation because to do so is merely to invite additional conflict. (We talk in more detail about the value of conflict to an empowering organisation in Chapter 4.)

The inadequacy of these formulations of power illustrates the subterranean influence of the mindsets that we describe in Chapter 3. Because the cultural 'paradigm' of the twentieth century regards hierarchical power as entirely legitimate, it has not been necessary to push beyond this as a definition. Now that this world view is breaking down, for the reasons described in Chapter 1, more of the picture can be seen. Whatever emerges as the new paradigm of power will no doubt itself be superseded in due course.

USEFUL DEFINITIONS OF POWER AND EMPOWERMENT

So human behaviour is the result of power, and power is the result of the interplay between individual consciousness and the forces and pressures of the external world. It is this relationship which gives us our starting point for a definition of power which in turn can be used to 'empower':

> Power resides in every aspect of the web of forces, values and beliefs which *determine human behaviour*.

Aided by this definition we can define the process of empowering as:

> The reorientation of all these forces, values and beliefs so that they support and liberate the individual, rather than diminish their range of thought and action.

The definition of empowerment provides a sound basis for the redistribution of power in a number of ways:

A basis for the redistribution of power

- It offers room to the whole menu of factors which influence human behaviour in organisations, and forces us to understand the sheer capacity and strength of the sinews of power in which we are all enmeshed. It enables us to look beyond and beneath the confines of formal structures or unequal reward systems and embrace other concerns such as sexism and racism, or the hidden messages contained in organisational rituals and myths.
- It locates power within the perception of the individual. It is not just whether there is a big stick waiting to fall, it is also whether someone *thinks* there is a big stick waiting to fall.
- Linking behaviour to power strikes a positive note. In effect we are saying that if you change the relations of power you will change behaviour. So if you remove the power of control possessed by tiers of hierarchy, people in the front line, including supervisors, change their behaviour of passive acceptance and begin to think for themselves and take responsibility. The power has shifted to them.

These points are vital ones for empowerment. Most of the influences listed in the previous workshop have force only because they are believed to be legitimate or unquestioned. We are caught up in systems which only have an existence because we believe they exist.

Power is in the eye of the beholder

The practical significance of this for empowerment is that if power, like beauty, resides in the eye of the beholder, empowerment will inevitably change the individual's perception of what is legitimate authority. Being empowered means becoming conscious of the forces that influence your behaviour. It is then for the individual to decide which of these forces he or she accepts as reasonable.

> Rule 1: Use your good judgement at all times.
> Rule 2: There are no additional rules.
>   *An executive's description of the management philosophy at Nordstrom's, a*
>   *department store on the West Coast of America (quoted in Peters, 1987)*

Power redistributed

Empowerment does not mean the end of power. Far from it. Liberated organisations will continue to have decision-making structures and rules, and will continue to enforce obedience to the general will.

What *does* change is that the structures and systems supporting the collective purpose are developed by the members of the organisation themselves, rather than being imposed from on high. Members of an empowered organisation give willing agreement to the organisational forces that bind them to a common purpose. The following case study is an illustration.

CASE STUDY: DEMOCRACY IN THE WORKPLACE

Mr Semler, the CEO of Semco, a Brazilian company making pumps, dishwashers and cooling units, 'has turned the (traditional) rule book inside out'. Instead of being a dispensable cog in the machine the worker *is* the machine which drives the company forward.

Guardian journalist Victor Keegan said of Semler: 'If empowerment is the buzz word of the 1990s, you couldn't empower employees much more than he is doing.'

The core of Semler's philosophy is to introduce real democracy into a workplace. The following Semco policies and procedures turn theory into practice:

- Workers take vital decisions previously made by managers. They reorganise their factories, come and go as they please, and many are encouraged to work from their own homes or to organise their own small factories.

---

continued

- A quarter of employees already fix their own salaries and soon everyone will.
- Based on an agreed formula, the workers themselves decide how much of the profits to share (which can be as much as 25 per cent) and how much to invest. However, being in charge of their own destiny like this involves heavy responsibilities. Their decisions are, in fact, tightly controlled by market forces. Setting salaries too high, giving themselves too great a share of the profits, or abusing the right to work from home and failing in a small business may all price people out of their department's budget, with disastrous results.

Nevertheless, the policy towards managers underlines that this worker decision making is for real. Semco's bureaucratic striptease involved shedding seven layers of managers, leaving the job of chief executive to rotate between six 'counsellors' including Semler himself.

From the beginning, all managers have been rated regularly on a scale of 1–100 by their staff. The second or third time a manager gets a rating of 50 or below he or she knows that they have lost the capacity to lead and they 'fade out'.

The second phase of this policy is even more radical – people elect their own boss. A manager imposed from above, Semler argues, starts at a disadvantage and if everyone has a financial stake in success, it seems sensible to him that everyone should also have a say in selecting the person they want as their boss.

The physical arrangements of the company mirror this democratic structure. An inner circle of six vice-presidents (including Semler) is surrounded by a circle of ten business unit leaders, which in turn is surrounded by the associates (workers). It is difficult to determine anyone's earning power since people wear what they like, practically no one has a desk, and power symbols, such as parking places, have been abolished. (In Chapter 8 and elsewhere we stress the importance of considering these physical arrangements.)

An impressive success story emerges:

- A fivefold increase in profits despite the hyperinflationary background of the Brazilian economy.
- Productivity has risen sevenfold and the company is not in debt.
- 23 per cent of its output is exported.
- Semler has twice been voted businessman of the year and his

continued

> book *Maverick!* has become the all-time non-fiction bestseller in Latin America.
>
> At a time when giants like IBM were experiencing fundamental problems, Semco aroused worldwide interest. Semler's book has sold more than half a million copies and the Japanese edition (in spite of making little sense to the traditional Japanese manager) commanded the largest advance ever given in that country for a business book.
>
> *Source: The Guardian*

A PROGRAMME FOR EMPOWERING LEADERSHIP

There are two separate but equally vital aspects to a practical programme of empowering leadership: empowering people and liberating organisations.

Empowering people

The first aspect is an understanding of the people and intellectual skills needed by everyone to be empowered to make a full contribution of all their latent talent and knowledge. It also involves people being supported in overcoming any physical or social disabilities which may trammel their abilities.

Liberating organisations

As the Semco case so clearly illustrates, the second aspect is the development of organisational structures which permit collective involvement in decision making. However empowered people may be in the skills sense alone, by definition they are not truly empowered unless they are also in control of the decisions being made around them.

We call this *liberating the organisation*. It involves a fundamental rethink of the nature of control and authority within all types of organisations – private, public and voluntary.

This book sets out a practical programme for empowering leadership which embraces both these themes. It is based on the belief that people work (and live!) in the midst of something which has been described as 'negotiated order'. All social institutions are a mass of conflicting power: conflicts of ideas, priorities and values as well as goals. Sometimes these debates are in the open with honest discussion about differences. This usually happens between two equally empowered groups or individuals.

More commonly, the real causes of an argument become submerged as the less powerful people or group turn to other tactics to express their unhappiness. This is often the explanation for one of the more common enigmas of organisational decision making: the time it takes to reach a decision about an issue is in inverse proportion to its importance. If your work group starts to struggle with small (but to its members symbolically vital issues) such as a fair method for collecting coffee money or where the office party should be held, then you might pause to examine what is really going on. You are witnessing the creation of a 'negotiated order' in microcosm.

In a negotiated order power is not evenly distributed, but it *is* distributed. In this sense, programmes for empowerment are not entering dangerous new waters, they are accepting reality. By recognising, enhancing and planning for the employees' ability to intervene you are potentially channelling their latent power into organisationally constructive flows.

Empowering everyone and liberating the organisation will not abolish arguments and conflicts. On the contrary, they will be more numerous and more varied, but also incalculably more productive.

WORKSHOP: NEGOTIATED ORDER

- At the next meeting you attend, either at work or within a social group, try to identify some of the hidden currents. Can you identify the strongly held objectives of the key participants? Are these their own objectives?
- Then analyse the decisions taken. Did they represent a compromise with a number of elements calculated to maximise support?
- Would it be fair to say that your own family represents a negotiated order in microcosm?

DOES EMPOWERMENT WORK?

In the last section we explained why our definition of empowerment goes much wider than the traditional view. Empowerment is not just about redistributing resources of various kinds, it also embraces all the psychological, physical and intellectual elements which make up each individual. The goals of empowerment are that people from every walk of life should:

- understand and feel good about themselves
- relate to each other with empathy and respect
- give voluntary agreement to the rules and structures that govern their lives
- have sufficient resources (of knowledge, training, authority, time,

tools, support etc. as well as money) to be able to contribute all the value they can to their chosen roles

These are the elements of self-determination. There are few political philosophers on either left or right (although excluding, for example, Christian or Marxist determinists) who would deny that such tenets are a reasonable starting point for moral philosophy and are therefore of universal applicability.

The arguments against such ambitions are normally more pragmatic, often echoing the sort of unconscious assumptions we described in the last section, in the mistaken belief that they are timeless truths. Thus empowerment is said to rely on a view of humanity which is too naive and trusting. Or it is argued that human nature is inherently unequal, that the strong will always dominate the weak. And in any case, while it would be nice to be able to put time and effort into an equitable and thoughtful distribution of resources, this would simply result in chaos and inefficiency which in the end would impoverish everyone.

Some of these arguments will be examined through a second example of empowerment in action. In order to test the theory we will take the extreme case of a collectively organised, voluntary sector body (studied by one of us in great detail over a three-month period) which has made the rejection of any form of oppression or inequality a core goal of its existence. Its approach is radical and all-embracing and yet it delivers a sensitive service to a gruelling daily schedule. To do this it employs people from all walks of life, from highly qualified university graduates to 'difficult to place' sixteen-year-old trainees on government work experience schemes, and even offenders referred by the probation service. If empowerment works in practice for this organisation, and to the benefit of its clients, then it should work in practice anywhere.

CASE STUDY: ORGANISATIONAL LIBERATION

The Airspace charity was founded in 1979 in Bristol, south-west England. Its purpose is to use games and movement with people who have severe learning difficulties (often enacted on large, stimulating but safe inflatable airbeds) in order to encourage the skills of self-awareness and communication. At the start Airspace did not have a conscious philosophy of empowerment. Its initial inspiration was based more on a deliberate rejection of two then current orthodoxies:

● the impersonal and institutionalised care that long-stay

---

continued

residential hospitals gave residents with learning difficulties (this is thankfully a thing of the past, but in the early 1980s there was no philosophy of 'caring in the community' and Airspace was for a while the only outside body which visited the grim Victorian institutions which surrounded Bristol);

- any form of organisation that gave one individual more formal or informal authority than another.

It was this pragmatic commitment to combining a vision of service excellence with an experimental approach to collective organisation which led Airspace, over time, to invent many of the features which we would now recognise as being aspects of empowerment. Some of these are described below.

Consensual decision making.   The interesting aspect of the charity's approach to decision making was that although it purported to be democratic, it was not so in the traditional sense of the word. In practice a decision was only taken when everyone was in agreement, so the only purpose of votes was to register disagreement. Indeed, considerable effort in meetings was put into empowering and encouraging disagreement. This was clearly functional. Once a decision had been taken there was no structure for enforcing its implementation beyond the voluntary compliance of every member of the charity, therefore it was vital to make sure that agreement was genuine.

Creating consensus extended into listening to the voices of the customers, the people with learning difficulties themselves. For example, they and their representatives were included on the management committee of the charity (otherwise made up of ex-workers, funders and community representatives such as local government councillors) which acted as the guardian of the charity's values and the quality of its service.

An ironic concomitant of the need to create consensus was the development of a very formal system of meetings for different purposes and a very strict approach to the distribution of briefings prior to meetings. If background information on important subjects for debate was not available, or was not in an easily understandable form, then the debate would be put off until it was. The onus was on the people responsible to ensure that they were understood, not on the listener to understand.

Equality of status and rewards.   Individual workers at Airspace were given specific roles to fulfil and had delegated authority to make decisions within these specific areas, but the roles carried

continued

no formal status beyond that. As a practical and symbolic commitment to this principle, all the core jobs were accorded exactly the same rate of pay.

The participation of everyone in the planning and review of services.   One of the most impressive aspects of the charity over the period we studied it was the investment of time in ensuring and improving the quality of the service. Every session with people with disabilities (of which there were several each day) was carefully planned, with every member of the team attending and contributing. Different themes and techniques would be adopted according to the particular capabilities of the clients at each session and their known preferences. At the end of each session successes and failures were carefully recorded so that general lessons could be analysed and discussed. In addition there was a major review meeting every six months when the charity shut down for a couple of days (despite the revenue loss that represented) and analysed in depth how it could do better in the future.

Emphasis on individual responsibility.   The only written rules at Airspace were two codes of practice. One governed matters of health and safety and the other detailed all aspects of an equal opportunities policy. Beyond these there was no formal set of rules to which members were expected to conform, but there were rigorous standards nonetheless. The overriding requirement was for a sense of personal responsibility which meant that if an individual took on a particular role or made an undertaking, he or she was expected to fulfil it without further question or supervision.

The sanction against anyone who was perceived not to be pulling their weight to the extent that they had promised was a formal disciplinary process in which three of the charity member's peers would attempt to establish the problem and in the first instance offer support to overcome it. During our research it was made clear to us that disciplinary meetings were by no means uncommon. Everyone, from the newest recruit to the oldest hand, had the right to initiate the procedure and it was seen as a valuable way of structuring conflict as well as offering support to someone who might not otherwise ask for it. But it also had the potential for hard action. On a number of occasions disciplinary hearings led to the dismissal of a charity worker if he or she had persistently failed to live up to the unwritten expectations of their colleagues.

However, there was also a more forgiving side to this emphasis

continued

on personal responsibility which accepted mistakes without a second thought so long as they were made in the right spirit. A quotation from one of the members we interviewed caught the attitude well:

> If you have made a mistake, but you have done the best you possibly can, the collective will then deal with the situation as it then is, rather than say you shouldn't have done this.

Acceptance of the whole person.   Perhaps the most shocking aspect of this working environment for a strait-laced Briton, used to the emotionally cramped conditions of traditional corporations, was the freedom with which people in the charity seemed to express their feelings. From both the men and the women we saw displays of tears as well as laughter, of anger as well as affection. Indeed, deliberate stress was placed on people showing and coming to terms with their emotions. The monthly collective meeting for which attendance was virtually compulsory, and which was often the site for intense argument and debate, often ended with the ritual of a game called 'huggy bear'. This involved the principal antagonists performing a curious dance which included a good deal of physical embracing.

Conclusion – did it work?   That Airspace was clearly a lively and thriving workplace which did good work was undeniable. Whether it worked better as a consequence of its pragmatic exploration of the tenets of empowerment is more difficult to assess. There were no immediate private or public sector comparisons by which to test the value and efficiency of the service. Three demonstrable and pragmatic arguments, however, suggest that the path the charity was following was in the right direction:

- It had clearly convinced its hard-headed funders in the health authorities and in the local council that it was doing a good job, since it had increased its income fivefold in ten years.
- The approach it had pioneered for people with learning difficulties had been copied by many other groups and by some therapists working within the health services.
- It appeared to operate with an incredibly low management overhead. At the time of our study the charity employed 37 staff, of which only three were not directly productive (one full-time fundraiser and one full-time and one part-time coordinator to maintain the administrative and management functions). All the other members of the charity had areas of

continued

responsibility but were expected to devote the vast majority of their time to direct sessional work with clients.

THE BENEFITS OF EMPOWERMENT

However imperfectly, the members of the Airspace charity certainly felt that they were building a very different working environment from that of a traditional organisation. Working empirically with a set of core values rather than a coherent philosophy, they had almost inadvertently hit upon most of the elements that have come to be regarded as intrinsic to empowerment. This is not surprising. Although it was clothed in different language they were reacting, albeit earlier and stronger than some, to the sense of frustration at the inadequacies of bureaucracy that is now felt by many people.

The Airspace case study also shows some of the benefits and costs of empowerment. Some of those identified in our study of the charity are described below.

Commitment.   At a subjective level, the interviews with the workers in the charity revealed an almost religious fervour about the organisation and the importance of its activities. A more objective test was the amount of unpaid overtime regularly performed. The charity itself did not use time recording, preferring to trust its employees to fulfil their contracts without supervision. However, as part of the research we monitored the actual hours worked over a period of three months. During that time the total number of unpaid hours worked was more than 50 per cent above staff members' formal contractual terms and conditions. This was not regarded as in any way unusual.

A better service for the customer.   One of the key arguments advanced by charity members for the empowering approach to their own organisation was that it enabled and accorded with the nature of the service itself. A contrast was continually drawn between their approach to people with learning difficulties (they were individuals like any one else to be treated with respect and understanding of their particular talents and foibles) and that of the institutionalised care of the state hospitals which they visited. To the charity members at least, it was clear that the primary goal of hospitals was maintaining order at the cost of individuality: for example, no attention was paid to residents' physical appearance and the primary therapeutic tool was an overwhelming reliance on sedative drugs. In contrast, the tools of the charity's work were intensive sessions of movement and games in order to teach core skills of communication and understanding, which in turn would help their users to become more self-reliant and empowered.

The transformation of individuals.   Members also spoke about the 'personal growth' they felt they had achieved as a result of the trust and responsibility that the charity placed in all its members without distinction. This was difficult to demonstrate in hard, measurable terms, but there was one interesting statistic which indicated such an effect. The length of service of the 'mode B', difficult to place 16-year-old youngsters which the charity temporarily employed (the maximum possible stay for any individual was a year) and trained with Government funds was approximately 30 per cent less than the national average. This puzzled the government agency administering the scheme, until they discovered that these youngsters were in fact moving to full-time, permanent jobs. It appeared that the self-confidence they were gaining at the charity was giving them a definite edge in the jobs market.

Embracing change and cost savings.   The world of charitable fundraising is every bit as competitive and ruthlessly commercial as that of business. There is a limited pot of local and national government grants and contracts and private philanthropy, which merely scratches at the surface of the potential demand. In the face of such financial pressures it was the commitment that came from empowerment that enabled the Airspace charity to survive successive financial crises. The salaries accepted by its workers were approximately 35 per cent lower than those paid for roughly equivalent work within the state sector. But more than that, on two occasions in the recent past the workers, when informed that income targets were not being achieved, had collectively decided to accept a general wage cut rather than see a colleague made redundant and the service suffer.

The downside – individual stress.   In case the benefits described above paint too rosy a picture of the potential benefits of empowerment, it is also salutary to consider the darker side of such an environment. The high level of stress that individuals experienced was seen as the direct corollary of the distribution of responsibility together with the absence of supervision. This created huge self-imposed pressures on members to live up to these positive expectations. Some could not cope and left. More seriously, some struggled on without adequate support. Two members of the charity had left with conditions akin to nervous breakdowns over the previous five years.

IS EMPOWERMENT FOR EVERYONE?

The last point mentioned above reminds us that empowerment needs to be approached carefully, and individuals need to be supported in coping with the stress of such new ways of working and thinking. However, it should also be clear that if implemented properly empowerment has something to offer to everyone and to every organisation. But are there any exceptions? Are there some 'business' conditions to which it is unsuited, or are there some people who are so vulnerable that they are entirely unsuited to such a programme?

We believe that the answer to these questions is an emphatic no, but this needs to be qualified by two important caveats.

At the core of empowerment is the principle that each person is considered in the light of his or her own unique capabilities and circumstances. Thus empowerment cannot be a set of monolithic principles applied regardless of the situation. It must be tailored to the needs and abilities of each individual. To push someone beyond his or her wishes or capabilities is probably the most disempowering and undermining experience that can be inflicted.

> When Alistair Wright became human resource director at Digital Equipment Co six years ago, he vowed he would set an example to the rest of the organisation by passing authority down the line and totally empowering his staff. But it was easier said than done. Mr Wright discovered that you can't hand out authority like luncheon vouchers. The motivation for taking personal initiatives has to come from the employees themselves. 'It took me a long time to reach a fundamental truth about empowerment. You can't give it; people have to take it.'
>
> David Oates, *Power to the People Who Want It*

Secondly, although we believe that every organisation can benefit from liberating the creativity of its members, it would be foolhardy to pretend that the process does not mean considerable investment of time, energy, emotion and money. Therefore the imperative for change is stronger where highly competitive business conditions make the demands for cost savings and innovation more intense.

Where competition is less of a factor (in some very stable and mature niche markets, or with public sector monopoly suppliers of services) it may well be that organisations could in principle struggle on for longer swimming against the tide. But just as mass production came to dominate so much of both public and private sector economic activity in the twentieth century, we believe that empowerment will become the prevalent organisational 'paradigm' of the next.

The benefits and costs of empowerment are considered further in Chapter 13.

3 The 'Common Sense' that Empowers

Empowerment represents a fundamental challenge to traditional thinking about how to organise.

In this chapter we show that this challenge goes right down to the level of our deepest assumptions about how people and organisations tick. In the same way that periods of history are characterised by particular paradigms or sets of basic assumptions about the way the world works, at the individual level people operate according to an unwritten 'mindset' of ideas about the world which they take to be self-evidently 'common sense'. A mindset is all the more potent because normally our conscious mind barely acknowledges that it exists, let alone questions it.

WHY MINDSETS ARE IMPORTANT

If these commonsense ideas – these mindsets – are articulated they are liable to be dismissed without discussion as being too obvious to justify, just as people used commonly to think that the world was flat. And yet the one thing we can say with absolute certainty is that all such mindsets are culturally bound and transient. Inevitably they change with changing historical circumstances. They also vary between different cultures. In fact, almost by definition a mindset is a number of relative values masquerading as absolute statements of fact.

These assumptions are vital to be aware of since they colour our perceptions of the world. They become self-fulfilling prophecies because the human mind is only capable of seeing what it expects to see. The evidence for whether the world was flat or round did not change with the speculations of Galileo, what changed was the mental ability of people to look at the heavens and see different facts from those which had been so obvious for the previous millennia.

The reason we want to investigate mindsets in this chapter is that the prevailing mindset within the traditional bureaucracy is almost entirely alien to ideas of empowerment. Only after we have challenged it and explained what can replace it will the rest of this book make any practical sense.

Two examples of the deep-down, 'commonsense' instincts at work in the traditional bureaucracy are:

- a lack of confidence in the ability or the trustworthiness of the ordinary employee
- an overwhelming psychological attachment to predictability, order and continuity

This kind of thinking underpins the 'zero sum' assumption that the total sum of power always remains constant. It is underlying attitudes like these that make it so necessary for the traditional corporation to centralise the 'brainy' functions of planning, coordination and command, leaving the 'doing' to the untutored front line. As we saw in the case study on Frederick Taylor in Chapter 1, this division of labour, with its rigid rules, strict supervision and the carving of the work process into small, meaningless bits which can be performed by rote, was found to be an unbeatable formula for maintaining order.

Traditional management disempowers

In other words, the primary purpose of traditional management processes is to disempower. This is a conscious strategy for maintaining control. For a brief period (now passed) it was also an effective strategy for commercial success: in Frederick Taylor's day it certainly helped to reduce unit costs and create consistency of product – the key elements of competitive advantage which prevailed in the early part of the twentieth century.

The process of disempowerment, and in consequence dehumanisation, did not occur just because the individual was not to be trusted, but because expressions of individuality were fundamentally dangerous. They upset the sense of order which took so much effort to create. Thus the careful manipulation of the work environment had to go beyond mere issues of who was in control and who made the decisions. Its deeper principles include:

- the separation of 'ownership' (whether real or psychological) from production
- money is regarded as the only (or at least the primary) source of motivation
- an authoritarian culture of rules, procedures and propaganda
- constant and institutionalised surveillance of people when at work
- a block on anything which expressed the whole individual (art, feelings or humour are a luxury to be enjoyed out of work time)
- the punishment of disagreement
- the presumption that the professional knows best

This is the mindset that empowerment must reject at the level of its underlying assumptions. Attempting to empower in practice while still struggling with such preconceptions is a futile exercise, as many of the early pioneers discovered to their cost. In the next section we describe the core elements of a new empowering mindset, a new common sense.

WORKSHOP: ANALYSE YOUR MINDSET

One of the best ways to understand your own mindset is to contrast it with different ways of thinking.
- Think of a period of history with which you are familiar and write down its typical mindset. How does your own mindset differ?
- Analyse a religious or political debate on the television or radio. Do the protagonists have different underlying assumptions about how things work?
- Observe the behaviour of people within an organisation you know well. Does this reveal the type of assumptions on which it may be based?
- Write down your own deep assumptions about the way the world works and show it to a trusted friend. See if he or she recognises your view of yourself.

THE CORE ELEMENTS OF EMPOWERMENT

If there is a consistent theme underlying the elements which make up the new empowering common sense it is that in empowerment the means *are* the ends. It is futile to separate the results of a process from the process itself: if you want a quality outcome you must take a quality approach to its production.

Therefore the core elements of empowerment focus on processes – on the means. This is in tune with the whole approach to empowerment: by definition, if you are giving individuals control of what they produce you must, in turn, rely on them to be the arbiters of the results.

> When you take a process view, you discover that the process can access and leave at any level in the organisation. So very often processes will go from somebody who is 'senior' in an organisation down to somebody who is 'junior' in an organisation. With empowerment, what you are actually saying is stop interfering with the process and let it happen as it should happen.
>
> *Eddie Obeng (in Oates, 1993)*

The three core elements of empowerment are:
- Expect the best from people
- There is no right answer
- Reunite the brain and the hand

EXPECT THE BEST FROM PEOPLE

Expecting the best from people is a view of human nature which emphasises the value of trust and positive expectations as the best way of motivating people. With a culture of trust empowering leaders can save all the effort normally wasted on control mechanisms and concentrate on gaining agreement to common purposes and goals.

'Human nature' is a difficult concept to pin down, and many esoteric monographs have been published on the subject. Meanwhile, those of us who are not philosophers have to get through life dealing with people hundreds of times a day based on our own intuitive assumptions about how to relate to others.

What we expect from others often varies, depending on with whom we are dealing and the situation we are in. Within families there is often a high degree of trust. Strangers from opposing sides at a time of war will have a different view of how much trust to place in one another.

Traditionally management has assumed the worst

Managers also have to work with intuitive assumptions about human nature. To an objective observer, it would appear that most senior managers behave as though their staff have been parachuted in by the enemy. The general presumption of the twentieth century has been that it is folly to put too much faith in your workers either motivating themselves or acting intelligently.

Organisational arrangements have presumed that people are 'naturally' lazy and selfish; they need to be surrounded by rules and bombarded with instructions. But the malaise goes deeper than the Taylorist division of labour. Not only was each task segregated in minute detail, but no compensating effort was put into giving each worker knowledge of how his or her work was combined with that of others to produce something of value to a customer. For some managers it was a point of principle that workers should be prevented from knowing the overall design of the product on which they were working, for fear of the consequent increased capacity for industrial sabotage. This was a double separation of the worker from the results of his or her labour: first, from any contribution to the quality of the particular function; secondly, from the final product itself. It is small wonder that the twentieth century has been called the century of 'deskilling'.

Nevertheless, there is much evidence to show that the expectations we have of people are self-fulfilling. Numerous experiments have demonstrated that, by and large, people behave as they are *expected* to behave. A modern parlour game which took place on a recent management course illustrates this very neatly. Each person was given a description of a social role (e.g. 'the joker', 'the person who stands in a corner being ignored') and this label told other people what to expect of them. It took five minutes for the normally serious-minded financial controller of a large manufacturing company to flower into a witty conversationalist. This (apparently unprecedented) behaviour was simply the result of being surrounded by a throng of attentive listeners who obeyed the sign on his forehead commanding them to laugh at the end of each sentence.

We behave as we are expected to behave

A more sinister example of the power of expectations is the famous experiment where students obeyed instructions to keep increasing the level of pain they thought they were inflicting on subjects who failed to answer questions correctly. Some were even prepared to inflict an electric shock that they were told by the white-coated experimenters would be fatal.

So expectations can be a vehicle for influencing human nature. Expect people to be lazy and they will be. Tell them in words and deeds that you trust them and they will be trustworthy. Empowerment assumes that what people are prepared to contribute to an enterprise is a result of what they expect of themselves, and what they expect of themselves is predominantly the consequence of what other people consciously or unconsciously expect of them.

Expect excellence and people will respond

This poses an enormous challenge for the empowering leader.

Creating negative expectations is easy; it is second nature for most of British management (or any other social institution). In contrast, reorientating every element of an organisation – its structures, systems and culture – so that they implicitly and explicitly reflect the message 'we trust you to do the best you humanly can' is a much tougher job.

But if you can show people that you *trust* them and *expect* them to produce an excellent performance, they will respond positively to your expectations.

CASE STUDY: ODDBINS

A good example of replacing negative expectations with a positive attitude was the novel approach of Oddbins, one of the most successful wine store chains of recent years. In contrast to the policy of other off-licence chains of employing low-status shop workers (whose main role was to take money and stock shelves), Oddbins realised the multiple benefits to be gained from staff who were enthusiastic and knowledgeable about wine. The customer would be encouraged to return for more advice and the overall market would expand if people were encouraged to experiment in new tastes.

Oddbins started to give wine away to its staff and empowered them to provide tastings for the customers. In one step the company reduced the cost of breakages, produced staff who could talk about their stock of wine with genuine confidence, and engendered an intensity of customer loyalty which was to win them *Wine Magazine*'s award for the best wine retailer for a historic five years in a row.

The practical steps that need to be taken to create trust look dangerously radical. But like all the actions required by empowerment there is no halfway house. For the new logic to work the old must be banished – even a residual safety net will undermine belief in the new attitudes and arrangements that are required.

Among other things trust is developed by:

- managers holding themselves accountable to their teams – explaining their actions and gaining agreement;
- clear explanations of facts – even (especially) when they are unpalatable;
- giving people responsibility and not checking up that they fulfilled it properly. Trust people to appraise themselves and report back problems;

- setting the highest standards possible for both yourself and others. Show that only the best is expected from people (and then forgive mistakes).

Trust and positive expectations are sensitive plants to nurture. They can only grow organically over a period of time as people learn that they are genuinely meant, and it only takes a momentary lapse to undo all the effort.

Above all, whether people feel trusted is a result of both the formal and the informal systems at work within an organisation. Reforming structures to create trust by delegating more responsibility is pointless if the informal culture of the workplace still condones, for example, sexist or racist behaviour.

Undoubtedly expecting the best from people is the part of the new common sense which requires the most emotional commitment to implement. To the worker on the front line it is also the most important.

WORKSHOP: EXPECTING THE BEST FROM PEOPLE

- Examine your own view of human nature. Do you trust everyone? Some people? No one? What distinguishes those you trust from those you don't trust?
- Think about an organisation you know well. Make a list of the ways it operates on a basis of implicit trust in its members. Then make a list of the ways it implicitly distrusts people. Which list is the longer?
- For three months, consciously behave more trustingly to people at work. Then review the results. What have you learnt?

THERE IS NO RIGHT ANSWER

It is important to think in terms of systems rather than mechanical cause and effect, in order to dispel the bureaucratic fallacy that there is always an optimum right answer. This is a major psychological barrier to devolving freedom and responsibility.

It is a barrier with a long historical pedigree. Ever since the Newtonian apple fell obediently onto the Newtonian head at a precisely calculable rate of acceleration, the Western world has laboured under the delusion that the onward march of progress would provide answers for all natural phenomena. It was an assumption that accorded well with the mechanical age. The regular and orderly motion of the steam engine became the metaphor for a civilisation.

The mechanical mindset

Effect followed cause with the same unfailing certainty with which the movement of the piston followed the build up of pressure in the cylinder. It was said to be only a matter of time before scientific reason completed the almost mechanical exercise of disentangling and describing all the elements of even the most complex of problems.

One consequence of adopting this mechanical mindset is that just as effect follows cause, so right answers obediently follow identification of the right problem. Science seemed to hold the promise of an optimum solution to every situation.

Indeed, the early days of the computer held out this same promise. A number cruncher was all that science needed to finish the job started by Newton. The conventional wisdom during the first years of the real development of computing in the late 1940s was that the world needed only nine computers in total – six in America and three in Britain. This was held to be sufficient to solve all known problems and fulfil all possible applications.

The belief in the eventual perfectibility of human reason and ingenuity accords well with the underlying hunger of the bureaucratic psychology for continuity and stability (perhaps ironically given its working assumption of human fallibility — or is this the reason?) It holds out the comforting promise of constant and orderly progress while justifying the army of clever planners required at the corporate centre. It is also one of the key foundations of the unequal distribution of power within a bureaucracy. The bureaucratic logic runs as follows:

Reduce uncertainty with rational procedures

- The key problem faced by any organisation is the uncertainty produced by the worrying array of variables which seem to confuse even the simplest of problems.
- Therefore the main goal of an organisation and its subunits is to reduce the amount of uncertainty it faces through the creation of rational processes and the application of specialist expertise or knowledge.

Centralise decision making

- In order for these processes to be optimised (something which is both possible and necessary) they must be coordinated and complementary. The surest way of achieving this is to centralise all significant decision making within the top hierarchy, where at least you could be sure that the proper procedure will be observed.

This, according to the mechanical mindset, is the way to get the optimum 'right' answer.

The cult of the professionals with their 'right' answers hangs like a millstone round many an organisational head. For example:

Unwillingness to experiment and innovate

- If there is only one right way of doing things, then the odds are that it is done that way at the moment. The reason for this happy coincidence is quite simple. The 'one right way' was probably invented by the boss whose success in climbing up the greasy pole was perhaps due to having developed this 'right' approach. Or people may believe that past practice must be there for a reason. Revans (1982) describes this idealisation of past experience as one of the four 'incorrigible handicaps' which prevent managers from learning and therefore from improving performance.

- If the 'right' answer must triumph, then all others must be vanquished. To *think* in this way (termed 'convergent thinking') is to *see* in this way; instead of looking for wider possibilities, especially in 'synergies' where the sum of the whole is greater than the value of the parts. A win/win outlook delights in the possibility that a gain for one view does not mean a loss for another.

  Only seeing win/lose possibilities

- If the mental framework to which an organisation is working is of the 'only one right answer' variety, then the organisation will be disinclined to look for feedback on how to improve systems or products. If it does not already have the best answer then it will have a team in a corporate ivory tower working on the replacement. Either way it simply does not see that its front-line staff have anything practical to offer. This sort of attitude actually considers empowering the front line to be not only dangerous but also irrelevant.

  Valuable feedback lost

The simple assumptions underpinning the mechanical metaphor of cause and effect, leading to the 'one right answer' syndrome, are breaking down in favour of a new emphasis on complex systems. The new science of *chaos*, as it has come to be called, is an indication of where current thinking is moving.

EMPOWERMENT SEES SYSTEMS NOT ANSWERS

Chaos theory demonstrates that even the most apparently random entities often contain complex patterns which help to explain their nature and their relationship with similar events or objects (conversely, even the most apparently ordered of events such as the movement of a pendulum, turn out to contain chaotic elements). Thus such diverse natural phenomena as the 'crinkling' of the seashore or the pattern of flooding of the Nile all share the same characteristics of a disordered order.

Equally, when the focus is turned on areas of human activity a similar picture of orderly chaos emerges. Computer analysis of a century of cotton prices in the Americas, for example, revealed this kind of chaotic pattern.

It is the triumph of reason to cast doubt upon its own existence.
Attrib. Federico García Lorca, Spanish poet and playwright

Perhaps the most evocative example of what all this means in practical terms is what is called 'the butterfly effect'. Chaos theory predicts that small perturbations in a non-linear system (any system which is not utterly self-contained) can quickly have disproportionate consequences as these variations become magnified by succeeding operations of the system. Thus a butterfly flapping its wings in one hemisphere can be said to create a storm in the other. This is a better and more contemporary metaphor for the workings of a complex organisation than that of the mechanical motions of the steam engine. It captures the idea of a complex play of different forces and events linked to probabilities rather than certainties.

Sociotechnical systems

It also has a high degree of resonance with one of the key theoretical advances of the twentieth century in the social sciences – the development of 'systems theory'. The Tavistock Institute first described organisations as 'sociotechnical systems', an attempt to convey the idea that the way we work is the result of the interrelationship of the two key elements of production, machines and people (with traditionally the latter being made to conform to the needs of the former). In their famous study of the longwall method of coal mining in a South Wales pit, Trist and Bamforth, both members of the Institute, demonstrated that production was improved when the social needs of the labour force were considered alongside the work patterns required to optimise the efficiency of the machines being used.

Some modern thinkers have developed this approach into a comprehensive attempt to explain many recurring patterns of human events (termed 'archetypes'). We describe one such archetype, 'the limits to growth', in Chapter 5 – a reinforcing cycle of growth and development (for example in an R & D division) is balanced by the countervailing pressures that its very success produced. Probably the most accessible description of how this evolving science can be applied to management is Peter Senge's *The Fifth Discipline*.

A powerful tool for understanding organisations

People who work with the concept of multidimensional systems, as opposed to the simpler but inadequate formula of a single cause leading to a single effect, are equipped with a powerful tool for comprehending how organisations work. In particular it provides a mental framework for understanding the interplay of the various forces in which you are enmeshed, and which you can influence.

Moreover, a change in one area of a system has repercussions throughout its interlinking constituents, not just those directly affected. It is impossible to anticipate all the consequences of a decision since, as we explained in the discussion of chaos theory, small initial variations can make huge differences a little further down the track.

However, the inability to predict detail should not lead to paralysis. Quite the opposite: the important consequence of systems thinking is that it liberates organisations to 'learn to love change'. Initiatives can be freely entered into, in the certain knowledge that they will have to be adapted at a later stage. Everything does not have to be worked out in painful detail before making a start because it is imperative to build formal times for project reevaluation into the development process.

Systems thinking empowers change

Nothing is as bad as consistency. There exists no more futile person than the manager who remarks, 'Well, you may say what you like but at any rate I have been consistent' . . . The manager who is consistent must be out of touch with reality. There is no consistency in the course of events, in history, in the weather or in the mental attitudes of one's fellow managers . . . The successful manager will not adhere to consistency, but will deal with each situation as it arises.

Lord Beaverbrook, *quoted in* Management Week, *6 November* 1991

WORKSHOP: SYSTEMS – NOT RIGHT ANSWERS

- Take an organisation you know well. Does it operate on the 'only one right answer' assumption? Hint: look at the role and power of the central professionals and at the capacity of the organisation to react to changing circumstances.
- Systems theory looks for patterns, not causes and effects. Look at an area in the organisation which is characterised by continual frustration or failure. Is there a *recurring pattern* in different attempts to improve the situation?
- Use the sociotechnical systems approach to your next important decision, analysing all the interacting variables. Later, study your decision. Was it a wise one?

REUNITE THE BRAIN AND THE HAND

There has to be an end to the artificial separation of 'brainwork' from manual work which has been the hallmark of production processes since the industrial revolution. Reuniting the brain and the hand is a vital precondition for involvement in decision making and therefore for empowerment.

Earlier in this chapter we described the disempowering impact of Taylorism, in part because his prescriptions represented the final severance of the link between the hand and the brain. But in fact the industrial division of labour, on which scientific management is based, has a much longer historical pedigree. A seminal description of its importance was in Adam Smith's *Wealth of Nations*, published in 1776 and regarded by many historians as the book that marks the birth of the Industrial Revolution.

Adam Smith described the benefits of the division of labour using the practical example of a pin factory:

> One man draws out the wire, another straightens it, a third cuts it, a fourth points it, a fifth grinds it at the top for receiving the head; to make the head requires two or three distinct operations; to put it on is a peculiar business, to whiten the pins is another; it is even a trade by itself to put them into the paper.

Adam Smith had grasped that the new technology of the Industrial Revolution was most appropriate to subdivided individual tasks and that, fully exploited, it could raise the productive capacity of individual workers not incrementally but by immense orders of magnitude.

He commented approvingly on visiting a small factory employing these principles where 10 people produced over 48,000 pins a day: 'But if they had all wrought separately and independently, and without any of them having been educated in this particular business, they certainly could not each of them have made twenty, perhaps not one pin in a day.'

Division of labour still occurs

Public sector or private, manufacturer or service provider, the organising principle of the division of labour has extended down to the present day. The craftsperson who constructed a product from start to finish has been superseded by the fragmentation of work. The overall process of production is broken into separate tasks. This enables workers to develop a special facility for their particular operation. Specialised machines can then be developed to automate production. As we have already seen, the whole approach reached its apogee with Taylor and the conveyor belts of mass production.

Adam Smith was not alone in recognising the critical importance of the division of labour. Karl Marx too saw it as the distinguishing feature of capitalist production. From his critical standpoint it was useful to the capitalists because it not only increased the quantities of 'surplus labour' that could be appropriated (roughly equivalent to profit), but it was, in itself, an instrument of control over workers because the brainwork was separated from the manual work. Marx regarded this as the ultimate division of labour with the early entrepreneurs maintaining power over the production process by exercising a monopoly on thought.

The division between brain labour and manual labour is profoundly disempowering for those on the wrong side of the divide. They are removed from:

Disempowerment

- control over their own part of the production process
- knowledge of the production process in its entirety or how it is coordinated
- any contribution to the design of the product or service
- any influence over wider decision making

Clearly empowerment cannot coexist with this division. But are there alternative approaches to production which do not require this split but which maintain competitive efficiency?

ALTERNATIVE APPROACHES

The last few decades have seen a good deal of experimentation on this question. The radical wing of the voluntary sector, the cooperative movement and some of the younger companies in America and Europe are in fact moving away from the traditional division of labour.

Total Quality Management (TQM) is a significant step down this path, but despite all the experimentation it has not really been taken seriously by the economic mainstream. Not, that is, until now (see Chapter 6). Just as we argued earlier that there is a certain inevitability about the advent of empowerment, so it appears that a tide of legitimacy is now running behind even TQM.

Total Quality Management

There is also now a school of management theory arguing the case for reuniting the brain and hand under the banner of 'business process reengineering' (BPR). Its most powerful and articulate advocates are two management consultants, Michael Hammer and James Champy. Their book *Reengineering the Corporation* is appropriately, if immodestly, subtitled 'A manifesto for business revolution'.

Business reengineering

At the heart of the BPR manifesto is a simple proposal. Traditional organisations organise around the various organisational *functions* (usually colonised by a 'professionalism' such as finance, marketing or personnel). Proponents of business reengineering argue that businesses, including public sector service delivery, should recreate themselves around their *organic business processes*. These are defined as the collection of activities that turn one or more inputs into the thing that is of value to the end user (the customer).

An example of this is to put a series of tasks, which once occurred step by painful step, into the hands of a single 'case worker'. One insurance company, for example, estimated that it took an average of

22 days to approve a policy – during which time the papers were worked on for a mere 17 minutes. The rest of the time was spent shuffling papers between specialists: from credit-checkers to actuaries to salespeople and back. We describe more of the practicalities of this powerful approach in Chapter 6.

Other organisational approaches

However, although it is a major step forward, reengineering the work process does not in itself fully bridge the hand–brain divide. Issues of organisational governance and culture also need to be addressed. Approaches which have attempted to cover the whole gamut of organisational decision making include:

- Taking 'vertical slices' of organisations (literally cross-slices from the front line to the executive board) to create time-limited project teams that have all the relevant expertise and authority to make recommendations on major operational or strategic issues.
- Rotating roles (i.e. chairs of committees, etc.) to ensure that people escape from the confines of one particular function and get the bigger picture and that positions of greater influence or knowledge are not monopolised to the disadvantage of others.
- The democratic election of managers.
- The investment of time and effort in collective planning, problem solving and review procedures in which everyone is expected to participate.
- Giving people greater spans of control through the creative use of IT systems which offer both data and menus of recommended options capable of interpretation by the layperson.
- Removing the mystique of professionalism by insisting on the use of plain language and by adopting forms of communication that everyone can readily understand.

Chapters 7 and 8 show how these organisational structures liberate people as individuals, teams and leaders.

Like all aspects of empowerment, these will probably feel like radical steps for most of today's organisations, and compared to the orthodoxy of the last hundred years they are. However, in many ways it has been the twentieth century which has been the aberration. It is the separation of the hand and brain which has been unnatural, not the reverse. Pre-industrial revolution forms of production did not recognise the separation. It is also significant that the reaction to the division of labour was the formation of the trade union movement by those otherwise disenfranchised. It seems that the human desire for self-determination will emerge in one form or another, however unpromising the circumstances.

WORKSHOP: REUNITING THE BRAIN AND THE HAND

- Examine your own or a friend's workplace. Are brains and hands separated? Is it an absolutely necessary division or is it more to do with history and maintaining the status and power of certain jobs?
- Using an organisation you know, take a product or service which is the end result to the customer. Trace backwards all the steps necessary from the beginning to its final form. What would be the implications of taking a business reengineering approach to its production?

Part I — Recommended Reading

Stewart Clegg (1975) *Power, Rule and Domination*, Routledge & Kegan Paul, London.

Michel Foucault (1979) *Discipline and Punishment*, Allen Lane, London.

J Gleick (1987) *Chaos*, Sphere, London.

Michael Hammer and James Champy (1993) *Reengineering the Corporation: A Manifesto for Business Revolution*, Nicholas Brealey, London.

Kinsley Lord, *Building the Empowered Organisation*, Kinsley Lord Ltd, 34 Old Queen Street, London SW1H 9HP.

Steven Lukas (1973) *Power: A Practical Approach*, Macmillan, London.

Ian Stewart (1989) *Does God Play Dice? The Mathematics of Chaos*, Blackwell, Oxford.

Max Weber (1947) *The Theory of Social and Economic Organization*, trans. Ann Henderson and Talcott Parsons, Oxford University Press, New York.

Part II
Liberating the organisation

4 Redistributing Control

Empowerment has two faces:
1. *Developing and enabling* each individual to unlock his or her abilities and full potential.
2. *Liberating* all staff by giving them more autonomy over their actions – in other words freedom to choose how and where they contribute.

In Part II we focus on the organisational consequences of empowerment. We consider the major policies, strategies and procedures which any corporate body must pursue in order to liberate itself. In Part III we consider the other side of the coin by describing the personal aspects of empowerment and empowering leadership.

We start at the heart of organisational empowerment with the issue of *control*. This is a harder and more indigestible word than some of its more palatable brethren such as 'involvement' and 'participation'. But the subject cannot be fudged. Empowerment does not, and cannot, happen without a real redistribution of control within an organisation so that all its members have a role in understanding, formulating and agreeing key decisions.

A liberating organisation redistributes control by:
- creating a common purpose
- creating liberating and supporting work structures
- distributing information, knowledge and decision making (and therefore power) by using the technical capacity of modern information technology (IT)
- encouraging constructive conflict

MANAGEMENT BY PURPOSE

The core purpose of the organisational process is control. By definition, an organisation exists to weld together the actions of its individual members to create a defined outcome. Hence individuals must be induced in various ways to play a part towards the organisation's goal.

In Chapter 2 we demonstrated that control through managerial hierarchies is both disempowering and cumbersome. 'Management by command' means that each rung in the hierarchy is subject to personal supervision from the one above. Exhaustive procedures and bulging rule books ensure that no one steps too far out of line. Elaborate pay gradations are used to reward those who observe the system, with the threat of dismissal reserved as the big stick for persistent 'troublemakers'.

These methods are out of tune with today's conditions and prevent empowerment. But is there an alternative? Doesn't the naked concept of control (of the group) as the *raison d'être* of all organisations sit uneasily with any idea of individual empowerment?

This is not necessarily the case. The cement that binds a liberated organisation is a shared understanding and acceptance of a *common purpose*. It is the *voluntary* agreement by individuals and teams to this common purpose, together with the strategies and tactics necessary for its achievement, which becomes the agent of (largely self) control. The task for an empowering organisation is to create this voluntary consensus.

Reconciling empowerment with control

> So much of what we call management consists of making it difficult for people to work.
>
> *Peter Drucker*

Creating the cement of a common purpose

So the key challenge for empowering leaders in the future is to find realistic ways of involving all staff in the formation of the common purpose. This is not to suggest that everyone gets a veto on the five-year strategic plan. But what it does mean is that everyone will have the chance to contribute their perspective on where the organisation is going and what they can contribute. All sections of an organisation must continuously create and recreate together the plans and culture which become the reference points that empowered staff will use in making the decisions that have been devolved to them.

The major purpose of an empowering organisation is to satisfy customer requirements. This external focus is of paramount importance to every organisation. All, including public sector bodies, exist only because they have customers, and if an organisation's objectives are not already aligned with the requirements of the customer, it is in serious trouble.

The common purpose translates into a number of practical strategies and approaches. It means:

- developing and sticking to agreed targets and decisions
- agreeing on cultural values
- maintaining a common purpose which demands a constant review and evaluation of success

The elements of common purpose are illustrated in the diagram below.

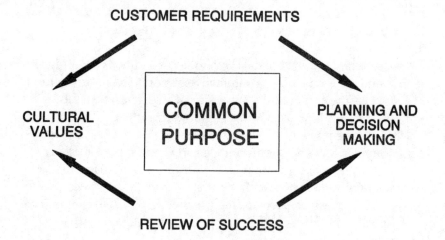

WORKSHOP: THE CONDITIONS FOR CREATING COMMON PURPOSE

Consider an organisation you know well. Write down the key aspects of its:

- customer requirements
- planning processes
- value systems
- processes of review

Do these work harmoniously together to create a sense of common purpose?

PLANNING AND DECISION MAKING

Planning is critical to empowerment because it is the process by which targets and goals are established. It is vital that everyone is involved. If people do not contribute when the plan is put together, gaining their voluntary agreement to its targets at a later stage is infinitely more difficult.

All plans should contain:

Crucial planning activities

- an acknowledgement of the strategic goals of the organisation and why the specific objectives will help to deliver these aims;
- some targets by which success can be measured with an estimate of any necessary resources;
- an analysis of the key threats and opportunities that the organisation (or subunit) faces and how to handle any contingencies which might arise;
- a clear definition for where the responsibilities and accountability for decisions rest.

There are three vital aspects to this view of planning:

1. Every part of an organisation should have a 'service' or 'business' plan with everyone involved in its formulation and able to understand not just what the targets are, but also why the group has set them. Staff will not be able to make suggestions for improvement unless they understand the full picture.

2. The plans cannot be set in isolation. There must be a process of both horizontal and vertical dialogue to ensure the coordination of all relevant activities. For example, strategy cannot be divorced from the realities of operations, nor can operational goals be agreed without an understanding of the strategies demanded by the future. A process of negotiation between the two is needed. It is a bottom-up, top-down and side-to-side process.

3. The process must be real. In effect the plans become a form of quasi-contract between the centre of an organisation and its subunits. Once a plan has been agreed the only measure of success is whether its targets are achieved. All too often, in our experience, this sort of process is adopted in an entirely symbolic manner. Once the paper exercise is over managers get back to the 'real business' of daily supervision, interference and making the decisions. Nothing could be more undermining to empowerment. (The following chapters describe many practical steps for turning plans and discussions into action.)

Whether acknowledged or not, all organisations operate on the basis of a distinctive culture and set of values. It is vital that these are made explicit – brought into the open and examined – not only because empowerment demands a particular set of core values, but also because a commonly accepted set of values is a vital ingredient in the creation of a common purpose. A recent report by Digital Corporation, prepared by John Hunter, states that 80 per cent of British companies put their values into words 'in order to capture the essence of the

CREATING COMMON CULTURAL VALUES

company – to tie people to a single goal and set of values'. This is essential since if you flatten an organisation 'people have nothing else to turn to when they make judgements.'

Companies vary greatly in the key values they state, from Ikea's business idea, which is 'to offer a wide variety of home furnishing of good design and function at prices so low that the majority of people can afford to buy them', to the declared intention of the Body Shop to make compassion, care, harmony and trust the foundation stone of its business. In general, however, recently more companies have been at pains to emphasise their ethical code – especially those with global operations.

The touchstone for judgement

Clearly and unambiguously stated, values become a crucial touchstone against which people can judge the appropriateness of their own behaviour and that of others.

This is a key feature of enabling management to let go. Decision making can safely be devolved in the knowledge that, while the precise decisions that will be taken at the local level cannot be predicted, there will be a common approach based on shared values.

Like the planning process, the values agreed by an organisation must be rooted in reality. Few things are more damaging than pious mission statements that hang on the wall as the doleful witness to thousands of daily infringements of their principles. Digital Corporation's report makes alarming reading on this point. More than 60 per cent of companies, it says, are not adhering to their value statements.

Once agreed, values must be turned into action. One company, Dun & Bradstreet, takes this so seriously that it trains every member of staff on the subject of company values for five days each year, and employees are rewarded for how well they live up to the values in practice.

Cultural values that empower

Each organisation will have its own unique culture and set of values reflecting its purpose and situation. However, there are some core values common to any organisation which believes in empowerment:

- Behaviour which must be oppressed is behaviour which is itself intrinsically oppressive. This must include any discrimination on the basis of gender, colour or disability, but it should also include less visible forms of oppressive personal behaviour, such as tactics aimed at destroying self-confidence in others. (Knowledge of the personal skills described in this book will help you to spot such tactics.) It is the duty of everyone to challenge such behaviour, not just its victims: a breach of this basic value makes a mockery of any positive attempts to generate a universal sense of trust.

- An empowering organisation goes out of its way to ensure that everyone's voice is heard, not only because participation in team planning and decision making calls for it, but because there must be equality of respect demonstrating that everyone's opinions, not just those of people who are most confident in group meetings, are valued and important.
- Finally there is a growing body of research which indicates that empowering organisations operate to a wider definition of what is *reasonable behaviour*. They seem to encourage people to express their emotions in a way that would be frowned upon in most strait-laced bureaucracies. Empowerment at work cannot be divorced from a wider acceptance of the individual as a whole person, consisting of emotions and attitudes as well as brains and hands.

> Questions, in a fundamental way, are inimical to authority. The question values change over tradition, doubt over reverence, fact over faith. The question responds to knowledge and creates new knowledge. The question initiates and reflects learning.
> *Shoshana Zuboff*

REVIEW OF SUCCESS

Explicit in the descriptions of both the empowering planning system and empowering values is that they offer statements of measurable precision. They can therefore:
- be continually evaluated for their appropriateness and for whether people are succeeding in meeting them;
- be kept under review if genuine life is to be breathed into 'management by purpose'.

When the planning system and values are 'for real' there will be nothing else on which performance *can* be judged. Indeed, they are fatally flawed if they are introduced merely as something 'nice to have' and so superimposed on existing supervisory patterns. There is no belt and braces in empowering. Unless it is approached as an intoxicating leap off the edge with no support, it will fail!

LIBERATING ORGANISATIONAL STRUCTURES

Structures define tasks and responsibilities and divide them between work roles. This clarifies relationships and provides agreed channels of communication. The structures exist *independently* of the person doing the work. Such clarity about roles leads to proper accountability and is therefore vital to empowerment.

> Structures of an organisation are 'the sum of the ways in which it divides its labour into distinct tasks and then achieves co-ordination amongst them.'
>
> *Henry Mintzberg*

However, structures are not an end in themselves; their importance rests on the way in which they enable an organisation to achieve its goal – to satisfy its customers.

Design flexible structures

Therefore structures must be *flexible* so they can evolve to meet new circumstances. They can be compared to the ever-changing patterns of clouds, rather than using the metaphor of 'mechanical' structures which occupies such a key place in the mindset of the traditional bureaucracy. Flexibility is also a natural consequence of empowerment. Self-motivated people voluntarily anticipating the future will be constantly networking in different groups as they react to new circumstances.

Empowerment cannot offer a blueprint for the structure of the liberated organisation. By definition, each one will be different from every other, and indeed different from how it was the day before. However, there are a number of guiding principles which will hold true for any liberated organisation. These are:

1. Organise round purposes and outputs, not functions.
2. Devolve management decision making to the front line.
3. Use time-limited project teams.
4. Design tight/loose structures.
5. Clarify roles.

ORGANISE AROUND PURPOSES AND OUTPUTS, NOT FUNCTIONS

In arriving at a definition of structures designed around purposes and outputs, the organisation needs to ask and answer two vital questions: 'What do we exist for?' and 'What key activities do we need to do outstandingly well?' Structures which fit the particular situation can then be designed around the answers.

Finance is not an activity which a motor car manufacturer necessarily wants to do well, although it is an important internal function. At the end of the day you cannot sell functions, but you do need to build cars well and be able to sell them.

Equally, public service organisations should focus on their key outputs: the direct services provided to the public not the departments representing professional disciplines. One local authority abolished the traditional central departments of finance, property, human resources and IT in order to create multidisciplinary teams focusing instead on service planning (uniting service priorities with the budgeting process), the review of service performance (combining the analysis of both service and financial management) and obtaining customer feedback.

The place of delivery of either a product or a service – the front line – must be given as much freedom and responsibility as possible. The creation of autonomous and self-directed working teams, described in Chapter 8, is the answer to the need for customising products (produced in units or small batches). Only in this way can both quality and flexibility be maintained.

DEVOLVE MANAGEMENT DECISION MAKING

In his latest book, *Liberation Management*, Tom Peters offers two examples of such new work structures which use project teams to develop production or design systems.

USE TIME-LIMITED PROJECT TEAMS

At the Union Pacific railroad in America, when prospective work comes in, a production brainstorm team quickly gathers. Headed by one board member, it typically contains three members, including a writer and a graphics person. Appropriate specialists are then added and the team organises itself – who joins, how they report, how the work gets done. Decision making, says the chief executive, is 'permanently flexible'.

'Business centres' are another type of project team which can function within a company or country, or widely across the world. They work as 'dialogue' or as 'shared minds', tied together by a 'soul of some sort'. The new information technology is able to link them in a more prosaic way, through electronic mail and other electronic devices, enabling them to become an international team if their purpose requires it. For example, Boeing in America and its partners in Japan jointly design aircraft through electronic links which enable both teams to remain in their own country.

Such a linked network can include world-wide company members, suppliers, distributors, customers, university think-tanks and accountants, all offering continually updated information, and unfettered by any hierarchical structure.

> It is an injustice, a grave evil and a disturbance of right order for a large and higher organisation to arrogate to itself functions which can be performed efficiently by smaller and lower bodies.
>
> *Extract on the principle of subsidiarity from the Papal Encyclical* Quadragesimo Anno, 1947

DESIGN TIGHT/LOOSE STRUCTURES

A tight/loose structure reconciles the need for both integrated central coordinating systems and the imperative of front-line freedom.

The 'tight' refers to a centre concerned with creating a cultural vision which defines the direction and objectives of the enterprise and sets standards for the product. In the late 1980s Harvey-Jones, the then chief executive of ICI, together with its board, set clearly stated objectives and then ensured they were fully understood right through that enormous empire. Matsushita, a large multinational Japanese company, has a tightly controlled six-monthly plan. Its companies are then expected to give it their total support.

The 'loose' is the devolution of day-to-day management control to operational units at the front line. In the fast-food chain McDonald's, a very small headquarters staff runs a global chain of shops with a common appeal and product, but with virtually no direct employees, since operations are contracted out.

> To think of ourselves and our position in the organisation, not as cogs in a gear, but as knowledge contributors . . . [to] blend the talents of different people around focused tasks.
>
> *Charles Savage*

CLARIFY ROLES

Successfully coordinating this tight/loose system to ensure the overall effective integration of decision making depends largely on analysis and detailed clarification of roles. These are not traditional descriptions focusing on the process of how a job is to be performed. Instead, they concentrate on the results or effects of each particular post.

CASE STUDY: NEW ROLE CLARITY

Traditionally, British county councils are huge and complex public bureaucracies, in which internal cohesion is almost entirely lacking, with semi-autonomous departments jealously guarding their position, their privileges and their power. One such council in southern England analysed and classified existing roles into the three distinct categories required by their situation as political bodies and service providers:

- strategists (assessing needs and allocating resources)
- commissioners (turning strategy into operational specifications for services)

continued

- providers (delivering the services)

This revealed that a great number of people were doing jobs incorporating all three elements, while big gaps in the council's activities were occurring in areas where there was a clear lack of responsibility (for example, many people who should have been strategists were bound up in the role of 'providers', making the day-to-day operational decisions).

Roles are now clarified, enabling this county council to be transformed into a flat and organic corporate body with only three levels of hierarchy, as opposed to the ten or more that was the norm before.

Once roles are clarified between the 'tight' centre and 'loose' day-to-day management (and within each of these categories) the groundwork for allocating accountability and responsibility has been done.

Accountability is a fundamental building block of any empowering organisation. It involves each individual, each work team, each department being absolutely clear about what is expected of them. It also means providing adequate resources – people, money, materials, time – and most critically the necessary authority. Hence the classic equation:

$$accountability + authority = responsibility$$

Accountability and responsibility

If leaders and work teams are to be held responsible, they need the authority to make production and staffing decisions, allocate and reward work, and view specialist functions as a service or absorb them into the line. If these conditions are not met, top management can only say 'do your best'. A canteen manageress once told one of us that she knew her chef was 'fiddling', but she did not dismiss him because she feared her bursar might not uphold her decision or, since she had no say in selecting a replacement, she might fare even worse with another chef!

Authority without accountability causes equally difficult problems. A common problem with many public services such as health care or social work is that decisions on action are made without reference to what resources are available. Access to these resources is then rationed through the use of waiting lists. Such a system places no discipline on the professional to exercise sound judgement on getting the best value for public money, and furthermore uses the customer's discomfort as the buttress against being responsible for awkward decisions. The case study of 'Care in the Community' described later in this chapter suggests one way of overcoming the problem.

Authority without accountability

Inappropriate structures

Inappropriate or rigid structures cause role clashes and destructive conflict which leads to damaged relationships and stress. A major finding from some famous research at Glacier Metals (Brown, 1960) found that inappropriate structures were the primary cause of deteriorations in relationships in spite of the best efforts of people to be socially skilled or 'nice' to each other.

Two main reasons make some structures inappropriate:

- They define roles and relationships which do not conform to the reality of daily operations.
- They can be unnecessarily constrictive. So, for example, structures which define boundaries too closely either prevent people from developing new relationships, or waste their time and energy as they search for ways of circumventing frontiers.

Thus structures should be like the skeletons of our bodies, supporting the living vibrant flesh and blood of organisations. They are *not* straitjackets. They should be designed around purposes and outputs rather than internal functions. The centre provides the vision and direction, while delegating accountability and authority to the operational units to run their own businesses with the flexible, changing systems needed to satisfy the ever-changing expectations of their 'customers'.

WORKSHOP: GUIDING PRINCIPLES OF STRUCTURES WHICH EMPOWER

- Which of the principles of structures which empower are present in your organisation, or in any other you know well?
- Estimate how much the introduction of one or more of these missing principles would liberate the people working in your organisation. Which functions would benefit most? R & D? Production? Marketing? Services?
- How much responsibility do you personally possess to make changes in the structure of your own area of accountability?
- Could your organisation make more use of combined teams to organise and run various practical projects?

INFORMATION SYSTEMS THAT DISTRIBUTE KNOWLEDGE

This section focuses on the implications of information systems and information technology (IT) because the flow of information in an organisation is a mirror of the flow of power. The individual, or team, which is getting top quality information quickly will be calling the shots, whatever the formal structure dictates.

> Don't automate, obliterate.
>
> *Michael Hammer*

But IT is even more central to empowerment than that. Modern IT has the technical capacity to distribute information, knowledge and decision-making tools to all staff within an organisation without a massive rise in costs. It is this that raises the potential for real empowerment and genuinely open participation in large-scale decision making.

Nevertheless IT, whether it automates a process or enables open communications to flourish, is a neutral tool. New technology does not inevitably produce empowerment as an automatic by-product: it can equally well support hierarchic control. The working assumptions of the people who design and commission an information system determine its use, as in any other aspect of management. It is not some 'value-free' technical issue in which there is only one right answer.

IT can empower or disempower

Indeed, because the new 'smart machines' are having such an impact on every aspect of the organisation of work, their design and the implicit work procedures they demand have become the new battleground for control. In her book *In the Age of the Smart Machine* (subtitled 'The Future of Work and Power'), Shoshana Zuboff describes four case studies of the implementation of major information technology projects. In every example the management tried to use IT to sediment existing information flows and management relationships. (We use one of these cases to illustrate counselling skills in Part IV.)

And in most instances, in the short run, the managers were able to achieve what they wanted. IT is a tool of great power and malleability. Design it to centralise all information and it will happily do so. If the commissioners of IT do not want front-line workers to have access to information, security passes can be built in or visual display units simply not installed. It is all a matter of choice.

However, for those who believe in empowerment there is a message of hope for the future since, as in other aspects of the empowerment debate, managers who cling to the old assumptions and the old ways of doing things are running out of time. As less hidebound organisations explore the immense new possibilities raised by new technology, they are finding that it opens up the prospect of quantum leaps in effectiveness.

IT that empowers

Organisations that use IT merely to reinforce current power relationships are likely to find they are unable to keep up with the competition. Zuboff locates the revolutionary potential of the smart machine in its capacity for 'informating' – a word she has coined to describe the way IT can produce information about processes or products over and above that generated as a mere by-product of mechanical automation.

This is new information that has never been available before. One of Zuboff's informants during the exhaustive research she undertook likened it to 'a vast crop and no one to harvest it'.

Need to empower the front line

Exploiting the vast potential of this 'crop' could lead to competitive advantage. But to do so, Zuboff argues, you must empower the front-line worker. This is for a number of reasons:

- To be fully exploited the information needs to be used when and where it is being produced. This demands what Zuboff calls 'intellective skills', and the need for 'critical judgement at the information interface' (so that this becomes the new front line for production, instead of the conveyor belt).
- What the use of information technology requires above all is a proactive approach to problem solving. Only empowered employees see problems before they become serious and have the capacity and commitment to suggest solutions, possibly straddling a whole range of systems.
- With the introduction of complex coordinating production systems comes the introduction of a new economic imperative. The costliest event possible is a breakdown in the system. The comparatively minor investment in a skilled workforce that can react quickly in such an emergency is a price that is likely to be repaid a thousandfold.

Even the most conservative of organisations will find it hard to resist the pressure to introduce IT that will in turn require empowerment. Competition will mean seeking to exploit information to the full, but the very act of exploiting information means posing questions about its impact on today and the future. And questions, as Zuboff points out, are fundamentally inimical to hierarchy. Like conflict, they are inherently subversive to a formal system based on status. In our view, therefore, IT can only be fully exploited within an environment of empowerment.

> Universal access [to information] provides a structure in which a redistribution of authority becomes possible.
>
> *Shoshana Zuboff*

Distributed information systems are ones that deliberately set out to give the widest possible access to the information they contain and process. They are sustained by an underlying paradox, since organisations which consider *decentralising* the availability of information (and therefore decision making) through the introduction of new IT, find that the same IT has an enormous capacity for instantly *centralising* information about the *results* of such decisions.

That is why IT, as in the cases described by Zuboff, is such a threat to traditional 'middle managers'. It removes the twin bastions of their authority. Not only does it allow front-line units to communicate directly, electronically transmitting results to headquarters as they occur for instant central analysis, but it also gives a front-line unit all the information it needs to do its own decision making. The traditional roles of middle managers as problem solvers and information givers or withholders is undermined at a stroke.

IT threatens traditional management

This is bound to make the introduction of new technology a highly contested arena of organisational politics. Since every IT system answers different problems within different environments, it is futile to try to formulate any general principles about the systems themselves. However, we can suggest some ways of implementing the process which should maximise the productive capacity of new IT and help to steer a route between the powerful interests which could be antagonised.

- The first and most important point flows from the discussion above. Information systems are 'political', so before any procedures can be designed a few strategic decisions need to be taken about what the *purpose* of the system is – who are its 'customers' and what do they need out of it?

Tips for implementing IT

- Our experience tells us that a new information system should provide an opportunity to introduce new working practices and relationships. Merely automating the current way of doing things almost certainly misses a big opportunity to empower and to maximise effectiveness.
- As a basic principle it is always better to start by building from the bottom up. Information should be collected at the point where it is used. If it is not useful at the point where it is generated, it is almost certainly not useful to the centre of an organisation. In general, headquarters should only require key summaries of statistics or indicators – they do not need to look at the whole shooting match.
- Involving front-line workers in the design of a system helps to ensure that:
  - things that would otherwise almost certainly have been overlooked are not;
  - the resulting system is more 'intuitive' to the real requirements of the job;
  - the system will be more user-friendly.

Apart from these immediate practical benefits, involvement also sends a powerful signal that you are serious about empowerment.

Clearly there is a close connection between power and information. In particular, information and decision making are almost inseparable. The empowering organisation must therefore exploit the full potential of IT.

WORKSHOP: IMPLEMENTING EMPOWERING IT

1. What information would you need direct access to in your workplace if you were to make the decisions that your boss normally makes? Would it be feasible to have such information collected and transmitted to a computer terminal at your workstation?
2. Would such a system enable you and your colleagues to become more effective and empowered? Would it contribute to your sense of ownership and commitment?

EMPOWERMENT THROUGH CONSTRUCTIVE CONFLICT

For most people, organisational conflict is a difficult subject. People behave as though it is to be avoided at almost any cost. It is seen as potentially explosive and therefore uncontrollable – something which hits at the very depths of the bureaucratic psyche.

Conflict seen as dysfunctional

Even if conflict is controlled it is seen as inherently 'dysfunctional', as distracting from the job at hand. But perhaps worst of all it is perceived to be subversive. Conflict between tiers of hierarchy cannot be tolerated. Its very existence undermines the legitimacy of the hierarchy, so the way most modern organisations have tried to avoid conflict is by pretending that it simply does not exist. (Check a few indexes of books written by modern organisational theorists and you will find that conflict barely rates a mention.)

And yet, whether we like it or not, conflict is all around us in our organisational lives. It is the dramatic and largely negative expressions of conflict which make the headlines – strikes, industrial sabotage and go-slows, for example. But usually it takes a more covert form – a passive inability to devise ways of improving a process, or deliberately misunderstanding the capacities of a new information system. Often it appears in an apparently irrelevant guise. A dispute over changes in shift patterns is in all probability about something more fundamental – how the change has been imposed, for example. When all else fails, bloody-mindedness is the traditional and legitimate weapon of the less powerful.

Thus despite its absence from the management textbooks, conflict has always existed and continues to exist. But it has been driven underground, or made part of the ritualistic manoeuvres of the industrial relations profession. This is not very satisfactory. Vast quantities of energy and ingenuity are expended on the elaborate but utterly unproductive game of arriving at a 'negotiated order' concerning the little things in life, as one way of expressing dissatisfaction at being excluded from the big issues. From this perspective it is the *suppression* of conflict which is dysfunctional, not the conflict itself.

Suppression of conflict is dysfunctional, not conflict itself

In fact, the practice of empowerment makes open conflict both inevitable and desirable. If you empower members of an organisation you are enabling them to voice their views, and it is highly unlikely that they will see eye-to-eye with their colleagues on all matters. But it is not just that empowerment makes conflict more likely. It is actually a fundamental aspect of the process of empowerment itself.

Conflict fundamental to empowerment

Conflict has three important beneficial consequences:

Beneficial consequences of conflict

- *Creation of consensus*. In the previous section we described how the empowered organisation must create a common sense of purpose in order to maintain control. Another word for this is consensus. To arrive at an eventual consensus all points of view must be aired and all disagreement or potential disagreement brought into the open before it is possible to develop a general approach acceptable to all. Consensus cannot be imposed.
- *Encouragement of continuous organisational learning*. Organisations, like biological organisms, survive changing circumstances through adapting and evolving. The seeds of this evolution are internal. Any entity should contain sufficient internal difference to enable it to evolve in any potential direction to suit changes in the external environment. Organisational learning is analogous to this process. A spirit of continual debate and challenge is more likely than any amount of passive obedience to stimulate the bright idea that allows the organisation to survive.
- *Stimulus to move forward*. Conflict and debate are also vital spurs to action. They harness the energy generated by the spirit of challenge and this becomes the motor force of the drive forward.

Approached in this positive and all-embracing manner, conflict becomes a recipe for continual organisational renewal.

CONSTRUCTIVE OR DESTRUCTIVE CONFLICT?

One of the difficulties of discussing conflict is that it is a many-headed beast. Taking a thoughtful and positive approach can turn many of the destructive 'heads' into a constructive dialogue; but equally there are some manifestations of conflict that can never be resolved to everyone's satisfaction.

In this section we discuss the more comfortable varieties of win/win situations where the resolution broadly satisfies all interested parties, and is a step forward. It is our belief and experience that, if handled adequately, the vast majority of intraorganisational conflict falls into this category.

Win/lose situations

One type of conflict at work does not fall into this category, however, since it is quite clearly of the win/lose type for its participants. This is where positions have become so entrenched that all common ground has disappeared. However well managed they are, this kind of conflict sometimes occurs in major change programmes aimed at clearing blockages to learning and development. The objective then is not to arrive at a constructive and generally acceptable solution: rather it is to win. (We discuss how to handle this type of conflict in Chapter 6).

One other kind of conflict this chapter does not address is the purely interpersonal tensions which arise between people everywhere, whether at work, within the family, or even in group leisure activities. Some comment we make and the personal skills we describe will certainly help, but the specific issue of purely interpersonal conflicts is beyond our scope. (A companion volume in this series, *Constructive Conflict Management* by John Crawley, provides a clear exposition of the main strategies that can be used to resolve such tensions.)

Contention fuels the 'engine of enquiry', and is a cheap and abundant fuel. Yet contention carries a stigma: managers are uncomfortable with it, and it is often misconstrued as a sign of organisational ill health. This need not be the case. Internal differences can widen the spectrum of organizational options by generating new points of view, by promoting disequilibrium and adaptation.

Richard Pascale

There are two broad and complementary approaches that organisations adopt in order to produce 'creative tension'. The first is to encourage a genuine culture of challenge and debate within a work unit. Where formal structures for team planning, decision making and review exist, there is ample room for conflict to emerge and be resolved within that unit.

However, this is not enough. Some of the world's best-managed companies, public institutions and charities are seeking to institutionalise conflict so that it permeates the operation of every aspect of the enterprise. For example, Honda has separated the company into three 'tribes' – manufacturing (including sales, marketing and administration), research and development, and Honda Engineering (responsible for all of Honda's proprietary manufacturing machinery). Each is a wholly owned but entirely separate company with its own president. Each is expected to stimulate the organisation from its particular perspective, and a good deal of creative tension results.

Institutionalised conflict

In his seminal book on conflict in organisations, *Managing on the Edge*, Richard Pascale describes the elements of constructive interorganisational conflict as:

Elements of constructive conflict

- fit
- split
- contend
- transcend

'Fit' is the basic organisational unity – the common values and goals that are Honda whichever section you belong to.

'Split' is the process for breaking down that unity into smaller subunits, the 'three tribes' in the case of Honda.

'Contend' describes the inevitable contradictions such divisions bring in their wake, the principal one being between the role of the centre and the role of the independent subsidiary.

As a result of this tension, Pascale argues that organisations are able to 'transcend' their present situation and move onto a new plane of complexity and vitality. This is analogous to the 'discontinuous' or second loop learning described in Chapter 5.

Constructive conflict is based on 'dialectical' thinking – the belief that the world is made up of opposites, and that truth and progress spring from the resolution of these contradictions. The new resolution then goes on to precipitate other contradictions and so on (which makes history look more like a spiral than a continuous straight line). This method of reasoning has a long tradition, stretching from the ancient Greeks to Hegel and Marx.

Progress springs from the resolution of opposites

As we saw in Chapter 3, modern systems theory also sees the world as a result of the continual flux of interconnected systems, some of which are in harmony with each other and some of which are in perpetual opposition. Bringing these systems into the open enables a judgement to be made about which to align and which to set up in opposition, in order to maintain a dynamic towards progress and effectiveness.

I like Bartók and Stravinsky. It's a discordant sound – and there are discordant sounds inside a company. As president, you must orchestrate the discordant sounds into a kind of harmony. But you never want too much harmony. One must cultivate a taste for finding harmony within discord, or you will drift away from the forces that keep a company alive.

Fujisawa, Honda's co-founder (quoted in Pascale, 1991)

CASE STUDY: CARE IN THE COMMUNITY

The reorganisation of the British social services into 'purchasers' (of social care) and providers under the provisions of the policy of 'Care in the Community' is an interesting example. Once monolithic entities, which both diagnosed need and provided the appropriate form of social care, Social Services Departments have now been split into two contending streams of activity, the *purchasers* and the *providers* of care.

These are now therefore to some extent in opposition, since the purchaser is primarily concerned with the needs of the individual client and no longer has any vested interest in the particular form of care which is provided by the local authority (because they are responsible for the care budget as well as care decisions they also have overall responsibility for the best use of the budget). If the local providers do not supply the appropriate service, in principle the purchasers have a budget enabling them to look further afield.

Where once there was only one system, there are now two. Where there was only 'fit' there is now 'split' and 'contend'. Continual structural opposition and conflict have been introduced as a new dynamic in the system, which should be to the ultimate benefit of the users of the service.

The effective resolution of conflict

The reason that conflict is mainly perceived as destructive is that people and organisations are unprepared for it. The key to the successful management of conflict is to expect and anticipate it as a normal part of the work experience. Argument loses much of its terror within a formal structure designed for the express purpose of its exploration and resolution.

There are a number of ways to ensure that conflict is safely and constructively handled:

- Conflict should be within the confines of a broad agreement on purpose, or at least values. If it is not, it is likely to become straight win/lose struggle.
- The parties to conflict should be broadly equal in strength, or at least one should not be dependent on the other, so that the dispute cannot be solved by *force majeure*.
- The terms of conflict should be such that protagonists have a way out while saving face. This is merely a sensible extension of standard negotiating strategy.
- Formal procedures for discussing (and creating) disagreement also help. These can include special 'no holds barred' sessions, perhaps even facilitated by an external mediator. (For an example of a formal structure see the description of *waigaya* at Toyota, in Chapter 6.)
- Managers and staff should be trained in debating and negotiating skills (Chapter 11). This helps to ensure that issues are brought into the open and depersonalised.

However, the most important element of ensuring that conflict is constructive, helping organisations to rise to a new level of understanding, is an atmosphere of *trust*. In this book we emphasise that without it almost every aspect of empowerment is doomed, but most especially the constructive use of conflict. With trust, almost any argument can be worked through and sorted out.

Truth springs from an argument amongst friends.

David Hume, philosopher

WORKSHOP: CONFLICT IN ORGANISATIONS

- Think of two examples of conflict, one constructive and the other destructive. What were the elements of the constructive conflict which led to a good result? Could the same elements have been applied to the destructive conflict in order to have turned that into a win/win exercise?
- Does your organisation encourage constructive conflict – if so, what policies and procedures support this approach?
- How would you handle a win/lose situation?

5 Empowerment and Organisational Learning

We have argued that the economic imperative which is driving the application of empowerment in the commercial world is the need to respond to rapid change. So in this chapter we show how empowerment is essential to creating the 'learning organisation' which:

- reacts instantaneously to changing circumstances
- endeavours constantly to improve on past performance

In linking empowerment and organisational learning we will be drawing on the principles and practices we have described in the previous chapters (and in particular the redistribution of control described in Chapter 4) to show how they apply to the management of change.

First we must be clear about what is to be achieved. Nowadays we are constantly being told to 'love change', but what does this really mean? Some change is for the worse, some for the better; some change is inevitable, some can be influenced. Most frustratingly, some change appears to take place in orderly and predictable steps, only to be overtaken by a cataclysm which rearranges all previous assumptions.

Do you really love change?

Are we supposed to love this rag-bag with equal intensity, or are we allowed some discretion in bestowing our affection? In other words, do you, as an empowering leader, believe you can influence the future – or are you resigned to the view that we are merely reacting to the inevitable unfolding of events which have their origin way beyond our ken?

The age-old debate about determinism (the theory that the pattern of history is preordained before it has happened – ironically, a view shared by both traditional Christians and Marxists) is no longer academic when the flow of change becomes today's torrent. Indeed, it makes the issue of how human agency can influence events more central than ever.

An empowered perspective recognises that there are some broad trends that can only be challenged with the same degree of success that King Canute experienced in ordering back the tide. However, there is still considerable scope for using ingenuity to influence events.

The trick is to find the 'levers' of change so that individual effort is magnified to have most impact. This is what we mean by *empowered action*: it is achieved through the conscious use of strategic leverage.

GAINING LEVERAGE OVER CHANGE

People are mentally and organisationally geared to slow, continuous, orderly change. We expect, for example, that the budget for next year will be the same as that for this year, give or take a few per cent.

Indeed, organisations expend vast effort in creating the illusion of order in the face of uncertainty. For example, the spires of mediaeval cathedrals were not only reminding the faithful to cast their minds towards heaven, they were also conveying a more temporal certainty. The institution that built them would outlast mason, bishop or supplicant. Traditional organisations tend to be built like those cathedrals. Huge edifices of procedures, structures and systems are created, not just because the goals of the organisation require them, but also to fulfil some deep psychological need for the imposition of certainty on a fundamentally unreliable world.

And, for a while, it has worked. Although the twentieth century has seen more change than the previous five centuries combined, in the business world it still used to seem that change could be anticipated and planned. In the jargon of the textbooks, change was 'incremental'. Production would increase by an average amount each year, as would the potential market. Such was the confidence in predicting the future that a new profession of fortune-telling was spawned. The *raison d'être* of corporate planning and operational research was the laborious tabulation of all variables into models of future conditions.

These comfortable assumptions about the nature of change no longer hold true. To warn of this danger, Charles Handy in *The Age of Unreason* tells the parable of the boiled frog. Placed in cold water which is then gently heated a frog will make no attempt to escape, even when the temperature reaches unsupportable levels. It remains comfortable with the continuous change past the point where circumstances call for a distinctly discontinuous leap to avoid being boiled alive.

Change is increasingly 'discontinuous'

In many organisations today continuous change has reached such a crescendo in so many areas that its cumulative effect has become 'discontinuous' – it is not simply more of the same but is creating whole new orders of activity. As we saw in Chapter 1, the regular improvement in the processing power of the computer is one example. It has been a story of gradual incremental improvement, and yet the total impact has been to unlock dramatic new applications for information technology in a comparatively short period of time.

> Change is not what it used to be.
>
> Charles Handy, The Age of Unreason

REVOLUTIONARY AND EVOLUTIONARY CHANGE

Other discontinuous or revolutionary change seems to come out of the blue, perhaps as the result of some dramatic technological breakthrough or major social upheaval. In fact, such developments often result from *foreseeable* underlying tensions and forces. The pressures trapped within webs of conflicting forces become so intense that they erupt into open opposition. This often resolves itself into an entirely new situation in which none of the revolutionary forces are recognisable. The way traditional ideas about how to organise for mass production are being challenged by quality management techniques is a case in point.

The very success of mass production has led to a situation where the only possible way to gain competitive advantage is to think radically about how to give the consumer the two things that would never be possible within a big corporate bureaucracy using mass production techniques – a real choice from among different specifications, and a step-jump in quality.

Today both types are the norm. Modern organisations have to liberate themselves to cope with both evolutionary and revolutionary change. This means an entirely new way of thinking about organisation. The cathedral-like edifices of yesteryear will no longer suffice. They were built for stability within a quiescent world. In a world which is no longer so quiescent, the successful organisation is one that continually changes its architecture to adapt to the different seasons, as well as to withstand the occasional earthquake.

> Change must become the norm, not cause for alarm. The bottom line, if you cannot point to something specific that is being done differently from the way it was done when you came to work this morning, you have not lived, for all intents and purposes – you surely have not earned your pay cheque by any stretch of the imagination.
>
> Tom Peters, *Thriving on Chaos*

So, unlike the frog, organisations must realise that continuous and discontinuous change cannot be contemplated in isolation from each other. The cumulative effect of evolutionary change is a discontinuous break; the effect of a revolutionary change is to create a new set of basic assumptions which, stage by stage, must be explored and developed.

Coping with change on this scale means everyone being enabled and empowered to react. The next section examines the scope we all possess for anticipating and controlling the process of change.

Determinists claim that we are little more than ticket-holders at the matinée of a play whose dénouement has already been revealed in the programme notes. If they are right, the scope for influencing the future is limited. Equally, if there is no pattern to the unfolding of events, we are all reduced to the armchair observation of a random and meaningless charade.

Systematic patterns of change

Empowering leaders attempting to steer a course which ensures the survival and success of their operations into the future can, and must, ignore both counsels of despair.

Over the last few decades, as the industrial world has seemed to be spiralling into more and more uncontrollable change, a considerable amount of intellectual vigour has been devoted to describing the patterns that underlie events. Understanding these patterns will enable a balance to be established between trends which are inevitable and developments which can be guided by human agency.

Argyris and Schon suggested the first 'systematic' model of change based on the insights of cybernetics. They claimed that most *physical* phenomena could be explained by the application of two mechanisms

Positive and negative feedback

– positive and negative feedback. Negative feedback acts to arrest a system (as, for example, a thermostat might turn off a heating system once it attained a certain temperature). Positive feedback has the opposite effect, accelerating a development by reinforcing the initial conditions – the same way that an amplifier works.

When this model is used as a diagnostic and predictive tool in the *organisational* field, many thinkers have discovered that both nature and society abound with a number of recurring patterns or 'archetypes', which can be broadly described in terms of positive and negative feedback.

The 'limits to growth' archetype

For example, most people will have (unknowingly) encountered the 'limits to growth' archetype. This describes a reinforcing process (positive feedback) which is set in motion to achieve a desired objective; however, its very success inadvertently creates secondary effects which serve to slow down that success (the negative or 'balancing' feedback).

Many of the new high-tech companies have followed this pattern. Initial growth comes from a dynamic R & D section which naturally flourishes with its success, engaging increasing numbers of engineers and research staff. But this in turn greatly increases the management burden on the senior engineers, whose attention is taken away from the technical tasks. Delays in development start to occur as this 'limits to growth' balancing dynamic comes into play. This can be shown graphically as two interlinked cycles of activity making up the complete system. The first is the reinforcing cycle which is linked at the appropriate point with the balancing cycle (illustrated in the diagram below, adapted from Senge).

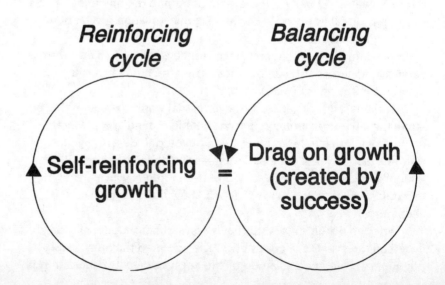

Reinforcing cycle   Balancing cycle

Self-reinforcing growth = Drag on growth (created by success)

Interestingly, many of the early, unsuccessful attempts at forming quality circles (described in Chapter 8) follow this pattern. There was often some early success which created front-line enthusiasm and demands for greater communication and collaborative problem solving. This very success posed a threat to senior management, who were unprepared to take the step of dismantling traditional power relations. Their half-hearted participation in quality circles became the balancing mechanism which slowed down the latter's success.

Thinking in this way about organisations as dynamic systems provides a powerful tool for maximising the impact of a change programme. Most people have probably experienced change campaigns which have gone off the rails. The impression which remains is of a morass of conflicting personalities, confused communication and well-intentioned misunderstanding; the only regular pattern is that no matter how hard you try and how many people you influence you always end up at the original position or worse. Nothing changes except the general level of stress.

Standing back from the fray and trying to perceive these events as the interplay of reinforcing and balancing forces helps people to maintain a rational perspective, and is also useful in deciding what to do. Having analysed the relevant systems, the choice is simple: either enhance a reinforcing mechanism or remove a balancing pressure. Either way disturbs the equilibrium of the system and exerts 'leverage' to move it in a different direction.

But this is *focused* leverage. It goes with the grain of the dynamic system it is trying to change. It is effective precisely because it does not try to change things on all fronts; instead, it looks for the key catalysts that make the system work for you. It gives strategic leverage because the system is now weighing in on one side of the fulcrum.

Strategic leverage

> The essence of mastering systems thinking as a management discipline lies in seeing patterns where others see only events and forces to react to.
>
> *Peter Senge*

None of this is particularly difficult or remarkable. Great leaders have always intuitively understood how to ride the tide of events, seizing and manipulating dominant forces with which they could achieve their ends. But systematising common sense in this way delivers this understanding into the arms of everyone. We can all share in the tactics and skill of empowering leadership. We can all plan effectively in order to make a difference.

CASE STUDY: LEVERAGE

A review team within a major public body was asked to look at the central support services (finance, property, personnel, legal, IT), to assess whether their organisation and size were still appropriate after three years of devolved management.

What became immediately obvious was that tinkering round with precise recommendations would be futile. The whole system was wrong. The central functions were ruled by the most powerful people in the organisation. These people were immune to many of the pressures felt by those actually delivering a service direct to the public, and in fact wielded a dominant influence on those services through the unquestioned imposition of their 'professional' judgement. The cart was not only before the horse, it was pulling it as well.

The effective answer, the one that exploited strategic leverage, was to introduce an entirely new dynamic into the situation. The budget for each professional function was disaggregated and given out to the departments that provided a direct public service, along with the freedom to buy services in future from wherever they wanted, so long as they observed some basic corporate standards.

This both reversed the power relationship and provided an almost automatic guarantee that expenditure on support services was at a level appropriate to the organisation as a whole. The introduction of a small amount of increased bureaucracy in the form of an internal customer/contractor relationship was a small price to pay for liberating the organisation by abolishing a number of entire hierarchies and removing blockages to further change.

This case study displays many of the aspects of strategic leverage worth looking for as you consider the most effective actions towards achieving your particular goal. Such action will often:

- introduce new relationships and new dynamics
- work on removing blockages rather than reinforcing positive forces
- identify key forces that reverberate and catalyse action within a number of systems

Strategic leverage can be learnt

Later in this chapter we suggest practical steps you can take to find such points of intervention and change. This is an art, not a science, but it is an art that can be learnt.

The next part of this chapter deals with how to turn your organisation into a *learning organisation* equipped to deal with continuous and discontinuous change. In a learning organisation everyone must be physically and mentally equipped to respond to change and contribute to effective action.

WORKSHOP: DISCOVERING AND USING STRATEGIC LEVERAGE

1. Analyse any change situation in which you are involved. Identify the positive reinforcing mechanisms and the balancing negative ones. What underlying influences do you discern?
2. What are the key leverage points that would enable you to influence the outcome? Would it be more effective to help with a positive influence or (often more productively) to remove an obstacle?

EMPOWERMENT AND THE LEARNING ORGANISATION

In the first section of this chapter we established that change was inevitable, but that managers and staff could make interventions at key points of strategic leverage in order to influence the direction of the change. In this section we consider how to decide which direction is best: in other words, how organisations learn that they must improve, and how they should go about it.

THE LEARNING ORGANISATION

Every now and again a phrase emerges from the organisational gurus which captures the spirit of a whole range of contemporary developments. One example is the 'learning organisation'. It is only through a process of learning that an organisation will cope with the unprecedented amount and level of change with which we are now faced.

The 'learning organisation' must be a liberating and empowering organisation. It requires all its members always to be looking to do things better, and to do better things. It continually poses the deceptively simple question, 'How well are we doing and what do we need to do to improve?' – and responds to the tough answers that come back. No aspect of the organisation is exempt from this sort of scrutiny: goals, systems, staff development, and so on should all be in a constant process of evolution to fit new circumstances and remain in harmony with each other.

This is an utterly whole-hearted approach to the improvement of performance. It can be distinguished from the traditional approach to performance review in a number of ways:

- It is systematic and comprehensive. Work on improvement does not just occur when a fault becomes obvious. The learning organisation *regularly* examines all aspects of its workings whether they appear to be in good shape or not – everything can always be improved.
- It is open and undiscriminating. It understands that lessons can and should be learnt from anywhere (competitors, customers, front-line staff, technological change, etc.)
- It recognises that, given the sheer wealth of potential improvement, it is counterproductive and futile to try to centralise all information. It must decentralise the responsibility for improvement to self-managing units in order to avoid terminal bureaucratic overload.
- It acknowledges that learning is continuous. The learning organisation has *liberated* itself to respond to change immediately; it does not have to wait for the next corporate plan before it reorientates its activities.

The learning organisation has embraced the search for continuous improvement which is the hallmark of Total Quality Management. It is as applicable to the public and voluntary sectors as to the world of business.

> The first step is for management to remove the barriers that rob the hourly paid worker of his right to do a good job.
>
> W *Edwards Deming*

Organisational learning is central to the theme of this book. It is inextricably interlinked with the empowerment of both an organisation and the people within it because:

- Staff from all areas and levels of an organisation need to feel empowered to speak their mind on any aspects of the organisation's workings if the entire reservoir of knowledge and experience is to be tapped.
- It is only within the *culture* of empowerment, described in Chapter 2, that people have the confidence and humility to accept voluntarily the possibility of constant improvement.
- Unless staff are clear about the organisation's goals and the purpose of their individual contribution, they will not be in a position to offer useful proposals for development.
- To learn, you must want to improve your performance and that of those around you. You must feel the commitment that only comes

from a sense of responsibility for the quality of what you, as an individual or team, produce.

Empowered people learn better, and people who learn better become more empowered. This is a virtuous circle. It is difficult to get going, but once in motion it generates a momentum all of its own.

EMPOWERED LEARNING

We have discussed the need for learning to be continuous, organised and comprehensive. It must be pursued in a conscious and systematic manner. It also combines understanding with action *in equal measure*.

Traditionally, understanding and action have either been seen as opposites – those with understanding (management) delegating action to the uncomprehending multitude (workers) – or the need for understanding has been underestimated, with management preferring to rush into action instead.

From this perspective, the elements of empowered learning are the same as those of empowered action. This approach to empowered learning:

Everyone must be able to turn understanding into action

- insists that *understanding* is a crucial precondition for learning, which comprises two separate elements – the 'big picture', and how individual goals and purposes contribute to it;
- turns analysis into action;
- specifically considers the issue of power. It evaluates its strengths and weaknesses and fills in gaps. It looks for allies, both metaphoric and real.

However, no action can be final. A particular answer may look successful but it will inevitably create repercussions of its own which will inexorably lead to yet another cycle of review and action. The trick is to understand and anticipate the repercussions (and the repercussions of the repercussions and so forth – the spiral is ever unfolding as the organisation continues to learn).

In the first part of this chapter we discussed the difference between continuous and discontinuous change. Although linked, these represent very different challenges to an organisation trying to anticipate the future.

Double loop learning

Coping with continuous change means liberating the knowledge and initiative of every member of staff to improve what is currently being done. Preparing for discontinuous change means completely liberating a few minds of all existing assumptions. These are two separate processes. Of course, one cannot be done in isolation from the other, but neither can they be fused.

The empowering organisation must apply the principles of learning to both processes, and it must make the link between them. Such

Each loop poses different questions

organisations apply another insight from the field of systems theory and cybernetics. This is known as 'double loop' learning. The loops mirror the distinction between discontinuous and continuous change, but they do so from the point of view of an organisation's (or an individual's) ability to cope with external challenges. In effect, each loop poses a different set of questions for an organisation to answer. The following diagram (adapted from Garratt) gives an illustration of how the roles should work:

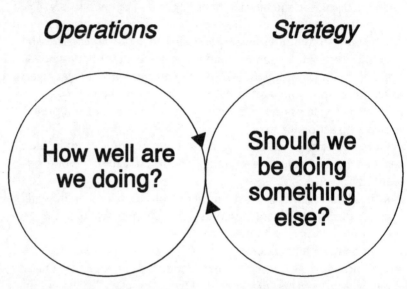

The first loop asks: How well are we doing and how can we improve our performance? This loop poses questions concerning current activity. It forces the systematic evaluation of the quality of what is achieved and of the efficiency and cost of current methods. It looks for better and cheaper ways of achieving broadly the same goals.

The second loop asks: Should we be doing something entirely different? This loop institutionalises a wider, more radical and perhaps creative analysis. Pursuing it takes many forms, involving abstract thought on future possibilities and forcing vigilance concerning the anticipation of external change. Second loop learning also means monitoring the continuous change enacted in response to first loop learning so that you can recognise when the cumulative effect of such evolution is bringing about a revolution.

The most efficient and effective route to bold change is the participation of everyone, every day, in incremental change.

Tom Peters, *Thriving on Chaos*

Bob Garratt describes first loop learning as essentially the preserve of the operational parts of the organisation. The mechanisms and information flows which ensure that these questions are asked and answered should be built into the productive processes of services or goods, since it is the front-line people who have the knowledge and experience to suggest valuable improvements.

Allocating responsibility for learning

> Extensive research has documented that when there is a problem, 80% of the time the core issues will reside in the system. Because the employees most intimately involved with the system are best able to spot its flaws, they need to be empowered to initiate fixes.
> Richard Pascale (*discussing the approach to empowerment and learning at Honda*)

By the same token, Garratt allocates responsibility for second loop learning to a small band of strategists (either part of or advising the main board, or public sector equivalent). These people must be freed from operational concerns so that they may turn a pure gaze on the future, untrammelled by current assumptions.

This is useful, but it is not the whole story. To locate sole responsibility in this way runs the risk of sedimenting one view when a range of perspectives might be of value and, although the two loops may look neat and self-contained when on the analyst's notepad, a fuzzier division between first and second loop learning may occur in reality. Thus without losing Garratt's clarity of role definition, the two loops must be linked in a way that allows each to feed off, and challenge, the other by deliberately creating a monitoring and challenging role somewhere else in the organisation. This ensures that no one loses sight of the big picture and also builds some healthy tension between the different learning loops.

Add a monitoring role

The diagram below illustrates these relationships:

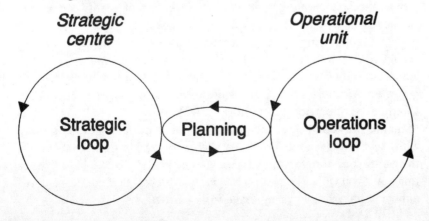

These relationships should be based on the principles of empowerment. Criticism and challenge should be constructive and delivered in a way that encourages, not demoralises. Yet not to have this tension would equally undermine attempts at empowerment, since strategists would not be linked to the practical problems of implementing dramatic change, nor would they benefit from the ideas of front-line workers who could well understand that the time has arrived to move on to something completely different.

EMPOWERING CONTINUOUS LEARNING

In this section, we suggest some ways in which the relationships between the two types of continuous learning can be achieved in any empowered organisation. The following guidelines outline some of the practical procedures:

Build learning into the actual work process (or 'you are responsible for what you do').   Traditional approaches to learning make it a separate stage of the work process, usually in the form of a quality inspection. This removes the responsibility from the workers themselves and means footing the bill for inspectors. As we have seen in earlier chapters, making staff responsible for the work they do is both more effective and more empowering.

Empower learning through role clarity.   To a traditional bureaucracy, placing responsibility for learning at the point where a process occurs feels like a terrible risk. After all, doing other people's learning for them was virtually the *raison d'être* of the traditional line of management. But, as we saw in Chapter 4, absolute clarity over roles and accountabilities replaces line management control and gives people the confidence to accept responsibility for themselves.

Measure (everything important).   Everything can be measured in one way or another. Even the most subjective aspects of quality can always be measured by customer surveys. In the absence of line management, having a 'feel' for what is going on necessitates more objective indicators of performance. Furthermore, by measuring something you start to consider the relationships within which it operates. Without such an understanding it is impossible to know whether or not proposals for improvement are valid.

Measure the right thing.   Deciding what is important should be done with great care. Pick the indicators of *key variables* and three-quarters of the battle for improvement is already over. Pick indicators of the wrong thing and you will never get off the starting blocks, or if you do you will almost certainly be heading in the wrong direction.

Two-way strategic/operational communication and planning.   In Chapter 2 we emphasised the need for strategists to agree plans with the operational front line. To take account of changes taking place there demands a radically different approach to planning and communication. Instead of a strategic corporate plan being handed down to subsidiary units, a 'bottom-up' business planning process incorporated within a strategic framework creates a dialogue and a consensus between the two loops of operations and strategy.

Nurture the organisational memory.   Just as people preserve what they learn in the form of memory (which becomes the foundation of further learning), so organisations have to institutionalise their basic understanding of what they are about and the best ways of doing things. This sort of knowledge is retained in a large number of diverse ways. Some examples are:

- the (much reduced) rule book
- processes and procedures
- management information systems
- training
- knowledge and experience of staff

The knowledge contained in the organisational memory must, however, be readily accessible to everyone. Thus all the structures and systems for continuous learning will need the sinews of *effective lines of communication* to hold them together as lines of management are removed.

Make data accessible

Communication is only as good as what is received, not what is sent. Voluminous and complex discussion documents are no use to a practically minded operations coordinator. It is up to the person trying to spread information to put it in a form that will be both interesting and understandable to the recipient.

> We're finding that people really love to know [what they cost and how much profit they generate]. A few years ago we had mechanisms showing how many parcels people were handling. And there was an uproar, people saying 'you can't measure our performance', etcetera. Now, when there aren't any, people want them. So the culture [after an empowerment programme] has become more positive in that respect.
>
> Pat Hedges, *head of internal communications and training at* Parcel Force
> (*in Jackson*, 1991)

Equally, much greater emphasis is needed on the presentation and active communication of policy and information to all staff, since operational units taking decisions must be aware of the goals and policies of the organisation. This is what we meant by the management by purpose described in Chapter 2. Previously it was only necessary for senior executives to understand the goals and policies, since they were the only ones who made meaningful decisions.

To achieve accessibility of this nature, the necessary supporting information needs first to be collected, stored and circulated effectively.

Collecting the data

In organisations not conscious of the need to learn, information is kept haphazardly. In contrast, the learning organisation systematically collects and records information on every important aspect of its workings. This is partly a question of extending the range of data recorded for many separate operations, but it is equally important to capture knowledge that formerly would only have been kept inside individual heads. This is a logical corollary of delegating responsibilities which meet acceptable standards to independent units.

The developments in information technology described in Chapter 4 come into their own here. 'Expert systems', for example, are a form of mechanised decision tree, and can model the complicated weighting and prioritisation that professionals accord to all the variables in their field of expertise and refine them in the light of experience.

Storing and circulating data

Thus to make use of these and other less complicated electronic systems, everyone needs ready access to the organisation's memory store. This, too, is a key practical issue for the learning organisation – how can this vast and potentially confusing wealth of information be stored, circulated and quickly accessed by the whole organisation? Two practical points are emerging, as different solutions are tried:

1. The emphasis on encouraging lateral thinking and the search for synergies (the bringing together of different elements which create more than the sum of their parts) mean that modern computerised systems are designed around the principle of open access and network cooperation. Anyone can access the main databases and different systems are expected to 'talk' to each other.
2. IT enables traditional information systems to be redesigned so that operational information 'trickles up', not cascades down. The priority of empowering systems is to help someone to do something better for the customer. So systems should be designed around the needs of the operational unit. There is nothing a headquarters needs to know about processes that is not also properly required by a well-managed devolved unit.

WORKSHOP: ORGANISATIONAL LEARNING

1. For an organisation you know well, try to identify all the ways in which it institutionally learns to do things better. How many of the aspects of continuous learning we have described does it regularly put into practice?
2. What practical procedures does it follow to ensure learning is built into the work processes and communication systems?
3. How is this learning passed on when key people leave?

CASE STUDY: BLOCKAGES TO LEARNING

There are so many obstacles in the way of learning that virtually every writer in this field has developed his or her checklist of those which fit particular themes and preoccupations. However, there is a remarkable convergence of views among four of the most stimulating writers.

The four corrigible handicaps
1. The idealisation of past experience.
2. The charismatic influence of other successful managers.
3. The impulsion to instant activity.
4. The belittlement of subordinates.

Reg Revans, *The Origins and Growth of Action Learning*

Blocks to change
1. The 'they' syndrome.
   Encourage the idea that it can be left to someone else.
2. Futility/humility.
   Shatter someone's self-confidence.
3. The theft of purposes.
   Disallow other people's goals and do not negotiate around your own.
4. The missing forgiveness.
   Record every mistake, and use them to threaten.

Charles Handy, *The Age of Unreason*

Ten rules for stifling initiative
1. Regard any new idea from below with suspicion – because it's new, and because it's from below.

continued

2. Insist that people who need your approval to act first go through several other levels of management to get their signatures.

3. Ask departments or individuals to challenge and criticise each other's proposals. (That saves you the job of deciding: you just pick the survivor.)

4. Express your criticism freely, and withhold your praise. (That keeps people on their toes.) Let them know they can be fired at any time.

5. Treat identification of problems as signs of failure, to discourage people from letting you know when something in their area isn't working.

6. Control everything carefully. Make sure that people count everything that can be counted, frequently.

7. Make decisions to reorganise or change policies in secret, and spring them on people unexpectedly. (That also keeps people on their toes.)

8. Make sure that requests for information are fully justified, and that it is not given out to managers freely. (You don't want data to fall into the wrong hands.)

9. Assign to lower-level managers, in the name of delegation and participation, responsibility for figuring out how to cut back, lay off, move people around, or otherwise implement threatening decisions you have made. And get them to do it quickly.

10. And above all, never forget that you, the higher-ups, already know everything important about this business.

> Rosabeth Moss Kanter, *When Giants Learn to Dance*

Does your organisation have a learning disability?

1. I am my position.
   (People are defined, or define themselves, by their role not by their abilities.)

2. The enemy is out there.
   (Always find someone else to blame.)

3. The illusion of taking charge.
   (Unthought-out action purely for the sake of appearing to be doing something active.)

4. The fixation on events.
   (Only focus on the immediate not on the longer term.)

continued

5. The parable of the boiled frog. (Only react to sudden threats not to a gradual deterioration.)
6. The delusion of learning from experience. (The real consequences of actions are too distant to be understood.)
7. The myth of the management team. (Skilled incompetence at collective enquiry.)

Peter Senge, *The Fifth Discipline*

The text in the brackets is the authors' summary of the original description by Peter Senge.

WORKSHOP: UNBLOCKING OBSTACLES TO LEARNING

1. Identify the common themes in the above case study.
2. Consider the blocks at work in your own organisation or one you know well.
3. Which blockages would still exist if the principles of empowerment were properly applied?

This workshop should help you to clarify your thinking about possible unblocking strategies. Usually the best approach is just to get started. That is the emphasis of the next chapter, where we look at some of the practical steps that can be taken to kickstart the process of transforming and liberating organisations.

Unblocking the blockages

6 Making it Happen

In this chapter we move from the theory of empowering the liberated organisation to the practical steps that need to be taken in order to get there. Organisational transformation is the name we have given to the process of changing from a hierarchic to a liberated organisation. We regard this as a special form of the management of change. It is a one-off event distinguished by the intensity of its challenge to the prevailing power relations.

The reason we describe transformation as a 'one-off' change project is that we dislike the connotations of the phrase 'management of change'. It is not a way of thinking that should be encouraged after transformation has taken place. Once organisational liberation has been achieved, future change will not need to be catalysed and 'managed' as though it were something unusual. Instead, the task will be that of facilitating and coordinating the endless stream of ideas and initiatives coming from all quarters. In the liberated organisation change is the norm.

Change as the norm

This is a different emphasis to that apparent in much of the current literature. The textbooks still speak of organisational change in a way which smacks of the old assumptions. It is seen as a specific answer for a particular problem; something for the manager to diagnose, nurse and ultimately cure, with the patient then returned to 'normal' stable life.

But if change is really accepted as the norm we need to reverse these assumptions. To the manager in a learning organisation it will be stability which is the unusual and disturbing feature. Perhaps the textbooks of the next century will have such titles as *How to cope with the usual!*

ORGANISATIONAL TRANSFORMATION IN PRACTICE

However, very few organisations can yet claim the status of being fully fledged learning organisations (PA Consulting Group, a top international firm of management consultants, estimates that there are currently 25 in the world – 19 in Japan and 6 in America). Therefore, the immediate practical problem that faces organisations thinking of adopting the philosophy of empowerment is how to get from here to there – how to achieve transformation.

> Major surgery must be accompanied by a character change.
> *Article in the Financial Times on the restructuring of a famous corporation*

Our model for transformation differs from the traditional view of the management of change in two important respects:

1. Empowerment and organisational liberation involve the redistribution of power away from some of the most senior and traditionally powerful roles in the traditional bureaucracy. Thus for transformation to work there must be open confrontation with the existing power relations within the organisation. To construct the future it is first necessary to deconstruct the present.
2. We have already made the point that in empowerment the means are the same as the ends. Because the goal is empowerment it must be achieved by a programme for change which is itself empowering. Everything we have said would become invalid if the process of change was alienating.

CASE STUDY: ORGANISATIONAL TRANSFORMATION

The most influential model of the organisational change process was first propounded by Kurt Lewin. He showed the process of change as a sequence of logical steps (illustrated below). The organisation was pictured as having a stable existence in a 'frozen state'. The role of the change agent was to precipitate the 'unfreezing' of the status quo in order to arrive at a better solution

---

continued

which more harmoniously suited the new conditions. The organisation then consolidated these gains by 'refreezing' into the new configuration.

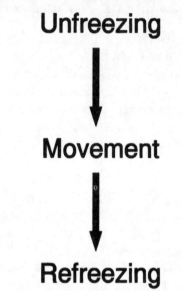

Unfreezing

Movement

Refreezing

This model, and all the other traditional models for the management of change which take this static view, are inadequate for modern purposes. Although freezing, unfreezing and refreezing is an evocative metaphorical model, it is only useful if the refreezing is conceived as becoming a permanently malleable slush.

Even more seriously, Lewin makes no overt reference to the issue of power in the change process. This is the rational model so characteristic of bureaucratic thinking – there is no room for conflict or disagreement.

Transformation as a 'political' struggle

Thus changing organisations to achieve empowerment will inevitably mean addressing the specific issue of power, in terms of both the end result and how that result is to be achieved.

Our model for organisational transformation reflects a view of the change process as dynamic and inherently full of conflict. If you are changing to empower then you are striking at the heart of the status quo, and threatening most those people at the top of the organisation.

This is not to revert to the traditional 'zero sum' approach to power which we described in Chapter 2, but it does acknowledge reality.

> Ultimately, we're talking about redefining the relationship
> between boss and subordinate. I want to get to a point where
> people challenge their bosses every day: 'Why do you want me to
> do these wasteful things? Why don't you let me do the things you
> shouldn't be doing so you can move on and create? That's the job
> of the leader – to create, not to control. Trust me to do my job
> and don't make me waste my time trying to deal with you on the
> control issue.'
>
> Jack Welch, CEO General Electric (quoted in Pascale, 1991)

Empowerment involves liberating new currents of activity and
enthusiasm – often from the people who have the lowest status in
the organisation. In turn this requires abolishing existing
differentials, awarding status on the basis of different values,
and challenging behaviour which oppresses. All this is a
fundamental threat to those who sit astride the traditional
bureaucracy. It questions their very existence. And there can be
no compromise. Empowerment and bureaucratic hierarchy cannot
coexist.

Empowerment is a threat to bureaucracy

So while the total *quantity* of power will rise with transformation,
there are still going to be powerful losers, which makes struggle
inevitable. The challenge is to the people who have the most to lose
and the greatest capacity to subvert the process. Indeed, this is almost
a test of the proposals for change. If they do not excite opposition they
are probably not changing anything very much; certainly not in the
fundamental ways demanded by empowerment.

A DYNAMIC MODEL FOR TRANSFORMATION

The recognition of this power struggle led us to develop our own five-
point model for organisational transformation (see diagram overleaf). It
is a dynamic model with the process following a sequence of different
stages, each with its own objectives and tactics.

Of course, the problem with all such abstractions is that they provide
a general pattern into which every particular situation is then forced to
fit, rather like a Victorian lady into the obligatory corset. So use it
intelligently to suit your own situation, which may well require a
different emphasis on various elements. Also, it is important to
remember that change is a moving process, and different points on the
model should be revisited time and again in the course of a major
review.

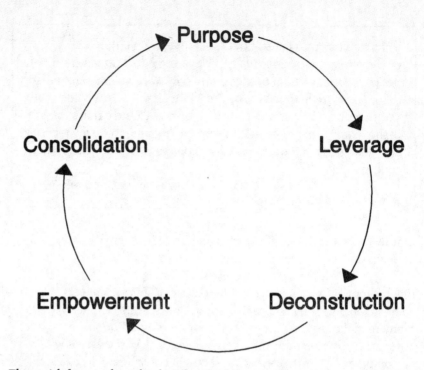

That said, for a truly radical and ambitious transformation programme to succeed, it will need to address all the stages in our model and we recommend that they are covered in the order given here.

DECIDE YOUR PURPOSE

It is not important to start the change process with all the answers; indeed it can be positively dangerous to do so. Inevitably you will be wrong, and you will not involve and empower others in the process. However, it is equally vital to start out with a clear idea of the direction in which you are heading. For this journey, you need at least a basic map which will allow you to discriminate between helpful advice and the signposts that actually lead to dead ends. Answering some vital questions will help to ensure that your purpose is robust enough for the journey.

Is the project aligned with your medium-term strategy?
Anticipating change in a radical and ambitious way means setting strategic goals and targets that span a number of years. However, setting priorities as a framework for action imposes a discipline of its own. All major investments in change should be able to justify themselves with a clear contribution to strategic goals, and going through this process is a useful way of testing the clarity of thinking behind a change programme.

What will be the benefits of the project?   It is vital to anticipate the benefits which will result from change and, with the help of some lateral thinking, to quantify the potential gains, either in terms of money, or quality, or perhaps increased production. The question is whether you can justify the investment against other profitable investments. If you cannot do this, then either the project is not worth it or you are not trying hard enough. Without ambitious targets, you and others will not be stretched towards the creative and challenging thinking which is the forerunner of genuine radical and empowering solutions.

Who is the 'customer' of the project?   At the outset, identify as your customer some powerful individual or group, ideally the chief executive and/or the top team, who will then become the sponsors of the initiative. This is helpful in a number of ways:

- In effect, they become your mentors (described in Chapter 7) – powerful allies who can move the project on if it becomes becalmed, and who will be able to give help and support in adversity.
- You gain the necessary top-level commitment right from the outset, with ready-made advocates when the time comes to 'sell' the proposals to the rest of the organisation.
- Identifying your customer and their needs forces you to clarify both your objectives and individual roles (who is doing what, and for whom).

In Chapter 5 we introduced the theory of 'strategic leverage' and we used a case study to illustrate how it finds the key dynamics in a system: enabling an initially small intervention to move mountains in the future. For example, a key dynamic was inserted into the system when front-line control was exerted over otherwise largely unaccountable central services through the creation of an internal customer – supplier relationship.

SPOT AND USE STRATEGIC LEVERAGE

There are a number of areas to consider in the search for leverage:

How to search for leverage

- The key points of leverage can often only be identified when the whole system (and other interrelated systems) have been understood in their entirety. Think laterally, looking beyond the obvious causes and effects.
- Find leverage by looking at relationships and dynamics, not by focusing only on structures.
- More often than not, you will find leverage in whole new ways of thinking, *not* in bright ideas which simply rearrange the past.
- Go with the grain of the existing system. Help a positive trend or remove a blockage rather than creating whole new systems. (Although it is sometimes counter-intuitive, it is often far more effective to remove the blockage – the balancing forces described in Chapter 5 – than to push futilely against it.)

How many points of leverage you will find necessary will depend on the scale of the programme and the nature of the systems being confronted. But it is rare to need more than two or three. Pick the right ones and all will fall into place; pick leverage points which do not fulfil the criteria and you will find endless effort rewarded by a complete lack of progress.

DECONSTRUCT THE PRESENT

Organisational transformation necessitates real shifts in power relationships and the adoption of very different assumptions and attitudes. These are two of the most difficult things to achieve, especially in a situation of apparent stability where the old ways of doing things have become deeply ingrained as common sense.

In such circumstances, it is foolhardy to rush straight to solutions. When you have identified the objective and the levers that will achieve it, your next step is to prepare the organisation both psychologically and physically by raising the level of dissatisfaction with the current state of affairs. Your task is more than half done if it becomes accepted that change, of whatever sort, is inevitable.

Force field analysis

One useful method for identifying the conflicting forces is called 'force field analysis' (illustrated in the diagram below). The analysis is carried out as follows:

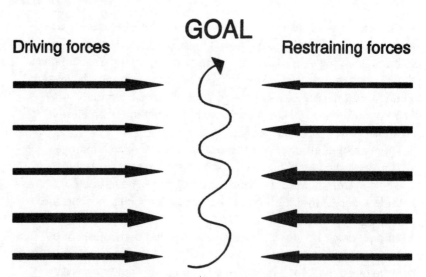

1. Down the middle of a blank piece of paper draw a line. This represents the status quo that you want to shift in a particular direction.
2. On one side of this line draw arrows facing in the direction you want to go, representing all the forces that are broadly helpful or sympathetic to your objective. Show the comparative strength of each force by the thickness of the arrow.

3. Think as widely as possible. Brainstorm around all the possible interest groups plus campaigns already under way and, above all, the major systems that the change could or will affect.
4. Now do the same for all the forces which are likely to oppose the change.
5. Conclude from this picture which factors are helping your position and which are holding you back.

Once you have established the nature of the opposing forces you are in a position to weaken them. Some tried and trusted methods (which can be varied to suit your own situation) are:

Weakening the opposing forces

- Circulate discussion papers setting out the arguments for change and listing the inadequacies of the current situation.
- Arrange a conference to discuss whether things ought to change. Make sure the debate occurs on your terms by providing the conference papers. Do not allow any premature decisions: remember you are still in the business of raising questions and doubts, not answers.
- Gradually raise the stakes. Start to provoke argument with those who are hostile to the proposals. Deliberately create uncertainty in the minds of staff directly affected. The impression must be that whatever happens, things are going to change. The only question is how.
- Marginalise any powerful voices that might speak against the change. Set up a project team that includes their representatives, but make sure they are in a minority. Find (or create) a decision-making body to legitimate the process of change that will support the objectives. Disenfranchise die-hard opponents from the debate by pointing out their vested interest in the status quo.

WORKSHOP: IDENTIFYING CONFLICTING FORCES

1. Think of a major change programme, either at work or perhaps within the social or political fields.
2. Use force field analysis to identify the conflicting forces at work for and against the change.
3. Think what you would do to get the change programme through (i.e. make your own plan to weaken the opposing forces and strengthen those which are moving in the right direction).

No doubt some of the steps which we suggest might be required by a programme of transformation appear somewhat heavy handed and Machiavellian. Perhaps they are. However, the point we are trying to emphasise is that such change programmes do not succeed because people automatically accept the self-evident reasonableness of the initiative. Much of this book is about how power pervades every aspect of the real world; and power does not work on the basis of reason, it works to protect itself. In that sense our prescriptions face organisational reality – empowerment is not some safe game in which no one gets hurt.

In order to empower you first have to disempower the powerful minority. Lewin's analogy of 'unfreezing' is apt in this context. To allow for the full liberation of new possibilities you must first loosen up the present. Done with sensitivity, enthusiasm and the skills we describe in this book, this can be a period of great excitement, even for those who are potentially the losers. Done with less sensitivity, or perhaps in less tractable circumstances, it can end with the withdrawal of senior people who continue to obstruct. Either way, if the process of disempowerment is not gone through you are merely storing up much more serious difficulties for later down the track.

EMPOWER

Laying down from on high a finished blueprint of the future never empowers. To transform an organisation, you must first empower staff to help to develop the new way of working for themselves. *The means are themselves part of the ends*. The question for the change agent is how to let go, while ensuring that the general principles of the transformation are maintained:

General principles for transformation

- The answer is the same as for most aspects of empowered management. The appropriate set of principles must be developed, agreed and communicated. Extensive staff consultation should be conducted around these principles to ensure that all possible difficulties are identified, and that people are given sufficient opportunity to influence the new approach.
- The process needs to be carefully constructed because it is in the nature of these principles to be non-negotiable once they are established. They are either accepted in their entirety, or it is likely they will not work at all. So it is important to ensure at the outset of the process of consultation that it is clear that everyone must accept the final result.
- Once the principles have been established, they become the empowering framework for all the more detailed organisational solutions. All potential areas of change can now be identified, and the relevant staff invited to bring forward precise proposals for implementing the new principles in their area.
- To ensure equity and a fair voice for everyone, ask someone external to each section to facilitate the process. This person, or if necessary a team, can then maintain the coordination and consistency of responses through knowledge of other discussions.

- Forming a 'dedicated' project team also helps by automatically creating champions of the changes: people who will simultaneously propagate the cultural and intellectual elements of the new 'common sense' as they are implementing the practical arrangements. It is also a way of including some of the younger and more junior staff who are probably the more natural allies of change.
- Your success depends heavily on your skills of communication. The atmosphere will be frenzied. Indeed, a by-product of having been through the stage of disempowerment properly will be a heightened level of anxiety. Anxious people do not listen carefully to what is being communicated. They tend to assume the worst, and will look behind the obvious to find obscure symbols which will confirm their own fears. Honest proposals for change are then judged as an elaborate pretext for some hidden agenda that will only be revealed at a later stage. Thus, everything you say or do must be measured, consistent and, above all, repeated many times. It should also be backed up by a similar approach across the whole organisation. This is the final stage in our model of organisational transformation.

CONSOLIDATE

> There is nothing more difficult to take in hand, more perilous to conduct, or more uncertain in its success, than to take the lead in the introduction of a new order of things, because the innovator has for enemies all those who have done well under the old conditions, and lukewarm defenders in all those who may do well under the new.
>
> *Machiavelli, The Prince*

You will already have focused on some important strategic levers. This is necessary in the first instance, but it is not the end of the story. The new ways of working will inevitably impinge on many aspects of the organisation if they are to be made both effective and enduring, so you need to sweep up behind the big changes with all the supporting action necessary to apply the new approach consistently throughout every aspect of the way the organisation works. This is necessary partly because the benefit of the changes will not be felt until this is done, and partly because consistency is of huge symbolic importance. When people see the new logic being applied in more unexpected situations, they really believe that something is happening.

Some of the areas that you will almost certainly need to examine are described below.

Leadership.   Real leadership shows itself within an empowering organisation. Stripped of any automatic right of obedience, is the leadership none the less nurturing the culture and values of the organisation on behalf of all its members?

Structures.   If the principles that we describe in Chapter 4 are followed, especially the need to organise around purposes and outcomes, new organisational imperatives will inevitably mean new structures.

Systems.   Systems should exist because they serve the objectives of the organisation, but all too often they impose a hidden set of assumptions about how things should be done which become obstacles to the process of change. Equally, therefore, new ways of doing things will demand new systems to work with the new arrangements. (For example, you cannot restructure management units if you do not also reorganise the financial system for providing relevant information to the new structure, and so on.)

Staff.   Any major change will bring a demand for new skills and new talents. Change cannot be facilitated without investment in training and, where appropriate, additional recruitment. The reward system should be brought into line with the changes, especially where this means acknowledging and therefore rewarding any additional responsibilities of front-line workers.

Symbols.   Do not neglect the potent power of the symbolic. Symbolism and myth are quite as potent as any practical measures that you take to bring in the new order. So choose new job titles, rearrange the accommodation, redo the corporate logo and the headed notepaper, abolish reserved parking places, come to work in something other than a suit and invent ways of mourning the passing of the old as well as celebrating the new.

WORKSHOP: RESOURCES FOR ORGANISATIONAL
TRANSFORMATION

1. Consider your own resources:
   - Do I believe strongly in empowerment? Do I have the determination to implement it in my own personal life?
   - Do I possess the required interpersonal skills to communicate effectively?
   - Do I need to transform my own leadership style?
2. If you are in work consider the resources of your organisation:
   - Has it a continuous learning policy and is it mature enough to support liberating changes?
   - Has it developed close and open communications?
   - Will it supply me with the authority I need to implement this transformation and back me up with some powerful mentors?

PRACTICAL PROGRAMMES FOR DECONSTRUCTING BUREAUCRACY

In the previous section we described a generic model for organisational change which deliberately addressed the issue of power. We argued that organisational transformation aimed at achieving empowerment would inevitably involve confronting and changing existing power relations. In addition, we emphasised the importance of looking for strategic leverage and that focusing on key fulcrums for change would have infinitely more impact than squandering scarce resources and energy in indiscriminately pushing on every front.

In this section we try to take this advice one stage further. We describe six specific tools of change which have strategic leverage and which actively challenge existing power relations. These strategies do not of themselves necessarily empower, but they can help create the conditions for empowerment and the liberation of the organisation.

Perhaps the most basic and common of current managerial initiatives is the drive to move operational decision making closer to the front line. Typically this involves moving to the front line the authority and accountability for matters of both internal organisation (expenditure, recruitment, administrative coordination, etc.) and the planning and delivery of the unit's functional purpose.

DEVOLVING MANAGEMENT RESPONSIBILITY

The philosophy behind devolving responsibility for operational decision making is to recognise that the staff and managers at the front line are closest to the customer and therefore know best how to resolve conflicting priorities. Moreover, locating as much decision making as possible in one spot minimises the number of layers of hierarchy necessary to authorise action, so immeasurably speeding up response times to changing circumstances. Finally, it has the benefit of locating accountability in one very visible spot, and cuts out the possibilities for the traditional bureaucratic game of 'back covering'.

The picture that is often painted of devolved management is one of changing an organisation from a supertanker with a turning circle of miles, to a shoal of fish which can change direction in an instant and in unison.

The key steps in a programme for devolving managerial responsibility are:
- Identifying or creating coherent and 'knowable' front-line management units.
- Appointing a new tier of team leaders or managers for these units who understand the new requirements and will act as the champions of change.

- Equipping them with the resources and the information (systems) necessary for managerial decision making (for example, without a financial system which accounts in terms of these units, managers will be unable to take charge of their own financial planning).
- Replacing the traditional bureaucratic chains of command for ratifying professional and managerial decision making with general standards to which front-line managers can refer when making decisions about such matters as recruitment.
- Putting a new emphasis on a coherent planning system, whereby each of these front-line units produces long-term and short-term 'business plans' with clear targets for how they are going to contribute to the organisation's wider goals.
- Making sure that middle management 'let go' of their traditional role of surveillance and supervision and change to coaches and facilitators (roles we describe in Chapter 7) by:
  - drastically reducing their numbers;
  - widening the span of responsibility of those that remain so that it is physically impossible for them to interfere operationally.

Moving managerial responsibility to the front line does not in itself empower, but it is a vital precondition. Once in place, organisations have an alternative infrastructure which allows them to dismantle the deadening superstructure of the traditional bureaucracy. Small, 'knowable' front-line management units also provide the necessary core organisational base for taking the next step of creating a culture and structures of participation.

SEPARATING SUPPORT FROM CONTROL

One of the distinctive features of the traditional corporation in either the public or private sector is often the disproportionate influence of non-productive central functions such as finance, human resources, estate management or IT.

Largely because of their proximity to the centre, these functions tend to accrete roles and positions which go way beyond the specific nature of their professionalism into the core business decisions of the enterprise. Furthermore, such professionalisms often have an air of unquestioned objectivity – they are merely ensuring sound professional standards, not representing a particular ideology of how power should be distributed. Nothing could be further from the truth. As we demonstrated in Chapter 4, those who control the information systems control the distribution of power. For example, how the financial management system is configured goes to the very heart of empowerment.

By reorienting these central functions the liberated organisation achieves two objectives – it creates a smaller strategic core which can escape from operational concerns to focus on the changing requirements of its customers, and it can turn the professional functions into a support to front-line units rather than a hindrance. One approach to this reorganisation is as follows.

Central functions are analytically dissected to establish those functions which are genuinely strategic or required to maintain essential corporate controls. Rarely will this require more than a few people per function, even in the largest corporate body. This is also an opportunity to organise those that remain at the centre into multidisciplinary teams focused on customer defined 'outputs' rather than professionally defined 'inputs'.

The reorganisation process

Most central functions can then be seen in their true light as services whose only role is to support operational units with whatever they require. Furthermore, in principle all such services could be bought in from external suppliers. For many professionals in a bureaucracy such a perspective is a radical change in culture. For example, the role of the payroll section changes from an enforcer of bureaucratic procedures into a service which concentrates on creating a process easy for managers to follow, while optimising its quality and cost (often completely untested).

A number of steps are open to organisations that want to institutionalise this change in power relations and consequently culture, as they must if it is to be maintained.

- The budgets for the central support functions should be disaggregated and distributed to their customers in front-line operational units which should have a choice over whether they have to use the internal functions.
- The organisational options for the support functions themselves are then to develop an internal trading relationship with their customers, to be 'outsourced' (contracted out) to specialist providers of such services, or in some cases to be physically broken up and devolved into operational units.

As with devolved management, reorganisation is a precondition for empowerment rather than empowerment itself. But unless an organisation goes through this process of freeing up the strategic core and reorienting the power relations implicit within professional knowledge and functions, all other steps towards empowerment will inevitably run into the sand.

CONTRACTING OUT FUNCTIONS

As both a logical extension of devolving management responsibility and as a tool for focusing on the core business and maximising value for money, many private and public sector organisations are increasingly looking to contract out (or in the jargon of the trade 'outsource') many of the functions that they had hitherto provided for themselves. The principle extends both to support services (for example, a specialist IT company providing a 'facilities management' service to maintain and operate an organisation's entire computing infrastructure) and to subcontracting parts of the business process itself, as car manufacturers have done for many years with their parts suppliers.

Where an existing function or 'undertaking' is transferred to a new employer, it is usual and good practice to transfer all associated staff on existing terms and conditions. To do otherwise invites opposition to what is already a major and unsettling change process. This principle is enshrined in European law as the *Acquired Rights Directive* and is applied in the UK by the *Transfer of Undertakings (Employment Protection) Regulations* 1981.

Benefits of outsourcing

Proponents of outsourcing argue that it brings a number of major benefits:

- It is a catalyst for the separation of support and control, and therefore enables the centre to free itself from operational issues to focus on its core business and its customers.
- It is a mechanism for dealing with the consequences for support functions of liberating the front line. With the erosion of their captive market, support functions lose economies of scale and become redundant. Putting them into the wider market allows them to expand their customer base.
- The process of testing the market by competitive tendering of the contracts for goods or services provides an automatic test of value for money in any particular area.
- Finally, it is argued that the mere act of having to specify in writing the required standards for goods or a service (as one must in a contractual relationship, since that becomes the only guarantee that you will be provided with what you want) is in itself a therapeutic process which reveals much waste and forces a reappraisal of custom and practice. In effect, functions are opened up for examination (and therefore accountability) in a way which is not usually possible within an internal relationship.

As contracting out becomes more prevalent, organisations have been experimenting with new types of contractual relationships which preserve the benefits but overcome some of the deficiencies of a traditional contract.

Partnering

Modern approaches have alighted on the concept of 'partnering' as a way of overcoming the adversarial nature of traditional contract management and its inflexibility if unforeseen circumstances suddenly require a completely different approach or service.

In a partnering arrangement the parties agree to share the potential risks and benefits of the arrangement. Both therefore have an incentive to focus on optimising the quality of the goods or services rather than wasting futile energy on mutual suspicion. These types of relationships have been pioneered in areas such as the oil industry or car manufacturing, where highly competitive business conditions put both client and supplier under particular pressure to cut costs, maintain quality and innovate continually to keep up with the opposition. We strongly suspect that this description will come to apply to most economic relationships in the near future.

In addition to its part in deconstructing the bureaucracy (as with devolved management, a necessary precondition for empowerment), the contractual relationship is in many ways intrinsically in sympathy with empowerment. Done properly it is a voluntary agreement between two equal and independent parties which brings benefits to them both. Moreover, it is a relationship which focuses on performance and outputs rather than operational processes. Finally the clarity of the contractual relationship, allied to partnering attitudes of trust, provides the basis for building a common agenda and agreeing common goals which are the hallmarks of the empowering approach.

The contractual relationship can be empowering

TOTAL QUALITY MANAGEMENT

One signpost to the type of work organisation which fulfils these new imperatives is provided by what has come to be called 'Total Quality Management' (TQM). Although initially propounded by Americans such as Deming, Crosby and Juran, it has been most enthusiastically embraced by the Japanese and many have seen it as the intellectual underpinning of the Japanese success story since the Second World War. More and more private sector companies in the US and Europe are starting to adopt this approach.

The quality gurus may argue about how to put TQM into practice (and even definitions – is quality 'fitness for purpose' or 'conformance to requirement'?), but they all share the same central insight. Enormous waste is produced by the traditional assumptions of bureaucratic management, typified by the minute subdivision of labour in pursuit of too narrow a definition of efficiency. Therefore, basic to total quality management is the drive to eliminate waste:

Eliminating waste

- Waste from work which is too good for its purpose.
- Waste from poor quality work that needs to be done a second time.
- Waste from quality control methods that are built into an organisation as a separate overhead, rather than being made part of everyone's job.
- Waste from production methods that require supplies of raw parts to be ordered and stored months ahead of when they will be used.
- Waste from management time spent supervising people who know better than the managers what should be done.
- Above all, waste inherent in treating staff like automatons rather than developing their full potential.

Constant innovation

The eradication of waste may not sound like a very exciting manifesto for organisational renewal, but its consequences are dramatic.

In place of the objectives set by a traditional corporation, Total Quality Management aims for *constant innovation* in pursuit of:

- getting closer to what the customer wants
- an unwillingness to accept imperfection
- the demand for constant improvement and innovation from everyone
- proper investment in both people and technology
- flexible and lean production systems
- short product development cycles which are closely identified with the needs and wants of the customer

Long-term programming to maintain momentum

These are objectives which are not achieved by short-term devotion to immediate financial results. They require a long-term perspective if they are to be implemented successfully. Recent studies indicate that the more mature TQM programmes take at least five years to show an improvement, and some companies have already been involved in continuous development for 30–35 years in Japan, 10–12 years in America and 7–10 years in the UK (which started later).

Our first case study on TQM shows how worthwhile this has been. And even six years ago a comparison between Honda and General Motors revealed the dramatic effect that TQM can have on the bottom line, as our second case study illustrates.

CASE STUDY: EVIDENCE OF SUCCESS FROM AMERICA

After 12 years' experience, the results from **Xerox** speak for their own success:

Launch costs	down 40%
Launch time	down 33%
Unit costs	down 50%
Errors (ppm)	down 70%

After 10 years' experience, the results from Hewlett-Packard (HP) and 3M are equally impressive:

Hewlett-Packard:

$50 million savings from one project	
Product failure	down 60%
R & D cycle time	down 35%
Unit cost	down 42%

continued

Productivity	up 90%
Profit	up 177%
Market share	up 193%

3M:

Justified complaints	1982: 16.3%
	1986: 2.4%
Complaint response	1982: 134 days
	1986: 17 days
Inventory	down $8 million

Unit costs reduced by estimated 50%
Productivity increased by estimated 90%

Source: PA *Consulting Group*

CASE STUDY: HONDA

Honda is a passionate advocate of all aspects of quality management (indeed, some commentators suggest it could claim the title of the best managed company in the world).

A comparison with General Motors illustrates the practical impact that quality management can have on company performance. In 1988 the two companies achieved the following results:

	Honda	**General Motors**
Sales	US$24 billion	US$102 billion
Market valuation	US$12.6 billion	US$12.6 billion
Profit as % of sales	3.6%	3.6%
Average cost per vehicle	US$8670	$10,170
Product development cycle	3 years	6 years
Number of employees	58,320	700,000
Employee hours/ vehicle produced	31	92

To achieve these results Honda has adopted an empowering management style which, in turn, creates new structures for the people constituting the workforce. An example of this is the way Honda has institutionalised the creation of free dialogue between

continued

> boss and worker through the ritual of *waigaya* (this translates
> literally as something close to 'hubbub' or the noise of active and
> excited discussion). In these sessions normal conventions are
> lifted and all are expected to contribute with straight talking.
>
> *Source: Pascale,* Managing on the Edge

TQM and empowerment

The example of Honda shows the close link between Total Quality
Management and empowerment. It also begins to illustrate the impact
of empowerment in practice. But empowerment is not synonymous
with TQM: it is both more and less. On one level, empowerment is
merely a particular human resource strategy used by companies going
down the TQM route. Once again, in itself it does not ensure quality,
but it is a vital precondition. At another level the sort of radical
empowerment described in this book also represents a step forward
from total quality. Even those firms universally hailed as being in the
forefront of the quality revolution tend to have one leg still rooted in
the old order. They have reduced hierarchic tiers, but there is still
hierarchy. Some front-line workers are involved in the design of the
product but not all, and certainly not yet each individual customer.
They use multidisciplinary project teams, but the disciplines they draw
on are still those defined as important in the nineteenth century. So
TQM is a step down the road but it has not yet defined the whole
route.

BUSINESS PROCESS REENGINEERING

In Chapter 3 we described the importance of business process
reengineering (BPR) for providing a way of reintegrating the hand and
the brain. This is because BPR advocates the need to organise around
what the customer receives rather than functions which are only of
internal or professional convenience. Thus as far as possible, the same
person or group should be responsible for the production of a good or
service right from its inception through to its delivery. Furthermore
they should have complete authority over all the resources and
decisions necessary for a successful result. (Team Taurus, described in
Chapter 8, is an example of this.)

BPR and empowerment

A look at the key elements of the approach advocated by Hammer
and Champy shows the practical as well as the theoretical connection
between reengineering and empowering. These key aspects include:
- Merging jobs and integrating tasks so that the involved worker or
  team sees a product through from start to finish.
- The workers make decisions.
- The steps in a process should be performed in a natural sequence
  for the operators (termed 'delinearising'). Then tasks can be done

simultaneously or according to absolute dependencies, not arbitrary administrative conventions.

● Processes should have multiple versions (for customised outcomes).
● Work should be performed where it makes sense (not around the specialist).

To these ingredients should be added what Hammer and Champy term the 'disruptive' potential of modern IT. Their refreshing approach asks people to discover how many of the old rules they can break with new technology – that is the way to think laterally about how to get the most competitive advantage from an investment.

Business process reengineering requires a radical reappraisal of traditional systems of production. It is the logical corollary of the sort of autonomous, team-based production we advocate and illustrate later in this book. It is also an essential underpinning factor for a programme of empowerment. Finally, as the case study below demonstrates, it can enable quantum leaps in improving production and quality.

CASE STUDY: IBM CREDIT DIVISION

IBM's Credit Division is responsible for advancing credit to organisations considering buying an IBM computer. It used to take two weeks between a request for credit and action: a period in which a considerable number of customers would lose interest altogether.

An analysis of the many stages of processing an application showed that in these two weeks there was a total of approximately 90 minutes' actual work.

The rest was the 'hand-offs' between different stages of the process made necessary because the menial work of administration was separated from the senior job of approving the money.

Answer – combine all processes into the role of an empowered core manager and improve production and customer satisfaction by a step-jump into the bargain.

Source: Hammer and Champy, Reengineering the Corporation

There is a school of thought which applies some of the language and techniques of psychoanalysis to the study of organisational behaviour. These commentators point to the almost paranoid attitude of bureaucratic organisations to their customers, who are often treated as an irritant and a threat to be kept at a distance (by, for example,

EMPOWERING THE CUSTOMER

making it very difficult to complain or by ensuring that the staff whose front-line jobs bring them into direct contact with the public have the worst wages and the lowest status).

In fact, the big corporations of the past had no need to 'get close to their customers'. The key to success in the private sector tended to be economies of scale and a big advertising budget. With sufficient publicity and a cheap product you could be pretty sure that your product would dominate that of your less financially powerful rivals, largely irrespective of which best fitted the needs of the customer. And in the public sector it was a positive disadvantage to be accessible to the user. Inevitably it is necessary to ration public services which are free at the point of delivery, and (whether consciously or not) one of the main tools in this rationing process has always been to discourage the customer through long queues and forbidding procedures.

Thankfully these days are passing. For the private sector firm, increasing competition and wider consumer choice have made it a matter of life or death to understand and satisfy the real wishes and needs of customers. But empowering customers to have a real voice in the goods and services they receive is not a matter of better training and more market research. It adds a whole new dynamic to the organisational power equation. If you empower the customer the people who deal with the customer need to be equally empowered so that they are able to supply the very best possible service.

Some of the obvious methods for understanding and empowering the customer are:

- everyone from every part of an organisation meeting their customers
- systematic feedback on product or service quality from your front-line staff and from market research techniques
- offering guarantees and warranties
- responding to and resolving every complaint
- innovation with new techniques which allow the customer to contribute to the process of design and production of the goods or services
- monitoring demand on a daily basis

Many best-selling books have been written on how to get close to the customer, so we are not going to labour the point here. However, we do want to touch briefly on the special circumstances within the public sector. The customers of a public service often face a particularly uphill struggle to get their voices heard:

- They usually cannot choose their supplier.
- They have no direct purchasing power, since the resources for the service are provided by a surrogate customer acting as 'gatekeeper' (the doctor, social worker etc.) or are allocated into the system at a

high level as a proportion of general taxation (means-tested welfare benefits, etc.)

In these circumstances the threat of a reduction in demand as people take their custom elsewhere has no impact.

In the place of money as a tool for empowering the public sector customer, there needs to be an exchange of information backed up by material means of redress in the case of dissatisfaction. As a minimum, public bodies should make clear to every user:

- *Who* is eligible for the service.
- To *what* quality standards the service should be delivered.
- *How* access to the service is gained.

Accountability for living up to this published information should be underpinned by systems of redress which ensure that unsatisfactory services are replaced and inconvenience recompensed. The comparative lack of customer power within the public sector has traditionally allowed it to manage in a more complacent manner than the private sector which faces constant competition. Setting customer standards (and introducing all possible choice over the supply of public services) will introduce the customer empowerment which is the necessary condition for accountable and responsive services.

Part II — Recommended Reading

Chris Argyris and Donald Schon (1978) *Organisational Learning: A Theory of Action Perspective*, Addison-Wesley, Reading, MA.

W R Ashby (1986) *Self-Regulation and Requisite Variety: An Introduction to Cybernetics*, Wiley, Chichester.

S Clegg and D Dunkerley (1980) *Organisation, Class and Control*, Routledge & Kegan Paul, London.

Bob Garratt (1987) *The Learning Organisation*, Fontana, London.

Charles Handy (1990) *The Age of Unreason*, Arrow, London.

Rosabeth Moss Kanter (1983) *The Change Masters: Corporate Entrepreneurs at Work*, Allen & Unwin, London.

Rosabeth Moss Kanter (1990) *When Giants Learn to Dance*, Unwin, London.

Rosabeth Moss Kanter, Barry A Stein and Todd D Jick (1992) *The Challenge of Organizational Change*, Free Press, New York.

Richard Pascale (1990) *Managing on the Edge*, Penguin, Harmondsworth.

Mike Pedler (ed.) (1983) *Action Learning in Practice*, Gower, Aldershot.

Tom Peters (1985) *Thriving on Chaos*, Random House, New York.

Donald Schon (1967) *Beyond the Stable State*, Penguin, Harmondsworth.

Valerie Stewart (1990) *The David Solution: How to Liberate Your Organisation Through Empowerment*, Gower, Aldershot.

P Watzlawick, J Weakland and R Fisch (1974) *Change: Problem Formulation and Problem Resolution*, W W Norton, New York.

Shoshana Zuboff (1989) *In the Age of the Smart Machine: The Future of Work and Power*, Heinemann, Oxford.

Part III
Empowering People

7 _Everyone is a Leader_

In an empowering organisation people take control of their own destiny and participate in the workplace to their full potential. An empowering leadership style is vital for everyone in this process. This allows organisational members to help each other to become committed to a common purpose in which they jointly believe, and this in turn enables them to become self-directed as they voluntarily work for the success of the enterprise. All empowered individuals provide leadership when required and teams need leadership to ensure they work cooperatively.

> Commitment is voluntary and personal. It cannot be imposed and initiated by others and can be withdrawn.
>
> ACAS _Research Unit Report_

This chapter is for everyone, since everyone in every walk of life plays a leadership role at some time.

EMPOWERMENT MEANS MORE LEADERSHIP

In the majority of work organisations, senior and other line managers are selected by their seniors but team or _ad hoc_ leadership roles exist at every level: some are chosen democratically, other roles move around as special needs arise. There are always things someone can do to make a difference, regardless of his or her official position, and so inspire and empower other people. In a nutshell, modern organisations require fewer managers but more leaders.

> The team which is dissatisfied with the way it is led will operate below maximum level.
>
> *Mike Woodcock*

Yet everyone needs to believe in the vision of empowerment:

Believe in the vision of empowerment

- To be people centred, expecting that everyone has something to contribute to the extent of their individual ability. To be, in the words of Moss Kanter (1989), a 'post-heroic hero' as you free and inspire people to accomplish excellence for themselves.
- To hand over control to others, and to support them as they exercise it through listening, influencing, enthusing and showing your trust.

In his seminal research into what constitutes successful team roles (described in Chapter 8), Belbin puts trust highest in his profile of successful leaders. They are 'trusting, accepting other people without jealousy'. As we saw in Chapter 3, developing trust starts with behaviour. Showing trust to staff is the best way to produce trust. The first step in gaining employee involvement, advised Donald Petersen, a past chief executive of Ford Motor Co, is to open up your books. He gave even sensitive financial information to union representatives in order to gain their trust, and said: 'Show your staff where you stand, what customers think of your products, and why you are asking for help.'

But mutual distrust between management and workers still exists.

Evidence of mistrust

Many managers believe that workers 'cannot think' and that people at the front line are not experts at their own jobs, giving rise to such comments as 'they get paid to work, don't they?' (Lane, 1989). This lack of trust is reciprocated by the workers – one American survey, for example, revealed that only 30 per cent of workers believed that their companies had their best interests at heart (leaving 70 per cent to think the reverse, or stay neutral).

According to Handy (1985) some of the roots of this deep seated

Workers – 'overheads' or 'assets'?

malaise lie within the fabric of our business society. Workers do not 'own' their company: shareholders – strangers to each other – do. Workers are still classed by many managers as 'overheads' not 'assets'. How then, he asks, can they think in terms of psychological ownership without physical ownership?

> Earn back the trust you give.
>
> *Martin John Yate*

Changing a culture of mistrust takes time and patience, and trust in a leader can be quickly destroyed. If, for example, you are constantly preaching change, but do nothing to encourage innovation, your team will soon lose confidence in you – only a windbag, they will judge.

LIVE THE EMPOWERING VISION

As well as believing in this philosophy of empowerment, you must live it, proving your sincerity by your deeds and showing that you are relinquishing one type of power for another. In return, you reap greater (sometimes total) commitment and cooperation – the most important element needed by every organisation. Successful organisations understand that this commitment is central to their very survival. With a committed workforce, enterprises have improved their performance in many vital areas. Productivity has increased, direct costs been saved, flexibility enhanced and relationships improved. Gaining this commitment is your greatest challenge. So follow the advice a coach gave to a world class tennis player: 'Have confidence in your own ability and you will succeed.'

> To be a good leader you need to give up control in a narrow sense in order to get control in a much wider sense.
>
> *Robert Waterman*

WORKSHOP: EVERYONE A LEADER

1. Keep a record for a month or a fortnight of the leadership roles you have played in that time.

   - At work: as your line function?
     ad hoc project leader or office holder?
     informal?
     other?

   - Away from work: within your family?
     at a social or other association?
     for your children's school?
     other?

continued

2. Analyse how you handled these roles:
- As an empowering and trusting leader?
- By controlling with orders?
- Each situation handled differently? If so, how and why?

3. What have you learnt from this exercise?

THE POWERFUL EMOTIONAL NEEDS WE ALL SHARE

To harness the power within people, however, we must first understand the nature and complexity of human needs. This section explains how to satisfy some of people's highest personal needs and therefore generate commitment. Research by behavioural scientists in the 1960s, refined in the 1980s, provides the guiding insight that people are not naturally lazy, uncooperative and stupid. When empowering leaders understand and satisfy their people's needs they are able and willing to take on responsibilities and deeply commited to fulfilling them.

Making it happen means involving the hearts and minds of those who have to execute and deliver.

John Harvey-Jones

The Japanese have a workforce which is turned on and excited about making cars.

British executive

THE HIERARCHY OF NEEDS

McGregor (following Maslow) offers a model which describes how people's needs at work can be depicted in a kind of hierarchy, similar to that in the diagram overleaf. At the bottom of the triangle are the needs of our animal nature for self-preservation – for sleep, for food and water, for shelter and warmth. These needs are basic; as someone aptly said, 'people do not live by bread alone, except when there is no bread.' Once satisfied, such needs cease to be strong motivators to action. Thus, as people begin to feel materially secure, their higher needs for self-expression (including the drive for achievement), for creativity, for an objective, for self-fulfilment, clamour for satisfaction. People become self-directed if they become committed to an objective

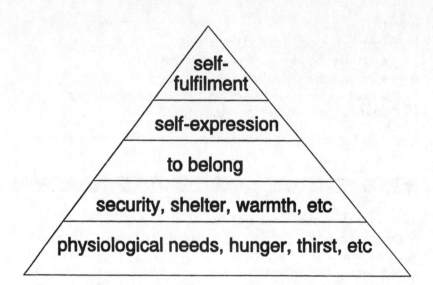

they value. (For example, a challenge such as the thrill of discovering something new or a chance to grow, as at Proctor & Gamble, where a cook grew to be one of their most qualified company-wide trainers.) They will not only accept responsibility but often seek it. Further, to work becomes as natural as to eat or sleep. Creativity is widely, not narrowly scattered among the population.

People are self-motivated

In short, people can be self-motivated. McClelland pointed out that some people are more self-motivated than others. These are the 'high achievers'. They like to set their own goals, which although challenging must be achievable, since they want to win. They also like to get immediate feedback. In the philosophy of empowerment, everyone must be enabled to become a high achiever in their own terms.

THE 'TRUE MOTIVATORS'

Another illuminating model depicting the relationship between motivation and work is offered by Frederick Herzberg. He interviewed 200 engineers to discover what determined their job satisfaction and job dissatisfaction. He found that they had been most satisfied on occasions which had involved them in achievement, recognition, taking responsibility for their own jobs, being afforded advancement or a chance to grow. They had also sometimes gained great satisfaction from the work itself. These factors are linked to people's higher needs to express and fulfil ourselves, and to *grow*. They are the 'true motivators'.

What makes people unhappy?

The engineers had felt dissatisfied when company policy or working conditions had been bad, or they had disliked their supervisor, felt their salary was low or their interpersonal relationships poor. Herzberg suggests that these latter conditions (which are linked to our animal needs) are 'hygiene factors'. They can make people very dissatisfied but do not positively motivate people to work hard. 'Job attitudes must be viewed twice: what makes employees happy, and then a separate question, not deducible from this first . . . what makes them unhappy?' So people work to a two-dimensional structure. If organisations fail to provide adequate 'hygiene' factors, people are dissatisfied, but however adequate such things as salaries and fringe benefits are, they do not by themselves inspire people to give of their best.

Empowerment has changed our understanding of some of the earlier lists of motivators, (those higher up on Maslow's triangle of needs and described as the 'true motivators' by Herzberg) without changing their essential meaning. Although some needs are now expressed in different terms, they still underpin and explain Maslow's concept of self-expression and fulfilment, what he called 'self-actualisation' (and we call self-fulfilment).

ESSENTIAL MEANING OF TRIANGLE OF NEEDS UNCHANGED

The six such needs which people frequently mention today as important to them are:

Six important factors

1. Respect and recognition
2. Welcoming challenges and chances for self-development
3. A belief in the value of their work
4. Equal treatment for equal competence
5. Autonomy and power
6. Affiliation

> Everyone wants to be treated as an individual.
> *Jan Carlzon, President, Scandinavian Airlines*

The models of human motivation which we have described are useful guides, not unalterable law. There are a host of individual and group variations. Broad research indicates that:

THE COMPLEX MODEL

- Needs change as people move through the age groups. Younger people seek advancement; security looms large for older workers.
- Every age group worried about job security feels discontented about all other aspects of work.
- Position in the traditional social hierarchy changes priorities. Professional people usually seek self-fulfilment. For others, status itself gives job satisfaction, even though the work may be dirty (e.g. doctors and geologists) or repetitive (e.g. royalty and diplomats). Many workers – especially those on assembly lines – were described as 'instrumentalists', primarily interested in pay rather than work or social satisfaction. Higher pay provides resources to satisfy needs outside work. A survey made in the 1960s in the dock industry

underlined these findings. The physical factors were more important to the dockers; the 'true motivators' most important to the managers and to a lesser extent to the supervisors. This is particularly significant, since it shows how narrow expectations can become under traditional management structures; whereas, as we have seen, a very different picture emerges when empowering leadership liberates the 'true motivators' in the work force.

- The nature of supervision is more important to women and the low paid.
- Some people prefer to work alone.
- Work in smaller companies increases job satisfaction.
- Finally, as a generalisation, people are not actively dissatisfied with their jobs but just not satisfied in any definable way.

One of my strongest impressions in all my years of consulting, is how many people seem mildly but widely dissatisfied with what they are doing but don't know what to do about their lot. Some remain where they are, putting in time, spluttering along like an engine, firing on half its cylinders. Others leave, go back to school, to a new company or into a new profession.

Robert Waterman

Such findings as these led Schein to coin the (unfortunately sexist) phrase 'complex man'. 'In the huge gamut of human needs and motivations,' he wrote, 'an individual's response will be governed by many variables at different times and in different situations.' Sargent developed this approach with a complex model which integrates the many motivational variables of complex man into the other general approaches. Sargent's model 'presupposes we are to a greater or lesser extent self activated'.

So we select our own goals to satisfy our needs and take the necessary actions to achieve our desired results. The strength of our motivation then depends on the value of the expected rewards.

The 'E' factor

To achieve these results, says Handy (1985), we decide (consciously or unconsciously) how much 'E' (= 'Effort', 'Energy', 'Excitement') we will expend. We cannot, for instance, calculate the amount of 'E' required unless we are clear about the results we want to achieve.

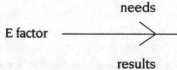

needs

E factor ————————————>   the motivational calculus

results

Expectations play an important part in motivation, as we described in Chapter 3. Suppose you are a high achiever wanting to see immediate results. You will *expect* these results and work hard, using a lot of 'E'. If they do not materialise your 'E' level may be lower for the next situation. Conversely, success will encourage the expenditure of more 'E'.

Expectations affect motivation

This brief summary of the research into human motivation, together with an analysis of your own complex motives, will make evident the link between empowerment and commitment. It will also help you to understand the many and different influences on other people.

WORKSHOP: COMMITMENT

1. What do you think would be the biggest changes in your working environment and people's commitment if you were working for an organisation seriously attempting to put empowerment into practice?
2. How does the concept of 'complex man' (and woman) help you to be an empowered leader?
3. How do the changing needs of people or yourself affect your leadership style?

So far in this chapter we have described the vision which underlies the philosophy of empowerment and shown how this is based on sound conclusions from a great deal of research over the years into the nature and complexity of human needs. In the following sections we outline the many practical steps you can take to make the fullest use of these insights.

The goal remains the same but, as we shall see, the key role of an empowering leader in attaining this goal has changed quite dramatically from the role of a leader in a traditional organisation.

ORGANISE AROUND PEOPLE

Staff who are regarded as units of production are disempowered, since they bring to work only a narrow element of their personality.

In contrast, enterprises which organise around people value their staff as whole human beings and treat them with dignity. This philosophy is an integral part of an empowering leader's actions and colours all his or her interpersonal relationships.

If you have a formal or informal leadership role, here are ideas for how you might put this policy into practice.

Be a mentor to your staff.   Successful mentors offer support, guidance and encouragement to each member of their team or department. A mentor guides and teaches other people to take on greater responsibility, to stretch their capability, and challenges them to make their own decisions. A mentor listens to their problems and doubts about their performance and encourages them to be persistent, particularly when things are difficult.

Fulfilling this role involves:

- building meaningful relationships with each person
- training and coaching them to cooperate with you and work with each other
- offering recognition for work well done

There is more on the importance of mentors in Chapter 9.

CASE STUDY: A MANAGER'S MENTORING ROLE

Waterman emphasises the importance of the mentoring role to empowering leaders. He describes the skills of Richard Steadman, who was thought by many to be the best knee surgeon in the world. He owes this success, thinks Waterman, as much to the mentoring role he plays, both to his staff and to his patients, as to his technical excellence.

While expecting his staff to work as a close-knit team, Steadman develops individual members to take on extra responsibility, always encouraging them to make their own decisions (asking questions such as 'What do you think is the best choice?' plus encouraging comments such as 'I like that').

Equally, a patient is not just a knee or shoulder to be healed but a whole person. Steadman therefore empowers them by transferring control over their recovery to them as soon as possible. This approach, he thinks, is as important to a successful recovery as the operation itself.

'Starting to exercise almost immediately after the operation', he says, 'replaces the feeling of hopelessness with something to shoot for.' Basic to his approach is the surgeon's accessibility as he wanders round his clinic constantly seeing both staff and patients. He fully realises the value of walking the job.

Build meaningful relationships.   Getting to know staff is a taxing job for a busy leader. It involves being generous with your time, ready to listen as people describe their hopes and expectations, always open to suggestions; willing, too, to support and counsel individuals who become overwhelmed by problems they feel they cannot solve (counselling skills are described in Part IV). Successful leaders have found that it is vital to take a systematic approach to this role or daily pressures will squeeze it out. One such structure is a regular performance review; another is to programme personal appraisal interviews (described in Part IV) with the members of your team.

Walk the job.   One of the best ways of talking and listening to people is to plan a systematic schedule for walking the job, allocating regular periods in your diary for it and sticking to them. For instance, visiting a team undergoing changes, turning up on the night shift (perhaps to work alongside people doing new or boring jobs) or being available by going round your department each day and talking to people on their own ground. The kind of questions people will appreciate will vary – Do you like your work? Are you getting enough training? Do you find team meetings productive? Where are you going for your holidays this year? and so on.

'Do not summon people to your office,' said one executive, 'it frightens them – instead, go and see them.' This advice is particularly important for senior managers. The chief executive of an American airline travelled 200,000 miles a year to express concern for visible management and to show he was an 'approachable guy'. His 15 top people were expected to do the same. Donald Petersen, the ex-chief executive of Ford International, says that at a plant he would have a lot of photos taken as he shook hands with people, and 'I always walked if possible; you don't want a picture of you riding a golf cart through a plant.'

Contact with your staff, either at their place of work or yours, helps you to discover the needs and expectations of team members and colleagues. With these satisfied, you can encourage people to commit their 'E' – Effort, Energy and Excitement – to departmental goals. So talk about your vision and listen to their reaction, and any discrepancies between the needs of the team or department and of its members will be apparent. Be patient until people's fears have been fully expressed. When they understand your leadership style and you take their reactions seriously, with a joint dialogue and maximum participation, a common vision can be created and with luck a consensus will emerge, as happened in the Airspace case study in Chapter 2.

Useful skills.   Try to remain objective and approach issues cautiously. Make no presuppositions, especially with people you know. Stay flexible, following the other person's lead. He or she may have grievances and allowing these to surface together is particularly important.

At an appraisal interview, one team member was described by a previous manager as having 'a fussy, schoolmasterly attitude'. He was seething with indignation. His team leader encouraged him to get the problem off his chest, using the skills of counselling and listening (described in Part IV). Encouraged by neutral and open-ended questions – 'Tell me about your likes and dislikes', or more directly 'Is your job too routine? Worrying? – the team leader revealed his own need for order and accuracy. This led to a constructive discussion about how his needs could be frustrated by some of the other team members' needs, and so on.

PEOPLE HAVE DIFFERENT NEEDS

Soon you will discover how people's needs differ – they have such different worries as a need for more pay to cover a crippling mortgage, or a black employee feeling that he or she is being discriminated against, and so on.

Even a need for achievement, advancement or recognition can be viewed differently. Achievement can mean greater challenge from present work or an expected promotion, or signal an imminent departure for greener fields. Recognition for one person is a bonus or a rise, for another a sincere thank you.

Assessing correctly the many expectations and needs of each 'complex man' (and woman) is a prerequisite for building meaningful relationships – a priority leadership responsibility.

CASE STUDY: WALKING THE JOB

One shy leader, Geoffrey Thompson, learnt the power of walking the job when the team of departmental managers to which he belonged made a new policy decision to visit all their departments frequently and regularly.

This decision offered Geoffrey a chance to do something positive towards attaining a target he had agreed with his senior at his last appraisal interview: to work at improving his staff relations. He was widely respected for his technical knowledge and skills, but regarded by his staff as unapproachable and aloof. The new policy offered an easy opportunity to overcome this barrier.

On each weekly round, therefore, he made a point of talking to someone different, if necessary about work, but also to discover more about their life outside work. At first, he felt very ill at ease and pushed himself to talk, but his confidence grew as he noticed

continued

that people seemed eager to respond when they saw him taking an interest in them. Slowly, too, he gathered a treasure trove of information, about outside interests, friendships, worries, future plans, present achievements, family life, holiday activities and so on. For example:

- There existed an interteam network of friends, based on a common home locality.
- One efficient and innovative team leader sang regularly in a choir, and also served as the secretary to her local political party.
- Another worker, regarded disapprovingly by Geoffrey as a 'clock watcher', had a pressing need to catch a certain fast train so that he could pick up their new baby from the childminder while his wife was working irregular hours.
- A surprising number of men and women regarded by him as 'ordinary operators' were nursing aspirations for a progressive future and began to consult him about possible avenues of development.

After several months, Geoffrey Thompson received a tangible sign of progress when he was invited by his team leaders to join them at the local pub for a birthday celebration. No longer regarded as aloof, by working regularly at a weakness he had developed it into a strength.

Coaching in cooperation.   Your own behaviour will signal the importance of cooperation. But it does not come naturally to everyone and, as their mentor, you can guide, train and coach your staff to work harmoniously with each other, with you and with other departments and teams, especially if you explain that their reward will be greater job satisfaction and increased productivity (see Chapter 8).

Holding frequent team meetings provides you with coaching opportunities, because face-to-face communication is one safe way to be sure that everyone has understood key information. It also ensures that everyone can add their own feelings, ideas and comments to the debate.

Coach in team meetings

Margerison and McCann give the example of one leader who holds five main regular meetings, one weekly, one fortnightly and three every three months. Members of his team felt they gained a wider understanding and 'a lot of the back-biting under the previous manager seemed not to occur although *all members were the same.*' This emphasis on meetings is an investment in generating consensus and common purpose. Achieving it puts great demands on your skill at running efficient meetings (described in Part IV).

Coaching a team all together can also be valuable. One senior manager organised teams with the aim of improving the service of their hotel. Every week she heard reports from each team, asked searching questions and made suggestions. The teams appreciated this while being able to get on with the detailed work themselves. In Chapter 5 we posed two different questions which a coach will find useful to ask: one about the present situation, 'How well are we doing now?' and the other about change, 'Should we be doing something else?'

> Senior managers at Digital and other companies, such as BP and Sherwood Computing Services, are being turned into coaches. Their job is no longer to control and command, it is to act as counsellers to the newly-empowered front-line employees. Costly training programmes have been introduced to help top executives make this often traumatic transition.
>
> David Oates, *Power to the People Who Want It*

Coaching through mistakes

It also helps greatly if you *genuinely* emphasise that making mistakes, and analysing them, offers a unique learning opportunity. (Peters (1988) recommends as useful questions: Can we itemise the main lessons learned? How can you/we do better next time? Are you/we repeating the same mistake as before? etc.) The closer this appraisal occurs to the actual incidents, the more powerful it will be.

> Experience is the name given to mistakes.
>
> *New Zealand farmer*

Team appraisal meetings are an effective training tool, since they concentrate on members giving feedback to each other about the process. How are decisions made? What roles do people play? How do people behave? The focus should be on incidents known to all and positive discussions.

VALUE PEOPLE BY SHOWING YOU RESPECT THEM

Today, people feel they are human beings first and workers second. They expect to be treated as adults, with dignity. Peters and Waterman quote a General Motors auto worker who expresses his frustration when he is not treated with respect: 'What is it that makes a child out of a man? Moments before he was a father, a husband, an owner of property, a lover. Salesmen courted his favour, insurance men appealed to his family responsibility. But that was before he shuffled past the guard, climbed the stairs, hung up his coat and took his place on the production line.'

> Everyone wants to be treated as an individual.
>
> *Jan Carlzon*

A redundant solicitor complained bitterly about the lack of respect in the way she was treated on her last day. She was supervised while emptying her office drawers, escorted by two partners to her car, where she was divested of its keys. She had hoped, she said, 'to leave with some kind of dignity.'

'How then', writes Yate, 'can we expect our employees to perform superbly for us if we don't perform superbly for them?'

> You see my dear Watson but you do not observe.
>
> *Sherlock Holmes*

The Japanese have developed egalitarianism in the workplace which signals to their workers that they are valued and respected. Signs of status are kept to the minimum. Everyone in a company wears overalls of a common design and colour and eats in the same canteen. Senior managers invite operators into their homes, spend a great deal of time on the factory or office floor, and help quite naturally if a team needs an extra hand. They keep to the same discipline and rules as everyone else.

Japanese egalitarianism

> The value of single status canteens 'does not come from actual mixing but from the fact that the company does not erect barriers preventing mixing.'
>
> *Peter Wickens, Director of Personnel, Nissan*

Progressive Western organisations are increasingly adopting similar practices. For example:
- Integrated wage systems, which unify all employees within a common pay system from management to cleaner, are being installed by many organisations. For example by 1990 70 per cent of manual workers no longer receive their wages in cash, but are paid by cheque.
- Performance related pay is a symbol of rewarding people who shoulder new responsibilities or learn new skills. When awarded by

a team to colleagues it has even greater symbolic importance. Profit-sharing schemes are also no longer confined to the ranks of management. They are spreading rapidly to other grades of staff and bring with them a greater sense of ownership and commitment.

- 'Clocking in' is either abandoned or made standard for all staff, reserved car park places are discontinued, and so on.

> Assembly-line workers jeered Terry Morgan, the chief executive of Landrover, when he addressed a factory meeting wearing grey overalls. They thought it was some kind of gimmick. That was three years ago, he is still wearing them, and people don't jeer anymore . . . Executives not wearing overalls are more likely to attract sarcastic comments today. When Bernd Pischetsrieder, the BMW chairman, visited the Rover plants immediately after BMW's takeover announcement . . . 'we had some overalls run up for him although the name tab was a bit of a problem. It almost ran down his sleeve.'
>
> *Richard Donkin*

White and Trevor's research shows that in British companies attempting to introduce Japanese-style methods, one of the main reasons for failure is a lack of association between production methods and good people policies. Where the latter do not exist, or are inadequate, the researchers conclude that it makes 'problematic the introduction of Japanese style working practices'. The lack of good working conditions and fair pay is offering a signal to the workforce that management does not value their wider commitment – they are not being treated with dignity.

EQUAL OPPORTUNITIES

Respecting and valuing people, however, go deeper than adopting egalitarian policies. The true worth of every individual has to be affirmed through a conscious policy of equal opportunities for all.

Equal opportunity is only a reality when everyone is working to the level of their competence and not discriminated against on the grounds of gender, colour, race, nationality, ethnic origin or disability (as four Acts of Parliament decree). The growing tendency to discriminate against older people when recruiting is also of concern. Equal opportunities policies should include:

Eight practical strategies

1. Collecting objective data on current practices. One Health Authority discovered that the black third of its workforce occupied the lower paid, less prestigious posts (one highly skilled radiologist was

CASE STUDY: RESPECT AND DIGNITY

The new chief executive of the Union Pacific Railway described how he was 'outraged' at hearing that at one branch people had been 'flattened on the ground and dogs used to sniff for drugs' with none being found. Taking two of his departmental heads with him he met these men and all three publicly apologised. The result was 'fantastic'; the men accepted the apology in 10 minutes. When they then described other unsatisfactory sleeping conditions, the CEO inspected these and said 'they were exactly like the guys described, they were unsafe and embarrassing.' His apology and care sent a message to the whole railroad – people were keen to be treated with dignity – a powerful empowering incentive.

Source: Peters, 1992

working as a cleaner). Another survey revealed that although an equal number of men and women qualify as doctors, only 15 per cent of consultants were women. Parkyn says that the disabled (better described as the differently abled) are often discriminated against through prejudice or through the lack of physical facilities.

2. Banning recruitment policies which consciously acknowledge and therefore reveal hidden institutional sources of discrimination – asking for inappropriate qualifications or physical requirements, or courses for interviewees to understand the approaches of different cultures, or rejecting people on account of their age.

3 Ensuring that a percentage of disabled people are recruited, trained and promoted. A 1992 report reveals that over 40 per cent of employers surveyed saw disabled people as 'unsuitable employees', and suggested that short courses or specific units should be established to deal with disability issues, and job interviews guaranteed to the disabled.

4. Providing training according to the needs of each individual – for example, assertiveness training for women. A study of 25 top American women reported by Henning and Jardim emphasises this need. All the women had fathers who taught them to become proficient at male activities, which gave them an inner confidence to get through the 'glass ceiling' and on towards the top.

5. Encouraging meaningful careers for women and installing systems for career breaks and re-entry which include career counselling and retraining. A 1992 report by the Equal Opportunities Commission

stresses that women have not yet achieved full economic independence since the big increase in the numbers of women at work has been in part-time, lower-paid jobs. Women require more flexible working hours and ways of solving the burning issue that the location of a job can become when both partners work and the need to care for children or elderly relatives must be met.

6. Promoting entirely according to ability.
7. Providing adequate and fair non-monetary and monetary rewards.
8. Challenging any perceived oppression. When oppression is seen to occur, open challenge and discussion must follow, otherwise it will become established. Furthermore, the oppressed individual should not be the one who has to blow the whistle – it is for a white person to challenge racism against a black person, for example, because it is the white person's culture which is the problem.

You may not possess the authority to create these policies but, however junior, you can lead others in treating everyone, especially the vulnerable, with the dignity they deserve.

OFFER RECOGNITION WHERE IT IS DUE

Positive and negative reinforcement

A word or action of recognition shows your staff that you do value them as whole individuals, yet most of us never realise how encouraging recognition or appreciation can be, especially from a leader.

The cultural norm in many countries is to assume we are working well until told the reverse; hence the feeling of satisfaction, often out of all proportion to the activity mentioned, when our superior or colleague offers a word of praise. This also explains the importance placed by Transactional Analysis on 'strokes'. 'Strokes' ('positive reinforcement' or praise) are powerful encouragements. We feel better, and so behave more constructively. After positive reinforcement, which is pleasant, we want to act in the same way again. 'Negative reinforcement' (blame or punishment), which is unpleasant, receives a negative reaction. Discouragement, not improvement, may follow – we produce an idea, our leader squashes it, we stop having ideas. We stay late and are told to use our time more effectively; we don't work late any more.

It's amazing how hard people will work for recognition.
Vice-president of human resources

Learn the skills of praising

Giving people recognition and encouraging them in this way may not come naturally. It requires considerable thought and attention, because it *must* be sincere. You can, however, make it easier for yourself by learning the skills of praising. Peter Honey outlines these very clearly.

Praise, he says, must be specific and immediate, citing the job which was done exceptionally well and giving the reasons: 'You calmed that situation very well, you listened attentively and offered help at the right moment.' If, as we suggest in Chapter 5, positive and negative reinforcement balance each other, a skilled approach is to praise strengths first and, once confidence has been built up during the encounter, then introduce areas needing improvement when these will be accepted less defensively. But too close a mix of praise and 'negative reinforcement' can be counter-productive. Most of us are conditioned to wait for the following 'but' ('I *am* pleased with this report – *but* there are two spelling mistakes and six words here when one would do'). Exit a depressed team member.

Remember to praise your boss – he or she also needs praise!

It is particularly important to give recognition and praise to people who have achieved some important goal – overcome new challenges, welcomed change, understood and used the new technology, learned extra skills or embarked on a different career path. High achievers, in particular, need the reassurance of a word of commendation.

Some organisations encourage and recognise achievement with conscious, far-sighted policies. Pat Dade, senior consultant with Futures Ltd, described how an American Bank which needs self-motivated people has a novel approach to developing them. Each employee is offered a six-month sabbatical every five years to follow his or her own vision. One older woman, not in the best of health, had always dreamt of running in the Tokyo marathon. The company gave her every assistance. She finished the marathon, successfully achieving something she thought was far beyond her capacity. She had seized a chance to develop herself and been given recognition for it. In that bank all employees achieve and grow and are empowered.

Some other companies place achievers in charge of new company business units, lend capital to develop a new product, or grant them a franchise.

Tangible signs of achievement are becoming more important in today's climate of flatter structures, when the chances of promotions are being reduced, yet people still want to be valued for their experience and competence. Some companies are responding by creating alternative career paths. Instead of a career in management, people can receive the same recognition, status and pay by following their own expertise. They become 'super' engineers, accountants, scientists, sales people, etc.

Giving public recognition is one of the most powerful empowering forces, even more so when it is given on a team basis. Moss Kanter (1989) tells how, to make innovation contagious, Ohio Bell staged an 'innovation fair' to display prize-winning ideas from staff taking part in their Enter-Prize Programme. The winners loved explaining their ideas. One man with 40 years' experience felt he was leaving a legacy after retirement. Another assistant manager was encouraged by her manager to submit an idea she had worked on at home. To her surprise, she was funded with $20,000. Displaying her system she made comments like 'I can't believe this is happening to me – I didn't realise how much interest there is.'

CASE STUDY: CORPORATE RECOGNITION

In the early 1980s Scandinavian Airlines gave a corporate thank you to all its staff. For helping to pull the company from its worst loss to its biggest profits in one year, all 20,000 of its employees received a Christmas present containing a gold watch, a memo offering more free trips, and a personal letter of thanks from its president. Said one employee, 'I stood in the Post Office and I was so happy I was ready to cry. It was the *first time* in all my years with SAS I had received a personal thank you for what I had done, and I felt I deserved it.'

Source: Jan Carlzon

BREAK DOWN BARRIERS

In earlier chapters we emphasised the importance of empowering organisations and structures, yet many conventional organisations disempower themselves by establishing structures which, by their very nature, foster separations, divisions and possible destructive conflicts, not only between the various constituent parts and functions which make up the whole but also with their outside contacts.

Hence, as you organise around people, one of your most essential tasks is to break down these barriers by establishing and fostering cooperative relationships. You become what Margerison and McCann call a 'linker'.

The linker's role

The linker's role involves many separate activities:

- Become a vertical channel of communication between senior management and staff, interpreting the opinions, expectations and needs of each to the others.
- Help to establish IT systems which distribute information so that everyone in the relevant communication channel has access to it, and learns to interpret it.
- Establish structural and personal links horizontally between different units and functions. In one company, for example, the team and departmental leaders spend a great deal of time visiting each other's factories, coordinating and informing: 'a flying newspaper' (Peters, 1988).

- Encourage communication between your organisation and its suppliers and customers. Give them a conducted tour, set up a demonstration centre for them and give training sessions to capture their interest. Involve them in joint activities such as appraisal systems or training programmes. In particular, work to eliminate functional barriers by incorporating specialists into product-centred teams which can then be held accountable for servicing the needs of the customer.
- Join outside training courses where you and your team can learn from others with different experiences.
- Foster visits by yourself and your team to other organisations.

Linkers sharing knowledge and spreading it to everyone who will benefit from it is one of the most effective ways of empowering people – their productivity rises and morale is high.

In this section we have suggested many leadership actions you can take as you organise around people. We finish with a case study describing how the chief executive of the multinational company General Electric is harnessing the emotional power of the staff, and how individuals are developing their own potential.

CASE STUDY: A CHIEF EXECUTIVE HARNESSING EMOTIONAL POWER

In 1992 Jack Welch, CEO of General Electric, succinctly reiterated his twelve-year-old vision of empowerment. 'Any company', he said, 'expecting to stay at the top of the tough global competition of the 90s must find ways to engage the mind of *every single employee* . . . If you're not thinking all the time about making every person more valuable, you don't have a chance. What's the alternative? Wasted minds? Uninvolved people? A labour force angry or bored? That doesn't make sense.'

So between 1980 and 1984 Jack Welch radically reorganised General Electric (which had become ailing, overfat and 'choked with bureaucracy') into a lean, competitive organisation. 'Neutron' Jack had insisted that creative destruction must precede renewal.

Henceforth, he insisted that the success of this lean organisation must, as a *competitive necessity*, be built on 'an energised, involved, participative work-force where everyone plays a role, where everyone counts.' This was his vision – a vision of empowered, inner-directed people.

Turning vision into reality involved encouraging all employees

continued

to shape and share common values through company-wide policies. Welch and his executives were creating an environment within which 'the mind of every single employee' could be won. He believed that General Electric would no longer depend for success on hierarchy or coercion, but on the power of common values, understood and shared by everyone.

Efficiency would come through consensus and a team of like-minded, empowered workers would not then require much supervision. Welch viewed subordinates as his intellectual equals: all capable of producing ideas. He wanted all people at local level encouraged 'to think for themselves and to find their own solutions'. By sharing *all* information, encouraging wide open debate and entering into a dialogue, he and his executives would 'lead by being led'.

What machinery and strategies helped Welch (in a favourite phrase of his) to win the hearts and minds of others? The following policies and practices evolved over the years.

First, 13 self-contained businesses were established, under the leadership of 13 like-minded executives who possessed complete responsibility for the productivity and financial success of their company. These executives, meeting frequently with the CEO in a Corporate Executive Council, empowered themselves by developing and living the values we have described. Open, truthful and sharing all information, they were stimulated and challenged by opposing views and the need for a final consensus.

They educated and empowered each other intellectually, becoming the company think-tank. Individuals, secure in the support of the others, were also empowered emotionally. For example, a costly mistake made by one company was shared by the team both financially and also with the offer of engineering help.

Yet by 1988 there remained a hard core of managers resisting this change of attitude. Welch launched another ambitious programme, called 'Work-out', described by consultant Noel Tichy as 'one of the biggest planned efforts to alter people's behaviour since Mao's Cultural revolution.'

In this programme, senior executives discussed company values and their problems with their direct staff, who repeated the exercise down the line until finally each junior manager had met his or her own team.

continued

In addition, local gatherings of 30–100 employees met in informal, off-site surroundings for three days with the brief to define their problems and develop concrete proposals for solutions. Only consultants as facilitators were present until the end, when managers appeared and were expected to give yes or no answers on the spot or within a month.

'When you've been told to shut up for twenty years and someone tells you to speak up, you're going to let them have it,' said one electrician. As frustrations were aired and confidence grew, ideas began to appear. For example, Jimmie, a shop steward, suggested how to improve a faulty screw. The consultant immediately flew Jimmie and others to the suppliers and Jimmie fixed the problem. No supervision is now needed in that department; an empowered Jimmie leads instead. At another plant, hourly-paid employees were authorised to write the specifications for $20 million worth of replacement machines which they tested and approved themselves.

By mid 1992, over 200,000 GE employees had participated in work-outs and with increasing trust more suggestions continue to appear. The company was healthy, flexible and successful but Welch envisaged still more changes – to remove boundaries between departments; to erase job titles which separate, such as manager, salaried and hourly; to create cross-functional teams; and an intended radical empowerment of workers.

Tichy commented: 'Effective competitors in the 21st Century will be the organisations that learn how to use shared values to harness the emotional energy of employees, who feel inspired to share their best ideas with their employers.'

Source: *Tichy and Sherman*

WORKSHOP: ORGANISING AROUND PEOPLE

1. Would you like to work in a company which organises around people, such as General Electric? Or as a member of such an organisation, how does your leadership role differ from your previous experience?
2. Do your staff feel you treat them as whole people, not units of production?
3. Are you a mentor to your staff?
4. Is your senior a mentor to you?

HAND OVER CONTROL

As we saw in the last case study, when people gain control over their own work and feel they own it, their higher needs – the 'true motivators' – are being satisfied and they become committed to a shared goal.

There are many stages in the control process, ranging from an autocratic style in which leaders retain complete control, through various intermediate steps when control is shared with the people concerned, to a point where individuals or teams make their own decisions and take full responsibility and accountability for their own work.

PRACTISE PARTICIPATION AND CREATE A COMMON PURPOSE

An early stage of sharing control is for leaders to encourage people to participate in the decision-making process to the full extent of their abilities. With open communication and trust, this generates a sense of purpose and a belief in the value of their work.

Some research by Rensis Likert indicates how this principle is translated into practice. Leaders set high-performance goals for and *with* their staff and believe 'with contagious enthusiasm' in their successful achievement, while continuously explaining what is expected and what achieved. This task must be supported with an atmosphere of approval, forewarning about changes, and defence against hostile outside influences.

Using Likert's methods, a district sales director dramatically improved the low performance of his 14 managers. At regular meetings he:

- trained them and supplied full information
- planned with them their objectives and strategy and analysed progress
- encouraged problem solving
- helped them to solve their interpersonal differences
- said he *expected* high performance

Within six months their district was leading the company by a large margin. Through his leadership skills the director had tapped unused sources of productivity.

Consulting people in this way and expecting changed behaviour helps everyone to feel they have contributed to the outcome and an undreamt-of liberation of energy, productivity and cooperation can unfold, as the next case study shows.

CASE STUDY: THE POWER OF PARTICIPATION

Tinsley Bridge Ltd, a Sheffield steel manufacturer which makes springs for the car industry, was part of British Steel until, in 1987, its managers became the owners through a management buy-out. At that time, however, the company was not competitive either in standards, quality, volume, delivery or price. Clearly, the attitudes of both managers and workers needed changing. Peter Wickens, the personnel director of the successful British Nissan Company, gave them good advice. To become a quality company, he said, people needed to believe in everyone being fairly treated through seeing what the managers did, rather than what they said.

By 1987 the company had established single-status staff conditions, with clocking-on abolished and employees arriving ready for work at a stated time, meeting in teams with their supervisors and starting the shift.

Yet the group of first-line supervisors were not prepared to play the crucial role this demanded of them – briefing their teams, taking responsibility for attendance and discipline, maintaining high quality standards (under a new statistical process control) and ensuring the effective maintenance of machines. The speed of change had been too great for them and they resented the need to manage not by giving orders to their teams, but by gaining their willing commitment and trusting them.

So the managers were facing a problem of mounting resentment. They realised this would never change unless they provided 'the training, the facilities and the system', since mentally it required a leap forward by the supervisors to recognise that they were now managers and stood 'at the critical point of management which makes things happen'. They were the key to the success of the new policy, but they had to see and accept this for themselves.

A seminar for all supervisors was therefore arranged at which the managers asked them to define their changed role. The final definition closely matched the one envisaged by the management, but instead of being a management decree the supervisors 'owned' their decision and 'it was as if something locked up inside them had broken out'. The managers provided a training programme on the understanding that the supervisors

continued

> were committed to the new approach and that management would support them as they implemented it. A new title of 'section manager' was introduced.
>
> The supervisors 'started managing in a different way', and on the appointed date for the change a group of very apprehensive supervisors, 'believing in what they were doing', briefed their single-status teams and started the shift.
>
> From then on Tinsley Bridge began to be successful, with profits up and order books healthy.
>
> *Source: Sargent*

BUILD A CULTURE OF SELF-DISCIPLINE

In the example we quoted earlier the sales director trained his managers in the skills of participation. When people learn to discipline themselves a further stage in handing over control has been reached. For example:

- Set agreed standards of discipline *with* each individual or team, coach them to keep these and *keep them yourself*. Because these standards are joint ones and so owned, they are not resented. White and Trevor report that at JEL, a Japanese factory in north-east England, waste and substandard work were simply eradicated. Operators made frequent checks on materials and production and reported deviations immediately. However, when the Japanese managers left for home and were succeeded by British managers, the workers complained that these new managers expected them to comply with the rules and customs of self-discipline, but did not keep them themselves. They felt that a traditional attitude of 'them and us' was being reestablished. The culture of self-discipline was being eroded because the standards were not kept by everyone, so were no longer *joint*.
- Set agreed standards of work performance with each individual, based on a joint agreement on the objectives, key result areas and targets which are required to accomplish the job successfully.

> People will work cheerfully if they know what to do and have the tools and responsibility to do it.
>
> *Bob Garratt*

What everyone needs to know

In order to perform effectively everyone needs to know:
- What is my job?
- What standards are expected?

● How am I doing?

Individual job descriptions may already exist. Ensure that they call for *results*.

The leader and team member should agree their main key result areas. Most managers find that job holders agree the objectives but will differ on key result areas – especially on priorities. (One study revealed complete agreement in only 5 per cent of cases.) When these disagreements occur they must be explored and agreement reached.

The next stage is crucial. Together, the leader and the team member *Set agreed standards* set the standards of performance required for success, so that an acceptable performance is objectively judged and job holders know where they stand. Some standards are easy to quantify – a sales representative or a social worker can programme so many visits within a set time. Goods produced to a specified quality and on time is a measure of production performance. A vicar promised 'faithfully' to acknowledge correspondence within two days.

For indirect work (functional, clerical, etc. and some aspects of every job) many standards cannot be so objective. Nevertheless you must agree and record an acceptable level for at least four areas occurring in most jobs:

● Numerical   figures for sales, production defects, complaints, etc.
● Deadlines   for completions, meeting dates, answers, etc.
● Financial   budgets, costs, stock levels, etc.
● Procedural   stages for giving information, writing minutes, settling complaints, etc.

Within these broad outlines set together some *targets* for completion to agreed time limits to:

● undertake a special project
● turn an innovation into action
● develop a new skill, etc.

Targets challenge and stretch people and, when met successfully, they *Set challenging targets* provide a great sense of achievement. The people concerned learn to take responsibility for their own work and their commitment is deepened. But if they are unrealistic or too difficult, targets demotivate and become counter-productive.

Each stage of defining together the job, its targets and the current standards it requires will involve asking searching questions which help the team member to explore his or her knowledge or skills development needs, and then coaching him or her to want to learn and develop and so meet these standards and surpass them.

Much of the value of coaching then lies in an ongoing joint *How am I doing?* discussion on how the person is performing and their attitudes and motivation towards self-improvement.

> Self motivation can be greatly enhanced by coaching and then coaching can be used to convert motivation into effective action.
>
> John Whitmore

One of your own targets as an empowering leader is to hold a progress review and monitor results with each member of your team consistently and frequently: once a month for some, once a week for a beginner or someone with problems.

DELEGATE WORK

The progress review lays the foundation for the next step in handing over control – to increase individual responsibility and accountability by delegating more demanding work to members of your staff.

Coaching them to become effective develops new skills and, as they achieve success in new tasks, they gain confidence, especially when you show confidence in them.

Delegating work satisfies both individual and corporate needs. When people increase their knowledge and skills their 'true motivators' are being satisfied, and it also allows you as the leader to concentrate on your empowering role – you *multiply* yourself.

> Delegation breeds commitment.
>
> Martin John Yate

Definition of delegation

Andrew Forrest defines delegation as 'when you deliberately choose to give to one of your staff authority to carry out a piece of work which you could have decided to carry out yourself.' The *whole* task is delegated, together with the necessary resources – money, time, equipment and authority. You as leader are, however, still accountable for its performance.

Make a delegation plan:
1. Write down your own key result areas and the tasks these entail.
2. Keep a record for a month of how you spend your time. Use some general headings such as 'meetings', 'discussing problems', 'visits', 'phone calls'.
3. Ask yourself some searching questions.

Find from your list *whole* jobs which will stretch the people who do them. (Delegation is not indiscriminate dumping, for example, of pieces of jobs which you may not like doing or which are time consuming.)

Decide to whom you will delegate. Who, for example:

- possesses unused skills?
- is most motivated?
- will benefit most?
- performs most successfully in their present job?
- is being underused?

Clive Thornton, for example, one of the top 19 leaders interviewed by Andrew Forrest and Patrick Tolfree, says he worked on the 'clear desk' principle at the Abbey National bank. When he took over as manager of three departments, he visited each one and found that everybody's desk was heaped high with paper, since his predecessor had to put the final endorsement on decisions. When he asked how often they had paperwork handed back as unacceptable, the answer was almost never. So he told them that now they would decide things for themselves, only asking him if they were unable to do this. If he found someone working late he would assume that there was something wrong or that the person was doing it from choice, and he would want to know why.

Delegation carries risks. You may have misgivings, yet you know it is right for the department and for the person. So choose someone ready for development and plan to proceed systematically.

How to delegate.   Discuss the process with the person concerned. Clarify the objectives and the limits of authority they carry, and ensure that you have made these clear and unambiguous – then you can stress that the individual chooses the *way* it is accomplished. You are delegating authority to *do*. Show confidence in success and offer encouragement and support.

Unfortunately, in many companies the only thing that gets attention is a mistake.

Jan Carlzon

Delegate in stages.   Decide together what steps to take from beginning to final take-over and possible actions if trouble looms. Andrew Forrest lists five stages, starting with you doing the job while they watch and ask questions and ending with a complete handover, supported by a feedback system and occasional spot checks.

Expect some failures.   At any stage there may be some failure. Reassure the person that you *expect* this: making mistakes is one of the best ways to learn. Using counselling skills (described in Part IV) help him or her to discover the reasons for failure and suggest solutions.

Some reasons could be:

- lack of planning (more coaching needed?)
- inadequate people skills (arrange training?)
- communication blocks with other departments (stress the importance of freeing these)

Slow down the process if necessary.   Use a weekly performance review interview to slow down hand-over stages and do more coaching. Only decide to continue or to hand the job to someone else when you are sure no further progress can be made. The person who failed needs counselling and help. Your skills of delegation may also have been at fault. In both cases, correctly handled, you can learn more about the skills of handing over control and the other person can learn more about his or her abilities and needs.

WORKSHOP: YOUR EXPERIENCE OF DELEGATION

1. Do you know what your job is, and what standards and targets are expected from you? If not, can you ask for a joint discussion with your boss to discover how you are getting on?
2. Analyse your boss's job:
   - Which aspects of it do you think you could do?
   - Which aspects should never be delegated?
3. Do you welcome the extra control such delegation would offer you?
4. Are there any appropriate circumstances in which you should delegate work upwards – to your boss?

HELP PEOPLE TO REDESIGN WORK SO THAT THEY CONTROL IT

In the last section we stressed the importance of delegating whole jobs. People feel in control of their own work when they follow a process through from beginning to end. They begin to own it and ownership brings control. So stimulate everyone to think creatively about his or her work and how it could be redesigned to give more individual control.

Waterman reports that 25 years spent by managers handing over control to their employees at the Lima plant of Procter and Gamble prompted one old hand to put this in a nutshell. 'There is one word', he said, 'which explains Lima's success – ownership.' In fact, Procter and Gamble developed this system of self-management over 30 years and considered it so strategically important that they had previously refused to talk about it.

Other organisations have achieved similar results. They report increased job satisfaction and commitment (sometimes 'immeasurably') and higher productivity.

- Carlzon describes how in one branch of Scandinavian Airlines, sales people are responsible for cargo and passenger sales. Everyone answers phones, sells tickets, checks in passengers and handles problems. Work has become 'more challenging and more fun'.
- A large insurance company has made even more revolutionary changes. An application which previously had to go through 30 different steps, spanning five departments and involving 19 people, is now processed by *one* case manager who has complete control from its reception to the issue of a policy.
- The train captain of the London Docklands light railway is similarly placed. With no driver or station staff, he checks tickets, collects money and controls the doors. He therefore relates closely to the customers.
- Some simple lateral thinking by the leader of a team assembling gas convectors transformed their job satisfaction and productivity. Instead of each assembler adding one part, restructuring the layout enabled the parts to move round the assemblies so that each worker assembled their own complete gas convector.
- Waterman gives the example of Levi's where, since 1991, teams of three to twelve people have been reorganised so that they are responsible for making jeans from cutting, through all the sewing steps, to shipping. They learn at least three of these operations and all have a big say in arranging their work flow and set their own production goals. This reorganisation resulted in jeans being shipped out of the plant in one day instead of the six or more that it took previously.

At the front line

If the work processes in your department cannot be restructured to produce whole jobs, many jobs can still have *partial* control built into them.

Add variety and extra responsibility

In Chapter 3, we suggested that rotating roles between functions develops responsibility, and that variety can be added by rotating people between different jobs or departments. This is common practice in Germany since workers learn all processes. (In semi-autonomous work teams operators often organise their own rotation.) Another approach is to enlarge a task by adding extra responsibilities. One supermarket manager turned boredom into interest for young trainees. Each was put in charge of an aisle of shelves. They stocked their own aisles, ordered new stock from the distributors and created special displays. Some even worked on their day off to ensure all was well.

Two other examples of enlarging jobs come from the secretarial section of the work community, where people are frequently underused. In two firms, interviews revealed that the cause of high labour turnover among secretaries was not working conditions but the absence of challenge in their work. In both companies work was enlarged. At one, secretaries were trained to write business letters, attend and report on press conferences, deal with advertisement copy and subedit press releases. They welcomed the challenge of self-supervision, morale rose and labour turnover dropped from 61 to 48 per cent.

COACH PEOPLE TO SOLVE PROBLEMS AND MAKE DECISIONS

In all the methods of handing over control we have described, one overriding precondition stands out – people must be able and willing to solve problems and make decisions. Yet although they do this quite naturally outside work and at home, in traditional organisations they have been conditioned to take orders and the manager may well have been conditioned to make all the decisions and to give orders. So staff may need to learn this new approach. Here are some suggestions:

Coach with searching questions

- The temptation to offer your own decisions needs to be steadfastly resisted. Instead, reframe them into searching questions. For example, have we got all the facts? what are the options? what would be the consequences of that? and so on.

Ask for solutions

- Ask for solutions, not complaints. Pegg describes a senior manager of a car factory who only received complaints and difficulties at problem-solving meetings. The manager changed his tactics, asking for no more unsolved problems but only solutions with options, for and against. In turn, he promised to give positive yes or no decisions. In time people began to solve their own problems. Self-management was on its way.

Introduce 'kaizen'

- Ask the question, 'How could we do this better?' – the Japanese concept of *kaizen* – so that continuous improvement becomes a cultural norm and inevitably speeds up the process. For instance, the Danish Railway did this by focusing on one particular area at a time, such as 'How can we tackle incoming telephone calls better?'

Lateral thinking

- Encourage staff to solve problems by thinking innovatively and so become used to lateral thinking. The best approach is to set an example, so start with yourself. Learn to think constantly about what you can do to change, innovate, create. Then ask the individual or team what new things did you consider? do? last week? last month?

Customer first

- Ensure individual accountability for customer services. A priority is to explain that each person will be held personally accountable for putting the customer first and must therefore be prepared to make decisions on the spot, with your support guaranteed. Emphasise that the customer can be internal within the same organisation or external. As Jan Carlzon put it, 'if you are not serving the customer then you should be serving someone who is.'

Front-line accountability

The Union Pacific Railroad in America reorganised its structure, in order to put its customers first, making a priority of reliability and a quick response by asking people working in the front line to take responsibility for rectifying complaints and failures. Five layers of management were removed and a cross-functional supply and demand committee composed of the heads of the day-to-day operations was instituted in order to match customer demand to carrying capacity (Peters, 1992).

> Mars pays well. But people are much more switched on by accountability. The thing I enjoy most is being able to do things for which I am accountable.
>
> *Locksley Ryan, Corporate Affairs Manager, Mars UK (in Jackson, 1991)*

Everyone is a leader

Getting closer to the customer and pushing accountability to the front line force you to train everyone, both managers and staff, to regard themselves as leaders. It is also your responsibility to ensure that all receive training in the people skills which enable them to treat customers courteously. The non-contact staff (cooks, accountants, computer staff, etc.) must also realise that everyone is their customer too – not clients or a nuisance.

> Take care of these people [customers] and they provide the service which gives you good returns and your profits.
>
> *Station manager with Federal Express (in Peters, 1992)*

The next case study illustrates how one British company changed their traditional hierarchic structure. Instead, the CEO and senior executives handed over control to the staff.

CASE STUDY: BARR & STROUD

Barr and Stroud, which designs and creates products as subcontractors to the British defence industry, completely changed its traditional hierarchic structure by reducing nine tiers of management to four. It created instead 12 self-contained teams, each dedicated to a specific project, encompassing all the activities to complete the project – designers, product planners, material purchasers, production controllers, plus a team leader. A

continued

policy decision that its major strategy lay in this designing and developing area led the company to contract out most of the manufacturing and production processes.

A move to a new factory aided this process and various measures aimed at reducing status barriers were introduced:

- An L-shaped open-plan office merged into the manufacturing area.
- The Managing Director sits in a desk space indistinguishable from the rest. 'This is where I sit', he said proudly.
- Six former canteens were merged into one, and so on.

These various measures met the most important needs of this talented staff. The involved teams were empowered to organise their work flow into a natural, sensible sequence and make decisions as a team. Most of all, they gained the deep satisfaction of completing their own whole job through from beginning to end.

Results underline the success of this strategy:

- In 1992 the company made its first profit since the late 1980s.
- Production lead time was cut from 15 months to 7.
- The amount of products delivered on time rose from 10 to 90 per cent.

Source: *Financial Times*, 12 May 1993

WORKSHOP: HANDING OVER CONTROL

- Which of the various practical ways of handing over control to individuals or teams most suit your own circumstances?
- Does your organisation possess systems for agreeing objectives and standards, delegating work, making everyone accountable for customer care and training people in decision making?
- How much control is being handed over to you? Would you like more? If so, what coaching or extra training would you need?
- Find an organisation or department which is putting these principles into practice and study it. How successful is it?

CONCLUSIONS

Skills of empowering leadership

This new leadership role, regardless of official titles, involves three distinct leadership skills:

- *Administrator*: helping individuals and teams to set goals, meet their objectives, solve problems etc.

- *Adviser*: providing the necessary technical knowledge, resources and judgement.
- *Coach*: shifting the emphasis from controlling to training; teaching the aspects now being handed over to the team and helping them to develop and mature, with the aim of eventually eliminating the need for coaching (one company calls this a 'weaning' process).

Handy (1985) describes this as 'a mixture between teacher, consultant and trouble shooter, requiring three types of skill: technical, social and conceptual.' 'Not a job for ordinary mortals', he concludes, tongue in cheek.

On the contrary, leadership *can* be a job for every ordinary mortal provided they are given the chance, because leadership can be learnt with training, encouragement and practice. Donald Petersen, when chief executive of Ford International, understood this. He described how he asked the Central Policy and Strategic Committee to find ways, with him, of 'pushing responsibility down to the lowest possible level' to empower the lowest level management team. So, 'if an engineer has the knowledge to make a decision, then let him make it.' The best way to show people that you do trust them, he says, is to let them spend more money; if, for example, a departmental chief knows the correct equipment for a job, he or she should be able to buy it. Thus a group of financial experts was asked to find ways of delegating more spending authority to levels closer to where the work was done, and significant progress was made.

Leading others to lead themselves

The job of an empowering leader can be summed up as: to lead others to lead themselves.

8 Empowered and Empowering Teams

There are two separate but equally vital aspects to empowerment:
- the possession of both people and intellectual skills
- organisations which liberate their members to take control of their own destinies and the decisions that are made

Successful teams help to supply both these aspects and are therefore vital to empowerment.

What is a team?

A team is a special kind of group, succinctly defined by Mike Woodcock as 'a group of people who share common objectives and need to work together to achieve them.' A group is a much looser association defined by Charles Handy (1985) as 'any *collection* of people who perceive themselves to be one.'

Group dynamics

Both groups and teams are examples of dynamic 'socio-technical systems'. 'Group dynamics' describes the multitude of interactions and inter-relationships within and between groups and teams; they are ever moving, always active. Indeed, both groups and teams have a mentality beyond that of the individual members, connecting them, according to Leroy Wells, by 'a process of unconscious machinery of inter-communications'.

A number of congenial people meeting regularly in the canteen are a group, but they are not a team. Supposing, however, they decide to write and perform a sketch for the Christmas show: they have a common objective, they write the script, rehearse and perform together. Accomplishing more than as separate individuals, they temporarily become a team.

THE POWER OF TEAMS

The power of teams is founded on one of the strongest needs depicted in Maslow's hierarchy of needs (Chapter 7) – the need to belong. Belonging gives us a sense of security and individual worth; isolation leads to stress, even for the most misanthropic. Asked what they would miss most when leaving work, the majority of people mention friends. Even when we belong to a group which is not a team and perhaps not of our choosing – a family, fellow prisoners or supervisors – we still need them and expect practical or emotional support when the going gets rough.

Equally important is the liberating effect of a team's organisation. The activities of its members towards a common goal develop a close network of interaction between members. They communicate about the task (being in one place facilitates this), consult over problems, and regularly rotate jobs. Just-in-time stock control (JIT) calls for team members to help each other with problems and over matters such as overtime at short notice. At Nissan, teams work before shifts and through their breaks to achieve their target, and in emergencies, office workers at another UK-based Japanese factory help out on the factory floor.

> The whole staff works as a family, it's close-knit, it's the atmosphere, man, it's great.
>
> JEL *employee* (*in White and Trevor*, 1983)

Structures such as groups or teams provide security and freedom, but *empowered* teams also satisfy Maslow's highest needs for creativity, self-expression and self-fulfilment and so capture the hearts and minds of their members. Research over many years shows that such teams possess great job satisfaction and high morale. Even when disappointments occur, they resist frustration, labour turnover and absenteeism are lower, and tests demonstrate that team decisions are better than those made by one individual and are more acceptable to others.

Teams satisfy the true motivators

Over 60 years ago, Elton Mayo conducted the famous Hawthorne experiments which still form the foundation for insights into the motivating power of teams. In a series of experiments designed to

The Hawthorne experiments

discover the effects of working conditions on productivity, he and his fellow researchers made changes in one group of six people, and none in a control team. In all they made ten changes – to lighting, rest breaks, shorter hours and to different incentives, etc. Each time the productivity rose in *both* teams – even when returned to their original conditions. Mayo's explanation of these findings was that communicating with the researchers made the women feel more responsible for their own and their team's performance, and their job satisfaction rose because they saw themselves as individual team members, not just cogs in a wheel.

Latent energy released

Further experience has enabled us to realise that our 'true motivators' are fulfilled by belonging to teams which have a common objective, and which are likely to be empowered to take responsibility and make decisions. In this situation people learn and *grow*. The latent energy of each individual is released – because we perceive ourselves primarily in relation to others, it is only through membership of a group or team that we can truly come to know ourselves. Individuals within teams can understand their own contributions and so gain a strengthened sense of purpose and commitment, which is a precondition for empowerment. The experience of 'new stream' innovative teams in America illustrates this vividly: their exhilaration and deep commitment meant that long hours and neglect of families seemed a small price to pay (Moss Kanter, 1989).

> Their shared need for success encourages ideas for improved performance, gains commitment and inspires keenness.
>
> ACAS *Report*

> Empowered teams improve quality, productivity and participation.
>
> *Richard Wellins, William Byham and Jeanne Wilson*

Teams satisfy organisational needs

Teams also play a crucial role in the wider organisation of which they are a part. Research suggests that organisations are more successful when the needs of the organisation coincide most closely with the needs of its staff. Successful teams satisfy both sets of needs. Organisational needs become radically different when, in order to remain competitive, companies recognised that satisfying customer demands was their major priority. Teams within an empowering organisation can fulfil this priority better than management by command.

This is because multi-disciplinary, empowered teams can respond rapidly to changing customer needs and avoid endless alterations as each change has to be cross-checked with other key players. They can increase efficiency and reduce costs, because they accomplish *more than the sum* of their individual members. They spark ideas and plans off each other which are better than any one individual could have produced on his or her own.

> A lot of little brains are superior to a few big brains.
>
> Konosuke Matsushita (in Pascale, 1991)

To do this successfully, *each person* must become multiskilled and learn to solve problems. Each, too, needs the skills of leadership, especially if the leader's role rotates.

Many companies in Britain's main competitor nations have already recognised the vital need for this type of strong team, and have established semi-autonomous teams at the front line. Japanese firms have developed this system most fully. Production is organised into self-contained cells – a 'mini-factory within a factory' with machines, people and operations arranged according to the work flow rather than departmentally. (The Toyota group has reorganised and builds all new plants to this system.)

In such teams each member, even the most junior, has the power to stop production immediately faults occur. At Toyota they call this *jikoda*. The Rover company, associated as it was with Honda, takes a similar approach. Teams are held responsible for the accuracy and quality of their product – organising their work, inspecting and improving it, solving problems, cutting waste and saving time. Functional people – setters, inspectors, quality controllers, etc. – become team members, and some operators even sign off their own work after self-inspection. Any extra management layer serves as a support – not controlling but sharing the burden.

Team responsibilities

Each semi-autonomous team has a team leader (the 'Meister' in Germany, the 'father' of the team at Rover). Together with the team, they possess full responsibility and accountability for producing complete parts of a large whole, whether a manufacturing process or a service. Rover describes the leader as the 'lynch pin'. White and Trevor explain that Japanese supervisors are usually responsible for both planning work and its execution, so team leaders meet their teams at starting time to:

- discuss production targets and the processes required to achieve them (at Nissan, team leaders discuss how to improve quality (*kaizen*), schedule changes and redistribute work);

- decide who does which job;
- solve problems;
- welcome and induct new members;
- at Nissan occasionally 'a great message from on high arrives'.

> In Nissan, if there is one aspect to be singled out as important in team building and commitment, it is the five minute meeting at the start of the day.
>
> *Peter Wickens, Director of Personnel, Nissan (1985)*

The JIT system allows no spare stock, and so such empowered teams actively anticipating future needs are vital to ensure that production flows smoothly.

German production methods

Some German manufacturing companies have succeeded by using similar production methods. Sorge and Warner explain that teams, trained when apprentices in engineering production processes, enjoy a large degree of autonomy. Meister and team cater for market niches, with individualised products manufactured in small batches by these highly flexible teams. The authors conclude that 'the prevalence of its culture has allowed the German machine tool producers to remain competitive despite a frontal Japanese attack.'

Teams in the Health Service

Management consultants Kinsley Lord quote another interesting example, which shows the creative possibilities opened up by multidisciplinary teams. Nurses in the Accident and Emergency Department of a children's hospital cooperated with the doctors to reduce the waiting time for seeing a doctor from 2 hours to a goal of 30 minutes. Plotting the types and timings of admissions enabled them to rationalise the troughs and peaks by making some changes in working hours, staggering meal breaks and creating a new admissions procedure. In 1991 they achieved their 30-minute goal for 99 per cent of their admissions.

An in-depth survey

Evidence that strong front-line teams are better at satisfying customer demand comes from a recent survey by Wellins, Byham and Wilson. This covered 500 organisations with in-depth research into 28 companies differing in type, location, size and function. In addition they reviewed 100 separate books and articles. Their conclusion is that there is a wealth of evidence confirming the success of empowered front-line teams.

Their survey shows that strong teams:
- Increase productivity – 45 per cent of respondents said that teams play an important role. One company using teams gained 40 per cent more productivity than other areas of the organisation which

operated without them. Another company increased productivity by 74 per cent in three years and another by 20 per cent.

- Improve quality and cut waste – one company increased service quality by 12 per cent, another cut customer waiting time dramatically; a carrier company reduced turn-around time from two weeks to two days. Volvo reduced defects by 90 per cent at its Kalmar factory.

Waterman describes how Rubbermaid, a supplier of plastic household goods, depends heavily on teams. A typical meeting is held monthly by the senior executive with heads of the departments for which he or she is responsible, e.g. cleaning products, rubber gloves or vacuum bags. Although decisions are reached by consensus, all members bring their own particular expertise to the discussions. Everyone therefore has a sense of individual ownership and is motivated by their own specialised tasks, yet they also depend on each other for the success of the whole section and so share in decisions about all its products. Rubbermaid is a company in the forefront of innovation and change, and a team structure encourages and supports this strength.

Rubbermaid

> With 12 people sitting round the table, if there's something missing, someone will catch it.
> *Peter Cockfield, senior product manager for cleaning products at Rubbermaid*

Teams at all levels

Teams can exist at many levels other than at the front line and can flourish equally well in powerful multinational companies and in small concerns. The consultants Kinsley Lord describe how two large organisations, Nuclear Electric in Britain and Esso, the multinational oil company, have successfully used *company-wide* teams to increase their efficiency and cut costs. In 1991 at the Wylfa power station staff at all levels working together cut closing time for maintenance from eight weeks to at most seven and thus increased electricity production by £2.5 million. The complexity of such a change was immense, yet by identifying new procedures and ways of working together, plus new skills, the teams eventually achieved the same result in just over six weeks.

Esso worked with its seafarers to improve productivity. Teams representing all the people in the fleet – officers, ratings and support staff – were involved in the process from 1978 to 1990. As a result, crews on the largest crude carriers were reduced to 42, then 30 and finally, although few believed it possible, to 19 in 1990.

> WORKSHOP: DO TEAMS SATISFY YOUR NEEDS?
>
> 1. Think of a team in which you have recently worked (or played).
>   How did it gain your commitment?
> 2. Was there a major problem that the team overcame or solved?
>   Was it the product of one member or did it evolve within the
>   team?
> 3. If you belong to a semi-autonomous team, with a leader, what
>   benefits for the team members and for your organisation have
>   you observed?

A note of caution. Strong, liberated and empowered teams may experience difficulties with other teams which are organised on more conventional lines. So it is important that all team members, as well as their leader, become 'linkers' to build bridges between other teams and departments.

SELF-DIRECTED TEAMS

Teams can be strong and liberated, but not yet completely autonomous and self-directed. However, *completely* autonomous and self-directed teams which have no official leader are becoming increasingly more common and important. They have reached the peak of Maslow's motivational triangle – self-fulfilment.

> The people closest to any task usually know more about it than their so-called supervisors.
>
> *Noel Tichy and Stratford Sherman*

DIFFERENT KINDS OF SELF-DIRECTED TEAMS

Below we describe some examples of teams which organise and manage their own work to illustrate how the system works in practice. These teams, representative of many others, are separated by thousands of miles and by their nationality, objectives and size. One is a restaurant chain, another is a manufacturing company making hoses. Another is a charity, others are *ad hoc* project teams or quality circles. Yet all possess two overriding common factors: they are self-directed and empowered.

Harvester

Jane Pickard describes the restaurant chain Harvester, where a branch manager works with a 'coach', who handles all the training and some other personnel issues. All the other staff are called 'team members'. Each team on each shift also has a coordinator, and apart from new recruits all team members will take on this role at different times.

Harvester has drawn up a list of what it calls 'accountabilities', special responsibilities such as recruitment, drawing up rotas, and monitoring sales against targets. Everyone in the team has one or more accountability, which are shared out among staff at the weekly team meetings. Someone who has mastered all the accountabilities is elected by the team as a 'team expert'.

The branch manager now spends more time on marketing than before the reorganisation, and also acts as a facilitator, encouraging people to believe they can work in new ways. Jane Pickard comments, 'It is not easy for waitresses or chefs to grasp that they were suddenly accountable for ordering their own stock, carrying out their own hygiene checks, sorting out their own problems, dealing with customer complaints, or cashing up.'

In *Liberation Management*, Peters describes the experience of Titeflex, a company making hoses, which is run successfully by a series of interlocking self-managing teams headed by a top administrative team called 'Genesis'.

Titeflex

All new orders are fed into this team which consists of five people from different functions – a contracts manager, a draftsman, engineers from manufacturing and a clerical support person. Their desks are arranged in a tight circle which enables them to talk informally, and make decisions with great speed – in ten minutes for routine orders and no more than two to five days for new or intricate work. They handle all the detail themselves with minimal paperwork (a complex order taking a page or so) and then pass the order for making the components to the factory which is organised in self-sufficient 'business development teams', each with six to ten members.

These are in fact small businesses which 'sell' complete hose-and-fitting sets to the Genesis team. The process is completed by final assembly teams. Astonishingly, these front-line changes were achieved in one weekend by the workers themselves. The first self-managed team was created between Friday afternoon and Monday morning, and in less than a month the whole factory was converted.

The teams consult directly with suppliers and 'have unlimited authority to do whatever is necessary for the customer' – so teams travel widely to consult customers and to satisfy their needs. Equally, customers work with Titeflex employees on new products resulting in a 50 per cent reduction in development time. Titeflex was then taking business from competitors since with growing efficiency their swiftness and ability to deliver custom-built hoses had increased.

Their output increased phenomenally – in one department, for example, from 300–400 pieces a month to 9–10,000 – yet in spite of this speed and pressure the workers said the work was more relaxed, and more 'fun'. Their liberation and empowerment had made it so.

> We believed in our vision, so we decided to do it all over a weekend, trusting that the operators would pick up the pieces and run with them.
>
> *Quality Assurance Director, Titeflex*

Cluster organisations

Peters also quotes the work of Quinn Mills who describes a similar way of running a complete operation with what is known as the 'cluster organisation'. A 'cluster' is a self-sufficient team of 30–50 people from different disciplines which accepts accountability for many administrative functions, for example:

- emphasising the paramount needs of customers
- pushing decisions forward into action
- sharing information widely

This large body is further subdivided into self-directed work teams of five to seven members, such as:

- a core team (top management)
- business units dealing directly with external customers
- staff units for internal customers
- project and change teams dealing with specific improvements or modifications to company strategy

Clusters, like all forms of devolved management, depend on the infrastructure which information technology can now supply. To succeed, their individual members need the backing of continuous, broadly based learning, the free sharing of both local and company information and, most importantly, says Mills, to 'know they are trusted'.

These clusters provide a fundamental alternative to the hierarchies which are so clearly failing to cope with today's business environment.

Airspace charity

In a different sector, the staff in the British charity Airspace, described in Chapter 2, provide a thought-provoking example of how the staff of a whole organisation can work successfully as a self-directing collective, through maximising participation and creating consensus over shared goals.

The success of the staff in fulfilling this exacting policy of consensus depended on a variety of empowering policies and procedures. For example:

- Everyone was expected to contribute honestly ideas, suggestions and opinions at their regular decision-making meetings. As a consequence, debates could become tense and full of fierce though constructive conflict (see Chapter 4) before a consensus emerged which all were prepared to accept. Any emotional damage was then repaired and healed by the ritual of 'huggy bear' before people left the meeting.
- All staff had equal status and were paid the same. Each person, deeply committed to the common goal, was then expected to fulfil his or her individual role *without supervision*.
- People supported and trusted each other to do their best, so did not condemn others when mistakes were made. Instead, a policy of continuous training and open discussions concentrated on improving performance.

Airspace provides an example of how a self-directing team produced successful results in spite of very meagre and uncertain financial resources. This participative structure satisfied the 'true motives' of each team member and created a sense of belonging and commitment to the charity's purpose so powerful that long working hours and poor pay were willingly accepted. Perhaps most encouraging of all, it demonstrates how 'difficult to place' 16-year-old youngsters developed and grew when they were trusted and given responsibility.

Manz gives details of an even more novel approach to company-wide employee empowerment, known as the lattice system. This is practised by WL Gore & Associates, a manufacturer of Gore-tex fabrics and other products, which has grown over a short time to become a worldwide organisation of 44 companies, each limited purposely to 200 'associates' (employees). The company has no formal managers other than one president and one secretary at headquarters. Instead, all associates have a sponsor who both guides them and helps them to choose *for themselves* the work they feel most fitted for; at times as team members, sometimes as initiators.

The lattice system

Thus a team created by one associate can have members who choose to belong to it from any part of the company. This 'lattice' structure leads to the constant self-development of temporary cross-area teams as the need arises, and 'associates' are expected to empower and develop themselves as they join the various operations they feel they can serve best.

Some 'associates' find the emphasis on self-management and individual initiative too difficult and so leave. This is the flipside of empowerment: it makes large demands on the individual and can cause stress, as we see in Chapters 9 and 13. Nevertheless, this egalitarian, participative approach has led to innovation, growth and success for Gore, and is a good signpost to the way many organisations may work in the future.

> Self-managing teams 'may be the productivity breakthrough of the 1990s.'
>
> *Fortune magazine*

DEVELOPING SELF-DIRECTED TEAMS

Describing his research into self-directed autonomous teams, David Barry says, 'There are several basic forces that will continue to make self-managed teams, with no official leader, an increasingly popular organisational device in the 1990s.' They appear at many different levels in both large and small companies – in front-line production, in service sections, as quality circles, or at the top, creating policies and strategies.

Why now?

There are many reasons for this:

- the need for constant innovation
- the information technology explosion, resulting in highly educated, self-motivated specialists who work best within participative flexible structures
- the need to eliminate the cost of interruptions to increasingly expensive equipment
- the importance of creating total staff commitment within organisations such as charities which cannot afford to pay high wages
- the growing evidence that these empowered teams save money, achieve conceptual breakthroughs, solve complex problems, increase productivity and introduce unparalleled numbers of new products.

Hand over in stages

Many organisations have found a satisfactory procedure is to hand over responsibilities in stages. Each new stage is introduced as teams gain experience and confidence. At the beginning teams usually find they can handle such responsibilities as maintaining safety, allocating tasks amongst themselves and monitoring quality (as with the *jikoda* system at Toyota). Next, as individual members are trained or train each other, the team could, for example, maintain its own technical machinery. The following stage involves *sharing* a wide range of duties with management.

Shared responsibilities

The in-depth survey by Wellins, Byham and Wilson describes some interesting findings concerning this in-between stage when teams are not yet fully responsible but are well on the road to being self-directed. Generally speaking, a large number of teams had a minority share of major management responsibilities, but as the table below shows, the split was becoming more even.

Teams with full responsibility	Teams sharing responsibility with management
29% set production goals	.49% share setting of production goals
38% select work methods	.54% share selection of work methods
42% make improvements	.51% share making improvements
34% work with external . . . . customers and suppliers	.44% share working with customers and suppliers

Fully self-directed teams can perform all of the following management functions:

- prepare and monitor their own budgets
- select team members
- handle performance appraisal
- allocate the total team remuneration between individual team members

Functions of fully fledged teams

Some teams, more mature than others, achieve this final point quite quickly. But once the process has started it is important to proceed rapidly since this demonstrates management trust and thus reinforces the empowering cycle.

One major issue remains for all empowering organisations – self-managing teams require an appropriate organisational structure within which to operate.

Baxi, a traditional manufacturer of boilers, provides a salutary reminder of this important point. Its CEO, Simon Carter, discovered that teams cannot be successful if left to function within a traditional corporate structure. In the late 1980s, Baxi was one of the earliest British companies to introduce team empowerment. But by 1989 the experiment was foundering because a strongly hierarchic, six-level, function-based structure was smothering all suggestions from the teams.

By 1990, therefore, the company had to go in for a wholesale redesign of the structure based on multiskilled teams which included functional experts, with only three management levels remaining. As a result, teams are now the core of the company and have taken on an enormously wide span of responsibility.

A second lesson can be drawn from the Baxi experience. Teams are not intrinsically successful. They need a lot of help and support and, above all, every member needs training in how to contribute to the team and in as many skills as possible. Baxi now devotes at least 1 per cent of turnover to training; the company's training programme throughout the recession has been impressive and the CEO seems in no doubt that Baxi will continue to improve.

The Baxi story re-emphasises the major importance of the team leader's training role and also demonstrates, as we saw in Chapter 6, that wider organisational transformation is fundamental for the success of self-managing teams and for empowerment.

WORKSHOP: DEVELOPING SELF-DIRECTED TEAMS

1. Analyse any team you belong to or know well. What scope has it to become self-directed?
   - As leader, what responsibilities could you delegate to the members at once and in what order would you continue the process?
   - What extra training and resources would this require?
2. What would happen if you tried to empower the team without adopting wider organisational structures? Would it be possible?
3. As a team member would you and/or your fellow members welcome more responsibility?

When we have a big problem, we grab ten senior guys and stick them in a room. They come up with an answer and implement it.

American chief executive

PROJECT TEAMS

What is a project team?

As we saw in Chapter 4, *ad hoc* project teams are a powerful liberating tool and they are being increasingly used to solve particular problems. Peters (1988) calls this 'chunking': problems are broken into several pieces and project teams, or task forces, organised to solve them.

The key features of a project team are:
- its existence is time-limited to the achievement of its objective;
- it should contain within its membership all the key skills, information and resources necessary for success (but be able to call upon additional resources when necessary);
- it will separate the work into discrete streams of tasks and clearly allocate these to appropriate team members;
- someone will be responsible for the timetable so that key tasks which need to be completed before others (called dependencies) are tackled in the appropriate sequence.

A successful project team in a loss-making British company was created with the objectives of changing management attitudes, introducing flexibility and reducing the work force from 1800 to 400 within four years. With strong teamwork and excellent communication across boundaries (especially with the unions) the team succeeded in making the company profitable again.

When Petersen was chief executive of Ford International, he 'gave power back to the employees' by establishing a new working structure based on self-directing teams. Steering teams in each factory were briefed to initiate 'employee involvement' teams, empowered to tackle any job-related problem they wanted and coordinated by one of their members as the facilitator.

**GIVING POWER BACK TO
EMPLOYEES**

At first progress was slow but, encouraged by the steering teams and by the examples of success elsewhere, eventually at least two-thirds of Ford's employees were participating in employee involvement teams. People had taken the process seriously when they realised it was a sincere desire for devolution and not just an exercise in motivation dressed up in radical language. These teams contributed thousands of worthwhile ideas: some improved quality, others saved thousands of dollars each year, and Ford was helped to turn round from some difficulties it was then experiencing.

The company benefited, but so did worker morale. A union survey revealed that 80 per cent of low-paid workers were satisfied with work at Ford, as against only 58 per cent before the employee involvement programme began.

You know, I used to hate coming to work here. But lately I have been asked what I think and that makes me feel I'm somebody. Now I like coming to work.

Comment to the chief executive by a worker from a Ford stamping plant

---

CASE STUDY: TEAM TAURUS

Realising that innovation was the key to success, Ford's employee involvement programme took a further step forward when it expanded from the factory floor to create multidisciplinary teams across functional lines. Car designers were combined with production departments, engineers with sales people, and so on. A design engineer would travel to a plant, collect together a team of machinists, assemblers and skilled tradespeople, then show them the design on the computer and ask for suggestions for improvement.

---

continued

A natural next step, therefore, was to commission a company engineer, Lew Veraldi, to organise and lead a team (called Team Taurus) which would create a new car by integrating all the processes from design through to marketing. The key departments of design, manufacturing and marketing were represented full time, others were co-opted or consulted on a part-time basis. This involved asking:

- dealers from sales and marketing how to make the car user-friendly;
- the manufacturing department how the car could be made easier to build – at the Atlanta plant the initial drawings were displayed and Team Taurus asked, 'Tell us what you want in a new car': there were thousands of suggestions;
- customers to test the prototype and make suggestions (instead of complaining afterwards);
- suppliers to become partners and produce high-quality parts.

The project was outstandingly successful, with team members motivated by pride in their workmanship and ownership. Costs were lower, especially those caused by post-production design changes, functional barriers were broken down, cooperation across frontiers was established and the needs of the customer came first. In 1985 the first Taurus and Sable rolled off the production line. Both models made higher profits than their predecessors. In 1986 they were named by two motoring magazines as 'best car in the USA'.

Petersen and Hillkirk describe how the Taurus approach was developed and refined in the following six years. Subsequent production developments identified clearly the team leader for each car and truck line. Ford of Europe was then the first to appoint programme managers who were completely responsible for leading their various functional teams seconded to a development programme. This structure was later applied to cars and trucks in Ford of North America. Each programme manager is given a lot of authority, so that the development team can make decisions without referring back to its functional boss.

Teams empowered to work horizontally are therefore replacing the traditional, vertical, separate functional groups, creating a unified effort to meet customers' needs.

These project teams aim for significant improvements to Ford's present models within 3½ years, instead of the Taurus time of almost 6 years.

In an atmosphere of what Henry Mintzberg calls 'adhocracy' – freedom to innovate without traditional constraints – many other companies foster successful multiskilled cross-functional teams to develop and market new products, reduce waste or improve the organisational process.

Experience of other companies

For example, the Japanese bring key people from different companies into a central project to develop a product. Each company then competes to produce it for home consumption. After that, world marketing!

QUALITY CIRCLES

Like Team Taurus, quality circles, although sometimes instituted by departmental managers, are often multidisciplinary and/or interdepartmental, and many consist entirely of volunteers, setting their own goals and being fully self-directed.

Quality circles concentrate on improving quality and include:
- improving production methods, and creating more efficient work structures
- solving specific technical problems (for example, all engineers in a plant working together)
- meeting senior management as equals to discuss overall strategy
- contributing new ideas for products or services

Quality circles are successful in America and Japan, but British companies have been slower to use this approach. In the early days of their existence, they failed at Ford's British company, said the union negotiator, because 'Quality Circles did not fit into the culture of hierarchy and authoritarianism which traditionally [and then] characterised Fords.'

However, one early success story came from Jaguar, after its privatisation. In 1980 Jaguar, losing £2m a month in lost sales, unearthed 150 quality problems. A multidisciplinary quality circle with no status barrier to membership was established to improve quality and reliability. By 1984 60 of these circles were operating and Jaguar's sales were double the 1980 figure. The circles were powerful and effective – for example visiting suppliers to improve their performance and producing action reports until the problem was solved.

A success story of the 1980s

If any company hopes to make significant improvement it has to take advantage of the knowhow of everyone in the company, not just the people at the top.

Donald Petersen

Success stories of the 1990s

There is more recent evidence of empowering employees through this kind of team. Kinsley Lord consultants describe it as 'a quiet revolution' led by organisations which have a tradition of respecting their employees and believe in their duty to them, such as British Steel, ICI and National and Provincial.

At Rowntree Macintosh, for example, quality circles consisting of six to ten employees are organised on a voluntary basis. As an example of action learning (described in Chapter 12) members choose a work problem with which they are familiar, meet once a week and finally present and justify a solution to management. They widen employee understanding of management constraints and gain strength from being part of the company's participation policy (IR-RR, 1985).

In the British public sector the entrepreneurial spirit is also stirring. Some smaller units in the National Health system, for example, are resisting the threat of closure by raising extra funds through various self-help activities. One cottage hospital, described by Harvey-Jones, has suggested calling in a property developer to build sheltered housing in its grounds. This would generate income from rent, while the hospital would care for residents if they fell ill.

Success within a participative culture

These various types of cross-functional, self-directing teams provide invaluable evidence of how barriers are breaking down and are an easily recognisable example of how teams working for company, individual and team goals succeed within a *participative* company culture. This revolution is no longer so quiet; instead, it continues to reverberate in all sectors of the British economy and to grow in strength.

Inspiring teamwork is a lot harder than bossing people around.
Jack Welch, CEO *of General Electric* (*in Tichy and Stratford*, 1993)

MAKING TEAMS WORK

Empowered teams do not occur spontaneously. As can be seen from the Baxi example, they require the correct soil and climate in which to grow. It is vital, therefore, that team members and empowering managers get the conditions right. If any *one* of these conditions is absent, or handled inappropriately, it can result in failure.

Yet the examples in this chapter show that when organisations are in the habit of using teams they can become the norm for almost every activity from the shopfloor to the boardroom.

> Team work is central to the whole idea of the entrepreneurial organisation.
>
> *Charles Baden-Fuller and John Stopford*

Experiments conducted by Meredith Belbin with those attending an executive management course revealed how much the success of teams depended on the correct balance of their roles. Over several years of his courses, Belbin and his observers compared the success of 'companies' (determined by financial assets) against the mental ability and personality of each participant, determined by tests and observation. Contrary to expectations, teams of people with similar personalities or high intellectual abilities were not necessarily successful – out of 23 teams composed of highly intellectual people only three won. Team members spotted all the weak points, but made few decisions. The total effect became one of disempowerment. Teams of conscientious but conservative members achieved only average results. They were inflexible and lacked ideas. A creative, imaginative person when 'planted' in a company would have ideas, but many were too unpractical to help.

Successful teams contained people who played complementary roles, for example a creative, imaginative type (who looks for available resources) teamed with a coordinator (who mixes well), plus a prudent person with good judgement. Two other roles added to the strength of the team – a loyal conservative person, able to manage awkward people, putting the team first; and someone who followed things through and reached conclusions (a completer–finisher).

Successful teams contain complementary roles

> Leadership is always vital and team leadership is no exception. Leaders are talented enough to listen to others, strong enough to reject their advice.
>
> *Meredith Belbin*

The final vital role was the team leader. The first 75 chairpersons were categorised as good, intermediate or bad. The profile of a successful empowering leader emerged:

- trusting, accepting other people without jealousy
- basic dominance (controlled by a strong chairperson the 'plant' became useful)
- commitment to goals external to themselves
- calm in controversy

An empowering leader's profile

● practical, realistic, self-disciplined
● enthusiastic and able to enthuse others

Although different people are temperamentally suited to different roles, we can all adapt to new ones as circumstances require.

Later descriptions of team roles

Belbin's findings have been a major influence on later practitioners who have followed his approach while using different descriptions.

Following this approach two experienced consultants, Margerison and McCann, describe four main work functions as 'Exploring', 'Organising', 'Controlling' and 'Advising', and assign two roles to each:

Exploring requires	'Creator–Innovators' (people with challenging ideas) and 'Explorer–Promoters' (who enthuse others and tap their ideas)
Organising requires	'Assessor–Developers (implementing ideas) and 'Thruster–Organisers' (organising procedures for people and systems)
Controlling requires	'Concluder–Producers' (setting standards) and 'Controller–Inspectors' (ensuring accuracy)
Advising requires	'Upholder–Maintainers' (providing support and stability) and 'Reporter–Advisors' (gathering and disseminating information)

A 9th role, 'the linker', coordinates (leads, empowers).

Consider personal preferences

Margerison and McCann also concluded that people sometimes very much *prefer* some activities and *dislike* others, and that whether these preferences were fulfilled had some impact on performance. Therefore they advise that when assembling a new team, individual preferences should be seriously considered.

> Each member has certain leadership qualities that will be needed by the team at some point.
>
> David Barry

Self-directed teams with no official leader

In self-directed teams a similar pattern arises. When one of the roles was missing, performance deteriorated, 'often dramatically' according to Barry. Even when all roles were represented, success depended on the linker–leadership role changing as the needs of the team changed.

A successful team

The results of one five-member team were considered by the team and by management 'to be an outstanding success'. Each person assumed the leadership role when his or her particular skill was needed. Ken, the linker–coordinator, started the group off by asking everyone to describe their backgrounds and making sure the quieter members, Henry and Chuck, contributed. Next Ann, fresh from a marketing course and so the explorer–promoter, led the team in exploring the potential market for its product. Henry followed by leading as the creator–innovator of the product, Jeff led when internal promotion subjects arose and Chuck, as the controller–inspector, monitored team expenditure and customer records. Ken remained the linker–coordinator, enabling the others to give their best to the team. As a result the prototype of the new product was quickly demonstrated and initial production commenced. These members empowered each other, resulting in a strong commitment to the team and its task.

By contrast, two strong creator–innovators in another team preferred to work alone and missed team meetings. This angered other team members so that they sabotaged or discounted the ideas produced. The management added a goal-oriented assessor–developer who at first led the team in launching three new products, but then began to stifle new ideas and low-risk projects were adopted. The team lacked a coordinating, empowering role, the negative behaviour went unchecked and the team was soon disbanded as a failure.

An unsuccessful team

WORKSHOP: TEAM ROLES

1. Using Margerison and McCann's definitions of nine team roles, decide which role you normally play. Is this your preferred role?
2. Analyse the teams you belong to. Do they contain a correct balance of roles? If not, what role(s) do you feel may be missing and what effect is this having both on team performance and on the feeling of empowerment?
3. Do the top managers in your organisation enthusiastically support teams? If not, what effect does their negative attitude produce?

Compatibility of the members of the management team is crucial to its effectiveness.

Charles Handy, Understanding Organizations

The last example demonstrates that teams containing people who are incompatible – not able to coexist with each other – do not succeed. Productivity and morale are low, members become frustrated, hide

Incompatibility disempowers

evidence, argue at meetings, grumble in private and score points against each other. Kakabadse found that incompatible boards make poor decisions since trust vanishes, relationships deteriorate and communication ceases. (Board members might not even want to enter into conversation with inflexible colleagues, 'feeling they were wasting time').

Causes of incompatibility

Incompatibility is caused by:

- Clashes of roles. (Too many critical thinkers spot the weak points and argue too much. Two thruster–organisers is one too many.)
- Explorer–promoters can irritate, and over-talkative people frustrate others.
- An inadequate mix of roles. (One concluder–producer supported by two upholder–maintainers can make poor decisions because they lack creativity. Belbin's 'plant' would require a team containing a judge, a diplomat and a strong leader to control him or her.)
- 'Group think', which afflicts teams composed of similar types, can lead to catastrophically bad decisions since the team feels superior to everyone else, fails to question its own reasoning, expects conformity and reject alls 'deviant' opinions.

Effects of 'group think'

Margerison and McCann give the example of a senior team in a computer retailing firm which, led by the finance director, agreed to a severe cost-cutting exercise when sales began to fall. Only the marketing manager proposed a big expansion into a new market. Instead of analysing his idea, comments such as 'outlandish' forced him to conform. A year later the firm closed down. The unanimous cautious attitude had led them all to agree. 'Group think' prevailed, and a disempowered team failed.

A team can also behave in ways that any one member would not contemplate (for example, taking risky decisions). The strong urge to conform publicly forces compliance with decisions which privately could horrify people.

> Team roles act as a brake on runaway specialists.
>
> *Meredith Belbin*

ANALYSING TEAMS

Existing teams can reap the many advantages of newly created ones if they first assess the roles essential to success, then discover role deficiencies and decide how these can still be balanced.

Balancing deficiencies

One senior management team decided that because of rapid market changes, they needed to be strong in creating, promoting and developing the roles of creator–innovator, explorer–promoter and assessor–developer. Yet their strength lay in organising, producing and inspecting – the roles of thruster–organiser, concluder–producer and controller–inspector. When another team faced this problem they decided to learn how to innovate and employed an expert to teach them lateral thinking. If the former senior managers had learnt this skill too, they could have redefined their business, perhaps revealing vistas of other markets which their production expertise could exploit. (Some time ago Shell, redefining its business as 'energy', opened wider possibilities such as the use of windpower.)

A 'SWOT' analysis is useful for assessing roles:

Analysing roles

S = Strengths of roles
W = Weaknesses of roles
O = Opportunities for improving roles
T = Threats minimised by role changes

Another approach, advocated by Handy (1985), focuses on positive compared with negative team behaviour, under eight headings: Goals, Participation, Feelings, Diagnosing Problems, Leadership, Decisions, Thrust, Creative Growth. For example:
- *Participation*: little interest, a few members dominate; or everyone involved.
- *Decisions*: not made, or a few made by some; or by consensus, and supported.
- *Creativity*: routine, rigid; or flexible with growth.

and so on.

Individual analyses can also be carried out through self-description or a structured questionnaire. One leader who wrote that he was a good listener learnt from others that he was not. Another thought she was allocating tasks according to individual preferences, but her team did not agree.

A leader and team members can help each other to discover and close role gaps through using a skilled team approach, for example by:

Filling role gaps

- listening to each other and showing understanding;
- considering their goals and deciding how their various roles fit into these – do some goals conflict with roles, such as personal goals clashing with team goals, etc?
- facilitating the closing of any role gaps uncovered through a team consensus, such as team members learning new roles, thus becoming more skilled and flexible as a result.

To learn these new skills, all need and must give support, trust and freedom. Describing teams of innovators, for example, Moss Kanter (1989) says they need freedom from bureaucratic controls and a feeling of security, since their work calls for speed and insights but contains unforeseen problems, uncertainty and a possibility of failure.

Learning new roles

Mida, a successful Canadian company making automobile parts described by Alex Stewart, gained great flexibility with a system of

Success through flexibility and 'team entrepreneurship'

'team entrepreneurship'. Raw recruits were given training in all Mida's technical and team roles and worked in any of these as required. These flexible teams, motivated and committed (the company's 'most important asset'), then completed all orders as a team, with the final responsibility for meeting the stringent demands of a few dominant customers. Mida flourished within a very exacting environment.

WORKSHOP: FILLING ROLE GAPS IN TEAMS

1. Analyse any team you belong to or have belonged to in the past. Make a SWOT analysis of the team and a description of yourself. Do you slot into a role the team needs? (or a past team needed?) Do your own goals clash with team goals?
2. Decide to increase your role flexibility:
   - by learning and practising the role nearest to your own, and then progressing to some others;
   - by linking with a member with opposite strengths to your own;
   - by joining other teams in a different role (a non-executive member of many boards soon acquired a large repertoire of roles).
3. As a team leader, analyse why your team has role gaps. Do some roles, for example, clash with team goals? With your team, make a plan for creatively filling the missing roles when practicable.

THE QUALITIES OF AN EMPOWERED TEAM

While working in teams is an essential precondition for empowerment, it does not make empowerment inevitable. Even where the roles balance, there are bad teams just as there are good ones. Empowered teams, however, have a number of other common qualities.

TWO-WAY COMMUNICATION

The ability and willingness to listen to others and to trust them underpin all other types of team behaviour. Listening behaviour (described in detail in Part IV) involves showing you are giving your total attention to other team members, through both verbal and non-verbal signals. Verbally, signals can be given through silence or encouraging comments: 'I see,' 'Could you explain a bit more?', 'Go on,' or 'In other words you are saying . . .' You can also convey a wealth of meaning through non-verbal signals, for example:

- looking intently at people instead of down at your notes (Michael Argyle says that we look at people 30 per cent more if we like them);
- leaning forward, and conveying interest with your hands;
- nodding and smiling;
- monitoring your unconscious gestures. One of us, with a colleague, regularly ran training courses on the skills of interviewing. An anecdote told by one was always signalled by the other (who knew it all too well) by an unconscious hand gesture of frustration – which told all!

People who listen are nourishing trusting relationships. Trusting involves mutual acceptance of each other's contributions, and thus frees people to talk about their problems, failures and successes, knowing they are understood. Lack of trust undermines a team's effectiveness more quickly than perhaps anything else. Morale sinks, openness becomes secretiveness, discussions become arguments. Trust is quickly destroyed: when, for example, a member – especially the leader – says one thing but does another, or criticises colleagues to friends in other departments.

MUTUAL TRUST

Kakabadse reports how rapidly chief executives can destroy board morale with a lack of trust. One chief executive held separate meetings with his non-executive board members. When one executive director attempted to tell him how much this annoyed the other executive members, he would not listen. Finally, industrial relations deteriorated into a strike and the chief executive was asked to resign. The others commented that if only he had listened to them, none of this need have happened.

So listening and trusting encourage communication. When asked how he managed his team so successfully, one chief executive replied simply 'I am open'.

Listening and trusting lead to open communication

CASE STUDY: WALKIE-TALKIE SUPPORT

The value of close communication is illustrated by Peters (1988). A Belgian manager installed walkie-talkies so that individual managers in his scattered team could talk to each other.

By accident, two faulty machines relayed everyone else's conversations to their owners and the manager noticed these two people becoming deeply involved at team meetings, offering solutions to problems in other departments and so on. So he

---

continued

purchased machines which allowed everyone access to all conversations. Gaining knowledge about each other's work greatly strengthened the team.

Teams may not possess walkie-talkies but they can still listen, learn to trust each other and become a better leader and better team members.

COOPERATION

People put the team's objectives before their own.

Mike Woodcock

Team cooperation grows with trust as everyone becomes more committed and ready to help others – sometimes to their own detriment. Handy (1985) reports research into 72 conference groups which showed that when individuals put their own needs first, team needs were neglected. At meetings fewer items were completed and dissatisfaction with decisions grew.

Cooperation leads to understanding

When people cooperate they begin to understand each other's attitudes and circumstances, learning what upsets, annoys or encourages. Team members behaving in these ways become respected as people 'worth listening to'.

Genuine consensus

Cooperation means working for a consensus. The Airspace case study shows that it does not mean arriving at unsatisfactory compromises to preserve team harmony. You express your opinion and others do the same. Although you may be tempted, you do not scorn them or retaliate with personal attacks or sarcasm. Such open discussion is an example of constructive conflict, yet if mishandled it can degenerate into open warfare. Reaping the benefits requires special skills, based on principled negotiation (described in Part IV). Discussion is depersonalised, becoming specific to the matter in hand. Available facts are pooled and each member tries to understand the views and needs of the others. The situation becomes a shared problem-solving exercise.

Majority decisions a last resort

Even if no consensus emerges, members should cooperate by being willing to follow the majority and give it a try.

PARTICIPATION

How and when to join in a discussion, in or out of a meeting, is a further refinement of communication and cooperation. People talk too much for many reasons, for example:

- they may have strong attitudes about a particular issue – for instance, including a disadvantaged person in the team;

- they may vehemently support existing team practices, believing a new proposal to be flawed;
- they may know they are the experts and expect others to follow their advice as the professional on financial or marketing points etc.

Other people stay silent because they lack the confidence to intervene, want time to marshal their thoughts, perhaps notice someone has snubbed them, and so sulk or are bored by the whole subject. When team needs come first none of these feelings influences behaviour.

Timing

Timing requires even greater skill. The total attention of someone with a hip-pocket solution is focused on getting their say in first. This intervention, being premature, irritates others who will state all the reasons why it is unworkable. But if someone waits too long the chance to speak may vanish forever. Once you recognise that contributing effectively is a skill, you are half way to improving it.

> The really effective team is constantly reaching out to others to ensure that its efforts are well received and supported.
>
> *Mike Woodcock*

Cooperating with other teams and across boundaries

In Chapter 7 we saw that a major job for the leader was to be a 'linker'. Equally, the team as a whole must take care of its boundaries, keeping communications open with its own department, other departments and senior or junior teams. Thus all team members are responsible for communicating with other teams, understanding their difficulties and offering help where needed. However, strong teams require the leader or someone else to take the role of explorer–promoter, a contact person who will keep the team informed about how its work is viewed by others and use a network of relationships to process problems and smooth away difficulties.

Regular joint team meetings

Where appropriate, regular joint team meetings encourage cooperation and serve many purposes:

- planning production together
- improving performance
- resolving differences before trouble arises
- helping both teams to reach their objectives
- supporting departmental managers and team leaders in their coordinating work
- maintaining a spirit of friendly rivalry

A charity we worked with ran 'It's a Knockout' games in which local business teams competed. Friendly rivalry was satisfied by the presentation of one trophy to the winner and another, larger one to the team raising the most sponsorship.

Be 'team oriented'

To be a good team person one basic attitude stands out. You need to be 'team oriented', since success calls for understanding and skill. Such people, says Belbin, 'with reasonable ability produce consistently good teams, covering between themselves, all the various functions that have to be performed.' (The role gap caused by the departure of a member from a 'team oriented' team can often then be filled by another member.)

A teamsman [or woman] is good to have in a team.

Meredith Belbin

PROXIMITY

An environment in which teams can see and talk to each other promotes close communications which empower and strengthen a team. Open plan offices, conference rooms, desks which touch each other Japanese style, senior managers in offices adjacent to each other and tables in canteens are all physical arrangements which promote what Peters describes as 'proximity power'.

When Reuters UK reshaped their structure into multifunctional account teams round their own desks and terminals (described in the *Financial Times*, 2 June 1993) the report from one of their number is particularly significant. The old atmosphere of fire fighting and buck passing had given way, he said, to mutual help and covering for each other especially as we '*sit around the same desk*'.

When people move together or apart by just 10 yards, enormous difference in frequency of contact occurs.

Tom Allen, MIT (in Peters, 1992)

STAGES OF TEAM DEVELOPMENT

Even if a newly composed team is well balanced and compatible, one hazard still remains. New teams progress through four stages. Handy (1985) itemises them as 'forming', 'storming', 'norming' and 'performing'; Woodcock's description is 'undeveloped', 'experimental', 'consolidating' and 'mature'. These processes can be speeded up, but ignoring them or rushing forward prematurely will hamper performance – possibly permanently, when the team will never be fully empowered. In a formal new team this process is best helped by a facilitator who can concentrate on the health of the team and ensure that the stages are properly tackled, with all emotions and ideas aired before moving on to 'performing'. A leader of a newly formed production or project team, however, may have to facilitate this process instead. Below, therefore, we describe the symptoms of each stage, since once they are recognised a leader can take appropriate action.

FORMING/UNDEVELOPED

At the forming stage, new teams are wary of their leader and each other. They question others but reveal little about themselves, play it safe, conform to the company line and frown on the unorthodox. They may conceal their mistakes but challenge others and do not listen. Expect this to happen and be prepared to work it through before moving on to the next stage.

STORMING/EXPERIMENTAL

Individual team members may be harbouring some latent attitudes. Some common ones are:
- fear (of appearing ignorant, or of authority) and lack of confidence
- resentment of the leader or some fellow members
- believing all meetings are a waste of time
- wanting to get quick results, etc.

If these or other negative feelings are present, it is best to encourage them into the open. The skills of listening, described in Part IV, are required. In particular:
- listening for emotionally loaded words, silences, hesitations
- looking for non-verbal signals
- asking searching questions about attitudes and feelings towards the task – do people think the task important? difficult? boring? not in their line?

The various negative opinions and conflicting feelings which emerge can then be dealt with positively, constructively and calmly. A team member may express a grudge against a fellow member, there may be a chorus of dissent against the task or the inefficiency of top management, and so on.

Handling the conflict

Some conflict will surface, and it will require a constructive and calm approach. Two common mistakes are to overreact and to pretend that it has not occurred, but conflict should be treated seriously as a problem to be resolved, and time allowed for a 'win/win' position to be reached.

When people have aired their emotional agenda and conflict has been handled constructively, a more positive approach begins to appear. The worst of the storm is over. Individuals feel more part of the team, more ready to study the process of their discussions and how they will proceed.

> They quickly learn that when the dirt has been put on the table and examined, the team becomes a healthier and happier place to be.
>
> *Mike Woodcock*

NORMING/CONSOLIDATING

Once the 'how' is beginning to be settled a general consensus begins to appear – a kind of 'oh well, let's get on with it as effectively as possible.' The norming/consolidating stage has arrived. Norming involves establishing standards of behaviour and agreeing rules of procedure.

The process is facilitated by searching questions to challenge people's intellect, and to encourage them to produce an agreed plan for performing. This plan will include norms for standards of behaviour, such as:

- ways of valuing each other's strengths (the quick finisher who speeds up action, the shy solving technical problems);
- agreement on time keeping and sharing homework fairly;
- deciding how conflict should be handled, and so on.

Process analysis

When this stage is reached an analysis of how effectively the team is operating should be made by the whole team. Handy (1985) suggests the use of a rating scale, 1–7 under headings such as clarity of goals, the amount of participation, decision making, listening, trust and creativity. A rating system aids objectivity – but open and honest discussions could provide more depth.

PERFORMING/MATURITY

This analysis indicates the stage the team has reached towards maturity and the improvements which are still required. When another storm blows up the team will possess the norms of procedure and behaviour to weather it and learn from it. The time and effort devoted to 'storming' and 'norming' will have been well spent.

WORKSHOP: ANALYSING AN EMPOWERED TEAM

1. Observe objectively a discussion in a team you belong to and discover:
   - Do team members listen to each other and respond?
   - How much mutual trust does the discussion indicate?
   - How does the team handle conflict?
   - Do some members talk too much, leaving others little chance

continued

to participate? Write down three examples of skilled interaction and three poor examples.

2. Observe the team's verbal and non-verbal unconscious gestures – encourage them to exchange information about these.

3. As a team leader, discuss ways of promoting cooperation with other team leaders.

4. As facilitator, leader, member or observer, identify the key moments when the team passed from one stage to another (norming, forming, storming and performing).

CASE STUDY: BUILDING SUCCESSFUL GLOBAL TEAMS

To succeed or even to survive, most companies will need to compete in the international global market. Is it possible to build successful global teams composed of possibly incompatible people, from different cultures, separated by geographical and language barriers and feeling they have little in common? The following case demonstrates that such a team can be created and become successful.

John Transi, Chief Executive of GEMS, a high-tech GE company making medical systems, created national teams composed of American and Japanese executives who had not previously met, together with a group of unhappy French managers from a newly acquired company. Said one American executive, 'Why should we give *them* the business over our own people?' 'We own Yokagawa Medical Systems. Them is us,' replied Jack Welch, GE's CEO.

Transi began to build his teams by regrouping the business geographically into three areas based in America, Paris and Tokyo. Each area would share the responsibility for developing and marketing and each had a world-wide responsibility for particular products.

Difficulties abounded. National groups all felt superior, time differences were up to 14 hours, language barriers demanded simultaneous translations, and even a global electronic mail system was difficult to launch.

Yet globalisation required an unprecedented level of teamwork, so Transi asked the consultant Noel Tichy, plus an international team, to teach the executives the ability to

continued

communicate, to be inventive and flexible and to work in global teams.

To begin with, seven small teams, each composed of Americans, Europeans and Japanese, were given major problems to solve. This helped them to get to know each other.

Next, 55 GEMS managers were flown to Portugal for five days where colleagues from all three countries met for the first time. The ice began to crack a little when multinational teams were given difficult training assignments calling for communication in spite of language barriers. For example, being forced to communicate by touch and voice tone as, blindfolded, they groped their way across wobbling rope bridges, or surmounted a 14 foot wall using only their bodies. This required trust and thoughtful teamwork, and a lot more.

Then, divided into seven teams, each was given problem assignments to solve with the brief to report results long after the training session finished. This entailed many communications with their team mates by fax, electronic mail, two-way video and personal meetings, flying across the oceans. They persevered through much stress (and complete failure at a second training session) because they began to recognise that globalisation was a winning strategy.

The teams presented their plans to Transi at a final meeting. The successful proposals were allocated millions of dollars between them.

By working together, all team members had formed lasting personal bonds and put a network of relationships in place. They had learnt, too, a great deal about the need to understand each other's cultural strengths and weaknesses, their ways of behaviour and their lifestyles. One participant said: 'To be global, you must know how the other Poles [areas] think, what their customers want, and basically what makes them tick.'

Much still remains to be done. The next stage is to develop multinational teams, each composed of eight people, to invent organisational systems to suit their needs and so to own them.

Source: Tichy and Sherman

THE ROLE OF THE TOP TEAM

The top team are critical to empowerment, for two reasons. First, they must support it; although by themselves they cannot force it to

> Managers do things right, leaders do the right thing.
> *Warren Bennis*

happen. Secondly, if they believe in empowerment it is vital that they live their belief. This means adopting a leadership style which is itself empowering. They are judged by their actions, not by their words. The top team must therefore learn to be themselves empowered.

> It doesn't matter what people say. What they do counts more.
> *Andrew Kakabadse*

The primary function of top teams is to offer a vision of the objectives and values of their organisation which have been created and agreed through discussions and consultation. This can then be turned into a 'mission' statement which changes vision into strategy and strategy into policies. The mission statement should be supported by explanations and consultations until the objectives are widely known, understood and accepted.

MAIN FUNCTIONS OF TOP TEAMS

Thus Harvey-Jones describes the main functions of the ICI board in the late 1980s as keeping a 'helicopter' overview, dedicated to the business as a whole not to any individual part, and to 'direct' not manage.

A top team taking an overall, helicopter view accepts that it is ultimately accountable for success and that it has many practical functions which only it can perform for the whole organisation. For example:

Translating thought into action

- creating, developing and encouraging a policy for empowerment throughout the whole organisation
- translating concepts like 'excellence', 'innovation', 'a learning organisation', 'a caring community', 'participation', 'self-managing teams' into strategies, procedures and behaviour
- maintaining financial viability
- allocating resources to priority areas
- managing crises
- building and using communication systems
- making creative decisions, unhampered by past solutions
- developing people for the future
- analysing and judging how global, economic, social and political affairs affect their organisation and thus maximising its position at home and abroad

- consulting and discussing these policies and procedures with their managers and workforce at every stage

Such a team is both empowered and empowering.

Problem for top management

Yet traditionally top management face a particular problem: nothing they have done to get where they are has prepared them for the role of thinker and strategist which they are now asked to undertake. It is their ability to *do* – to make things happen – which has usually brought them to their present top role.

Not surprisingly, many managers arrive at board level with little understanding of this role and how to fulfil it. Andrew Kakabadse, researching into 11,000 senior managers in 740 organisations in Britain and Ireland, confirms this situation. Over 60 per cent of business concerns are thought to be badly managed, 52 per cent of chief executives are unhappy with their team's efficiency and 76 per cent of general managers 'feel negative' about their seniors. Another survey revealed that 37 per cent of respondents from companies contacted could not identify with the vision described in their mission statement.

> Many directors think it better to be seen doing something than thinking.
>
> *Bob Garratt*

To take a helicopter overview to work out an overall strategy, to think rather than do, top teams need to develop some special intellectual skills

- *to ask wise questions*, searching for information from every source and recognising that many of the answers will emerge from the people with practical work experience. There is enough knowledge in the system which can be tapped when the right questions are asked. Garratt suggests three useful questions: who knows? who cares? who can?
- *to think as a generalist*, seeing the wood not the trees
- *to focus on the essential issues*, to encourage innovation and to welcome change and discontinuity
- *to challenge assumptions*, for example, the chief executive of Toyota continued to question the need to stockpile large quantities of components and the solution of JIT finally emerged
- *to synthesise*, to use creative insight, defined by a Japanese guru as 'the ability to combine, synthesise or reshuffle previously unrelated phenomena – to get more out of the emergent whole than you have put in' (Kennedy, 1991).

> The best way to keep power is to give it away. The best way to retain ownership is to share and the best way to influence is to listen.
>
> *Paul Thorne*

Chief executives can help their teams to develop the intellectual skills required for a helicopter overview. Following the example of Alfred Sloan, the great manager of General Motors in the 1920s, they can develop 'creative dissent'. At one meeting Sloan asked, 'All in complete agreement?' – 'Yes' came the unanimous response. 'In that case', said Sloan, 'I propose we postpone further discussion to the next meeting to give ourselves time to develop disagreements and perhaps gain some understanding of what the decision is all about' (Kennedy, 1991).

Using these intellectual skills enables the top team to clarify and define its main functions, but like all teams, it only becomes truly empowered and empowering when its members also cease to behave as individuals and work harmoniously together instead.

Learning to become good team members

> Incompatible Boards make poor decisions . . . learning how to react with team members is crucial.
>
> *Andrew Kakabadse*

A key function for chief executives is to coach top team members in their new roles.

This coaching should help newcomers to:

Key subjects

- unlearn the narrower, now insufficient, horizons of their departmental jobs
- recognise their need for extra team skills
- learn to understand their colleagues and to nurture relationships with them
- learn how to relate to team decision-making processes

These new skills take time to develop, but slowly, by trial and error, individual members become accustomed to a wider vision and to people-oriented attitudes.

Kakabadse describes the process as a learning curve, from false confidence through relearning to competence. It takes, he says, 20–30 months and cannot be rushed. Helping them to recognise these stages and defining the skills speeds it up.

Board meetings devoted entirely to team processes play a powerful role in this training exercise. In one company for example, all directors,

Top team honesty

including the chief executive, agreed to help Kakabadse and his researchers by completing questions about the team and about each other posed in a 'team grid'. Interviewed before, the functional directors described their managing director as a 'difficult and ineffectual leader'. He believed they saw him as 'out of step, unreasonable and holding back progress'.

The grid results showed the opposite. The team was the real problem. Their colleagues judged three functional members to be highly specialised with low strategic insight and a poor understanding of marketing. All had poor relations with the other members of the top team and their own staff. The two other functional directors were seen as poorly disciplined and distrustful of colleagues.

The managing director emerged as supportive, well disciplined, trusting, good at managing people and positive. This feedback at first created shock, then denial. Eventually, with the help of the consultants, it was owned and empowered the people concerned.

WORKSHOP: RATE A TOP TEAM

1. Imagine you were asked to join in a survey similar to the one carried out by Andrew Kakabadse. Rate the top team of your organisation or any other you know well on:
   - their strength in directing and taking a 'helicopter view'
   - the clarity of the policies you receive from them
2. Analyse which intellectual and interpersonal skill gaps you currently lack to fulfil a top team role.

Poor quality relationships need not exist. To create an effective team is entirely in the hands of top management.

Andrew Kakabadse

Behaviour that inspires

The behaviour of the chief executive and the top team sets the tone of their organisation. They project a hopeful, enthusiastic, encouraging image when they act and look that way. Sagging shoulders and downcast features send signals of gloom and spread worrying rumours. Charismatic leaders believe in the capabilities of their staff and inspire not only their own dynamic team but the whole organisation.

Empower 9
Yourself

We have shown how empowering organisations liberate and encourage staff to use all their talents and to reach their own potential. Everyone is valued for themselves and as a consequence all are expected to become leaders at times. We have also shown that leadership does not have a particular mystique possessed only by some people, typified by a report John Adair once read stating 'Jones is not a born leader – yet'. In fact, average 'Jones's' can *learn* leadership with training, encouragement and practice. The empowering approach concentrates, therefore, on *action* – what an empowered individual and a leader *does* rather than any innate qualities of such people – and when it has been learnt, ordinary people can produce extraordinary performances.

Empowerment must then be inclusive and involve everyone learning the appropriate skills and participating in leadership.

DECIDE ON A LIFETIME OF SELF-DEVELOPMENT

If you want to learn to become empowered, attaining new attitudes, extra strengths and the skills this requires, be prepared to act as your own mentor. Although finding a mentor to help is very useful, such a person will not necessarily be around. So take charge of your own development – you alone are responsible for it.

> 25 years ago I was a student. I will always be a student.
>
> *Luciano Pavarotti, opera tenor*

Examine your motivation

Begin by analysing whether you *want* to be empowered. Building on our list on page 23, do you possess or do you want to acquire the following attitudes, qualities and resources:

- To empower people and help them to grow.
- To be empowered within yourself, and to possess the self-motivation which makes you confident and 'feeling good'.
- To feel capable and keen to tackle new challenges, to set development goals and to attain them.
- To understand your own strengths and weaknesses.
- To be objective about your feelings and attitudes, to control them and to be able to express your requirements to others.
- To make decisions and to be innovative.
- To become multiskilled and flexible in your own field.
- To be a good team member and a good team leader.
- To possess the necessary resources (knowledge, training, time, support, memory, etc.)

WORKSHOP: SELF-DEVELOPMENT AND CONTINUOUS LEARNING

If possible, collect together a group of colleagues, friends or fellow members of a training course and ask them to help you to analyse your attitudes.

1. What qualities, abilities and experience do you need to develop to empower yourselves? For example:
   - technical knowledge and skills in your chosen field
   - business skills
   - intellectual skills
   - interpersonal skills
   - flexibility
   - team membership skills
   - leadership skills
2. What gives you the most job satisfaction? What frustrates you?
3. Do you value people and want to help them to grow and to develop themselves?

No one can make you feel inferior without your consent.

Eleanor Roosevelt

Many major industrial countries already have a head start over British institutions in developing these new empowering skills. Their school education lasts longer, the level of qualifications gained is higher, and there are more opportunities and provisions for acquiring further education and training afterwards. More children stay on longer at school in Germany, America and Japan than in Britain, and their standards of achievement in core subjects at 16 and 18 are significantly higher.

PREPARE YOURSELF FOR EMPOWERMENT

The 'Handy Report' (Handy, 1987) and a comparative study of *Management and Labour in Europe* by Christel Lane both make this very clear. Workers and executives alike are less well prepared in Britain.

Self-development, either through higher education or on-the-job qualifications, is the key to learning, and 'the beginnings' are crucial. They also make a life in business seem exciting and worthwhile. Most of Britain's competitors ensure that a large proportion of young people receive a broad education to the age of 18. Americans believe that education is an investment and that each person is responsible for his or her own destiny.

Early education in other countries

In Germany there is a very strong apprenticeship system containing on-the-job and off-the-job training, which provides a highly trained workforce and prepares a large number of men and women for an understanding of leadership, grounded in the shopfloor.

In countries other than Britain development opportunities are available for people who want to become managers and, in time, senior executives. 50 per cent of Americans enter higher education, and 85 per cent of their senior executives are university graduates. A business qualification and career are widely valued and the majority of future executives acquire a Master of Business Administration (MBA) degree. In Germany, people aspiring to a career in business study a relevant discipline for seven to nine years and are aged about 27 by the time they start their first job. 62 per cent of top executives have had a university education and many have doctorates.

Thoroughness and relevance is taken seriously by young and old [in Germany].

Handy, The Making of Managers

Although the French education system turns out large numbers of university students, some highly educated, as a generalisation it does not help them to be naturally sympathetic to the philosophy of empowering leadership. This attitude is changing, but as Barsoux and Lawrence document some students from the prestigious *grandes écoles* still believe that workers have no ideas of interest to contribute.

Early education in Britain

By contrast, British young people do not gain so advanced an education. 52 per cent leave school at 16 with no academic or technical qualifications and, until recently, 45 per cent of shopfloor workers received no further training. Furthermore, the demand for unskilled labour is falling. As employing and supervising them becomes less cost effective, the need for people with further qualifications and skills is rising – one calculation concluded that it takes four unskilled people to produce the same output as one skilled person. Although some British workers have qualifications in various technical skills, many are semiskilled. The unskilled are also becoming more disempowered, especially financially.

British preparation less thorough

British preparation for producing empowering leaders does not, as yet, come up to the general level of the competitors we have described. One poll reveals that 50 per cent of the executives sampled left education before degree level. Many received no subsequent further education and only 24 per cent of British top executives were graduates.

Traditionally the élite from public schools or Oxbridge are considered (often erroneously) to have a natural talent for leadership. They are often gifted amateurs, managing 'by the seat of their pants' (which probably plays its part in the dearth of leaders suited to modern conditions in Britain today). So graduates from the few British business schools are regarded with suspicion by some existing managers, and the verdict on executive training is summed up as: 'Education is too little, too late and for too few' (Handy, 1987).

Acquire more qualifications

Although technical and academic qualifications are not the 'be all and end all', equipping yourself with them, whatever your age and needs, will help you to empower yourself. After the publication of the Handy Report many new initiatives occurred in Britain, so the chances of a more adequate further education are becoming brighter. 'What is clearly evident', says Handy, 'is the new enthusiasm for business education.'

It is never too late to catch up. Part-time or full-time courses leading to valued diplomas are available and many are government backed. A degree course can also be taken part time. One senior executive, for example, feeling she was missing something vital in her past education, is now taking an Open University course.

Among 19 very successful leaders, Andrew Forrest and Patrick

Tolfree describe two top leaders who left school at 14 and 16 respectively but 'took immense pains to make up for this later on'. One, Clive Thornton, set a pattern with no let up of two hours' study from 7–9 pm each day and every Saturday morning and Sunday afternoon, in order to qualify as a solicitor.

> The old world of pragmatism and nothing else has gone forever.
> *Charles Handy, The Making of Managers*

If you already have a degree, analyse what extra knowledge you need and aim to fill the gaps. Others are doing just that. One arts graduate has taken a business school course; another added an accountancy qualification. In fact the latter is a very common form of entry to a business career in Britain. The comparative figures with other countries are significant. 120,000 trained accountants work in British management; Japan has far fewer and Germany has only 4000 (Handy, 1987). Although thorough, will the accountancy approach equip you adequately to be an empowered leader within a liberating organisation? Accountants are trained to be cautious, yet modern competitive business calls for initiative and enterprise. A more rounded education would lead you to an MBA or other courses of that kind. These are now proliferating, so seize your opportunities.

Nevertheless, Professor Anne Jones, one of the successful leaders interviewed by Forrest and Tolfree, warns against collecting qualifications for the sake of getting a better job. You should learn because you are *interested* – it is the learning itself that counts.

> Control your destiny or someone else will.
> *Jack Welch, CEO of General Electric (in Tichy and Sherman, 1993)*

CONTINUOUS LEARNING EMPOWERS SELF-DEVELOPMENT

To continue developing yourself, however you plan it and wherever you work, calls for a continuous learning programme. If you work in a learning organisation, you can recognise it as an organisation which:
- regularly examines its position
- learns new ideas from all quarters
- desires to improve every aspect of its operations

Chapter 5 gives a fuller description of a learning organisation.

Practise setting goals for your own empowerment so that you become capable of greater achievements, greater insights, greater potential than you thought possible. And by leading others to learn in the same way you empower them to work for goals you jointly share (as we see in Chapter 7 and Part IV).

> The door to development is locked with the key on the inside.
>
> *Peter Honey*

Definition of self-development

A positive approach to a lifetime of self-development is vital whether you are working on the shopfloor, progressing to more senior posts, becoming a chief executive or joining a board of directors.

Peter Honey defines self-development as 'the development of yourself by yourself, through a deliberate process of *learning from experience*.' Self-development does not happen by chance, but because you plan it and put it into practice. No one else can do it for you; only you have the key to your own development door. Making an inventory of your development needs will provide this key, especially if you concentrate on the gaps you discover.

Learning from experience.   All experience teaches us, but here we are concerned with work experiences. According to Charles Handy (1985), real learning takes place when we solve our *own* problems. Four steps facilitate this process:

- Ask what is the problem is.
- Find a theoretical answer (why, and how could it be solved?)
- Act on the theory and test it.
- Reflect and think about the process and learn from it.

For example:

1. Your *problem* might be: I have an autocratic boss.
2. The *theoretical answer*: I must help him to listen more.
3. *Action*: decide to start a quality circle to show the boss that the staff have ideas too.
4. *Reflect* and think. Did you:
   - give him some good ideas?
   - persuade him to put them into action?
   - follow the ideas through?
   - get him to attend the meetings on a regular basis?

Reviewing and setting targets.   This rigorous test is most useful when, concentrating on your gaps, you consciously and methodically apply it to the events of your daily life, as soon after they have occurred as possible. This involves making a review each week, analysing what you have learnt, and setting targets for improvement.

Learning from mistakes.   Many newly promoted supervisors in European countries often find themselves thrown in at the deep end to sink or swim, with no previous training in leadership. If this happens to you, profit by learning from your mistakes. A Japanese worker, when complimented on his performance, is likely to respond: 'how could I have done things better?' Seniors, skilled in empowering techniques, will help you by giving encouragement, withholding censure and depersonalising the issue; you can emulate their methods. Thus one manager opened a team meeting by describing the worst mistake he had made in the last week and ended, 'Can each of you now tell me yours?'

Finding a mentor.   Your review will reveal specific incidents and enable you to isolate the behaviour and skills involved, which will help you to repeat successes and avoid failures in future. A 'stroke' (described in Chapter 7) from someone else is all too rare in British business life, but it works wonders for your empowerment, so, if you can, find a mentor to support and encourage you. This person needs to be someone objective, perhaps from some other function, often a senior prepared to play a mentoring role. Mentors have long held a respected position in Japan; their use is growing in other industrial countries. For example, many of the successful leaders interviewed by Forrest and Tolfree say they owe a debt of gratitude to mentors who helped them on their way. At Crosfield's, a Unilever soapworks company, for example, Sir Peter Thompson obtained his first management experience as a trainee because 'it had a very good cadre of foremen and managers who took a pride in training people and bringing them along.' Effective apprenticeship schemes employ a similar method of allocating a trainee to a single craftsperson.

Paddy O'Brien gives additional practical advice. Find a *partner* at work, she suggests – to share your emotions, discuss your problems, commiserate with your failures and share your successes.

Learning from your experiences inevitably involves you in coming to terms with your own leadership style. The diagram below (adapted from Blake and Mouton) can help you to analyse your own style and discover if it empowers others or not.

ANALYSE YOUR LEADERSHIP STYLE

The 9,1 style is management by command. It concentrates on the task, ignoring individual needs and regards people as 'units of production'. A typical saying is 'I plan work *for* my subordinates.'

Description of the styles

The 1,9 style runs a cosy 'country club', looks after people and values friendly relationships more than productivity. (Said the superintendent of an engine repair shop, 'We have a cheerful crew, but we haven't repaired many engines!')

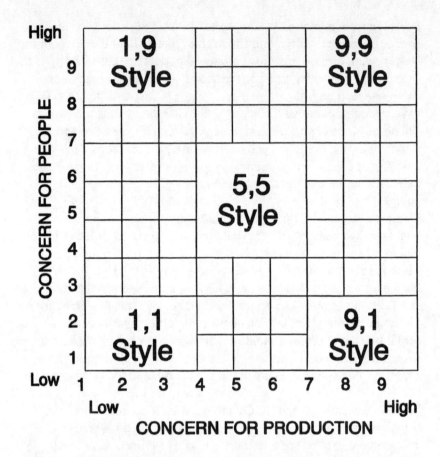

The 1,1 style has little concern for people or production. ('I've only 5 years to go towards my pension. I don't want to rock the boat.')

The 5,5 style compromises between people and productivity, sticks to rules and procedures and aims to produce as much as possible without trouble.

The 9,9 style is used by leaders who obtain high productivity through gaining commitment, harnessing individual and group motivations and making fullest use of the energy released.

Develop a flexible style

No one style is appropriate to every situation. Modern conditions require a *flexible* style, adapted to the demands of the moment.

WORKSHOP: LEADERSHIP STYLES

1. Study your behaviour in any leadership roles you have undertaken. Which of the leadership styles we describe do you normally use?

---

continued

2. Which style do you think will most effectively empower you and others?
3. Can you adopt this style in all circumstances? If not, how would you behave instead?
4. Plan a continuous learning programme which will help to develop leadership habits to change your past style or reinforce your present empowering one.

Another way of gaining experience is to seek out new ones which will offer greater challenges. You take the initiative: you know best what circumstances challenge you.

Actively seek new experiences

WORKSHOP: NEW EXPERIENCES

On your own or, better still, with one or more colleagues or friends, analyse the empowerment experiences you or they feel they lack. Set targets for actively seeking situations which will provide the relevant experience.

To start you thinking, here are some possible circumstances.

1. You are at the moment unemployed. What can you learn from this position? For example:
   - Find a course which will teach you a new skill.
   - Work as a volunteer for a local society on a variety of organising and fundraising jobs.
   - Consider founding your own company as Tim Waterstone did in 1982 when he was fired by W H Smith. (Some years later Waterstone's employed 600 people, and was recently acquired by W H Smith!)
2. Although in employment you are on the lookout for new opportunities.
   - Your organisation advertises jobs internally. Would any offer new skills and challenge?
   - A Japanese company working with self-directing teams or a known 'learning organisation' has local vacancies. Might you apply?
   - In your own department or company there are vacancies for volunteers – for example, to sit on a safety committee. Would these offer new empowerment experiences?
3. Analyse the leadership behaviour of your team leader and/or

continued

> that of senior management, and learn from their strengths and weaknesses.
> 4. Are you involved in a change project? If so, what key leverage points (described in Chapter 5) can you apply to control or learn from this?

> If you have a clear vision of what you want to do . . . and a huge amount of self belief you can get money to do anything.
>
> Tim Waterstone (*in Forrest and Tolfree*, 1992)

OTHER CHANNELS FOR CONTINUOUS LEARNING

Books and relevant management journals.   These have a growing market. The printed word alerts you to new ideas and reading can be fitted into spare moments. One manager reported to us that reading his newspaper seriously on his commuter train offered several items useful to his work every day. The Japanese are voracious readers – are you?

Videos and television programmes.   The special channels supporting management training and others reporting on world business trends are particularly useful.

Training courses.   These may be run by your organisation or outside agencies. Research indicates that managers, in particular, make little effort to discover what is available, but a relevant course may fit your own empowerment or leadership needs.

Decide which of these channels of learning you might find helpful to use on a regular basis.

Smaller organisations

If you work for a smaller business or charity where facilities for learning do not exist, shop around from the available external options. In France and Germany, local Chambers of Commerce offer training facilities, and French businesses believe that small concerns will fail unless their managers learn the professional skills and know-how of larger companies. British businesses should take heed.

One small company, Riverside Electroplaters, took advantage of the Department of Employment's programme 'Investors in People' (IIP) to gain training. They achieved IIP status by meeting its requirements, which are:

● Goals have been set for the company and explained.
● Workers have the right skills to meet these needs.

Their training was related to their business plan and involved, for example, holding a meeting between the management and the six staff every Friday evening to discuss progress. Measuring improvements proved difficult; however one successful scheme which involved the employees in measuring their own rejects resulted in a drop in the reject rate from 25 to 2 per cent.

The IIP programme is supported and facilitated by local technical colleges. A useful step for you might be to influence your employer to join a local IIP programme.

TAKE CHARGE OF YOUR CAREER

Only you can continue to maintain and develop your knowledge and skills, and gain ever more experience. Modern organisations no longer *owe* careers to people in their employ. There are fewer high-level jobs but there are more people below wanting to climb a shorter ladder.

> The corporation ladder is collapsing because it can no longer carry the weight.
>
> *Rosabeth Moss Kanter, When Giants Learn to Dance*

Base your security on employability

As we saw in Chapter 5, much change is so fundamental and rapid that it becomes 'discontinuous' and possibly, therefore, your own position could become discontinuous too. Therefore, manage your own future, and look for a new kind of security based on your experience, your ability to empower and your own employability in the market place; not on your length of service or position in a hierarchy.

> There are four kinds of people in the world:
>   People who watch things happen,
>   People to whom things happen,
>   People who don't know what's happening,
>   And people who make things happen.
>
> *Liz Willis and Jenny Daisley*

CAREER ADVICE

An independent management consultant (quoted in Peters, 1992) described how, at the end of his first consultancy year, he realised that, although he was incredibly busy and making a lot of money, he was doing the same work for a variety of clients, yet not adding to his abilities. Hence his market value was declining as he had no contributions to make to new assignments. 'Keeping my career moving forward, even staying level, was going to take conscious effort' he concluded.

He offers helpful advice to others. Whether you are 25 or 55 you should always be worrying about the future direction of your career. Ask yourself such questions as:

● In which ways am I more valuable this year than last year?
● What specific new skills will I set out to acquire this year?

> Our employees look at change and learning as job security.
> Henry Quadracci, *Chief Executive of Quad Graphics* (in Peters, 1992)

Build employability

To remain employable calls for a fundamental change of attitude to your future. It means continually gaining retraining in case your present job or skills become obsolete, and as a leader, instead of climbing up, ensure you move *horizontally*. You may find this a very difficult attitude to change, since traditionally career success has meant going *up* a ladder, progressing to more responsible and senior jobs, offering ever higher salaries and more attractive status symbols. Today, however, success for many is achieved not by going up but by doing something which is more in line with their interests and needs and more challenging than they have yet done, and so learning new knowledge and new skills.

> Responsibility = response-ability – the ability to choose your response.
> *Stephen Covey*

Japanese and German customs

Since it is their custom to move people upwards by seniority, the Japanese provide learning by planning a continuous development programme which begins with everyone gaining front-line experience. A mix of on- and off-the-job training follows, all integrated into the company's staffing plans. They also rotate people from job to job – from line to staff and from one function to a different one. Sumitomo Electric Industries rotate jobs twice a year. In January 1990, 500 managers were moved, 30 per cent going to another division.

Equally, under the German apprenticeship system people are given a series of specific jobs across a wide range of functions.

Early experience of some top British leaders

Forrest and Tolfree give examples of how British leaders often have to make opportunities for themselves. One chief executive found in his early days that he had too little to do in BP, so he 'made it very clear he wanted to move' elsewhere in the group. Another said, 'I liked doing something new, something that the company hadn't done before.' An employee of a large printing firm summed all this up: 'I take as many courses as I can, it's a matter of survival.'

Baroness Tessa Blackstone, now Master of Birkbeck College, turned combining a career with bringing up a family into an asset since 'this required the development of organisational skills which many men don't have to develop in the same way . . . and helped me to develop a real sense of how to use my time productively.'

Ann Burdus, now a senior vice-president, has risen through the 'glass ceiling' in the public relations profession. Twice in her career she ran up against a career block; once when her supervisor left, his job was offered to someone she considered less qualified than herself, and once when the head of her department and his deputy, both brilliant men, were the same age as herself. To her interviewer's summary that, when she saw a career block, 'she did something about it', she answered, 'you should act positively, you should assess the situation . . . if it's in my nature to say I'm unhappy I had better do something about it and get on with it.' Her view is that 'we are responsible for our own lives and indeed for other people's.'

CASE STUDY: ENHANCING EMPLOYABILITY

Menconi, a secretary with computer manufacturer Apple, felt that her role presented few chances of personal development. She therefore asked a career counsellor for advice on what to do next. Tests showed she had mechanical abilities and liked working independently and out of doors. She eventually found one department in Apple which was looking for a woman electrician to balance its mostly male ranks. It seemed to fit her needs but she, of course, lacked the experience, education and technical skills it called for.

So in October 1990 she set out to acquire them by entering a union-sponsored three-year apprenticeship and then enrolling on a two-year educational course sponsored and financially supported by Apple. At the same time, she moved laterally in Apple from her secretarial 'grade 27' to the same grade as a mechanical technician. 'I'm incredibly happy', she said. 'I wear jeans, I'm outdoors a good part of the time, I'm doing something different every day, in my own van' (Waterman, 1993).

A woman who already possessed a PhD and is a mother of two small children decided to change from her job as a researcher

---

continued

and university coach to become a vet. On her own initiative and in spite of all the problems this created she applied for, and obtained, a mature student grant and a place on a four-year full-time veterinary course. She passed all her exams and in 1993 started her new career as a veterinary surgeon with a wide general practice in the west of England.

Working in an international team

Tom Peters (1992) describes how the experience of going overseas broadens the knowledge of global competition. He advises: 'I'd also urge all students, especially MBA sorts, to get the heck out of the country, whichever your country is. A little global experience goes a long way.' In particular, this gives practice in the difficulties of working in an international team.

As the European single market gains momentum, more and more European jobs will appear. Eurotunnel is an example of such a trend. To meet the company's priority of service to customers on both sides of the Channel, it is establishing a single management structure with a new breed of cross-Channel executives selected for being the best people to do the job, whether British, French, German or from another country. In this culture, safety and customer service, not nationality, are the driving forces – the company affirms that it does not want any competitive nationalism to develop. Engine drivers and traffic controllers must be bilingual, managers and engineers attend intensive language courses, and people in contact with customers have a two-week course in the basic phrases required for customer information (*Financial Times*, 4 June 1993).

In the UK an increasing number of larger companies have at least one foreign national as a non-executive director on the board, in order to gain a more international perspective. A survey by headhunters revealed that 60 per cent of these companies were looking for a European to fill that slot and the *Financial Times* estimates that the number of foreign non-executive directors could rise to 84 per cent in the foreseeable future.

All this suggests that a career move to Europe or further afield may be one way of remaining employable.

We are responsible for our own lives and indeed for other people's.

Ann Burdus

CASE STUDY: ONE GRADUATE'S EXPERIENCE

A graduate whose experiences we have followed, described as having rather itchy feet, built a wide base of experience by moves into many different fields. His jobs after business school took him from running a French subsidiary (and perfecting his French) to Nigeria (gaining African experience) and back to a company in England. This was acquired by a larger company which assimilated its product and made everyone redundant. Our graduate was the last to leave and wrote his own redundancy notice. As he had also gained an accountancy qualification and become an expert in information technology on the way, new job opportunities soon presented themselves.

WORKSHOP: EMPLOYABILITY

1. Imagine yourself on the day you 'retire'. Write down what you would like to claim you have achieved. Did you take sufficiently into account:
   - the unprecedented rapidity of change over your employment years?
   - if you thought you were a high flyer, the difficulties of mounting a rapidly disappearing ladder to the top?
2. Now write down the future moves or the types of experience and skills which would help you reach your goal:
   - *Within your organisation.* For example, to a team training to be multiskilled, or already on the way to being self-directing? to run a profit centre?
   - *Moving to a different organisation.* For example, one already empowering people, or dynamic and growing, possibly with overseas connections.
   - *If you are unemployed.* How will finding employment affect your future? Will you aim for the same goals as above?
3. Set yourself five key empowering challenges to accomplish over the next 3–5 years.

LEARNING TO HANDLE STRESS

Stress and empowerment are closely linked. Deborah Clarke defines the conditions which create stress as 'High Demands plus High

Constraints plus Low Support.' Feelings of stress occur partly as a result of our own emotions and temperament and partly through the effects of our environment and circumstances. For example nurses, social workers, caring charities and carers all face high demands and make high demands on themselves, but often lack the resources to meet them. If they do manage in spite of this, their reward is job satisfaction. If not, frustration and stress can result. Reducing your own stress, therefore, increases your ability to empower others.

But equally, anyone being empowered may be put under greater stress, since empowerment gives them greater responsibility and authority, and expects greater results in return. Perhaps this is a factor causing stress at a more senior level, since the effects of stress on some senior executives is now so serious that they are beginning to question their corporate lifestyle.

According to a BUPA survey, many directors suffer from stress, feeling insecure through ignorance about their new role as directors. 'The very specialists who bumped into mountains because they kept their heads down are suddenly expected to leap them at one bound' (Garratt, 1987).

> If I'd known what little fun it was to be a director, I do not think I would have accepted it.
>
> *International banker*

Employee assistance programmes (EAPs) are becoming increasingly popular in British industry, especially in banking, pharmaceuticals and financial services. It is estimated that 61 per cent of companies employing over 1000 people offer this professional counselling service. EAPs identify stress symptoms and help people through difficult periods. One senior bank executive started to develop headaches and eczema and became so demoralised that he began to look for another job. Counselling discovered a difficult relationship with a superior; the executive stayed with the bank and was soon promoted. Since the late 1980s, 150 companies including Whitbread and Mobil Oil have instituted EAP programmes. Whitbread's community investment manager says EAP has been a major factor behind its success in retaining managers, and Mobil's medical adviser points out that if you are not 100 per cent fit in the offshore industries you are a safety risk. Other companies run courses on stress management. For example, United Biscuits runs a programme based on the results of a comprehensive stress test. People are then offered counselling or advice (IBS, 1990).

Proper training reduces stress

People who have been properly trained and are confident that they are doing something worthwhile, in work or when unemployed, can withstand more stress.

One further key to empowering people without causing stress lies in giving them solid support. As we saw in Chapter 4, a major skill of empowerment is showing supportive behaviour. The techniques we describe for controlling stress, particularly if your senior is caring, can help you to understand and to be in control of yourself, which is a vital component in your own self-development and empowerment and liberates you to support and empathise with others.

Support reduces stress

This makes sense of one view that it is the *lack* of a challenge which causes most stress. So shopfloor workers suffer more stress than their executives: the monotony of their jobs is the biggest frustration they complain about. Being unemployed and without occupation is an even greater frustration. Empowerment for these people would be the answer to reducing their stress.

For whatever reason, stress is an ever-increasing by-product of our modern, fast-moving, ever-changing world. Whether your job is within a large organisation or outside (a freelancer or part-timer, running a business, etc.) surveys show that stress can have serious effects on you and your organisation and your skills of empowerment.

Stress can affect everyone at work

When you are suffering from stress you can become irritable, anxious, depressed, lose concentration, miss appointments, avoid others and become unable to solve problems or make decisions. When physical symptoms appear, a person often becomes one of the absentees which cost British industry £2 billion a year. (One estimate considers 25–50 per cent of all absenteeism from work in Britain as attributable to stress.) A 1992 survey by the mental health charity Mind found that stress at work has replaced personal problems such as death, divorce or moving house. Nearly 90 per cent of the people surveyed put redundancy, recession and pressure to perform as the main causes. So, from director through to shopfloor, stress can strike.

Stress symptoms

CASE STUDY: STRESS

A team of production workers acquired a new supervisor. He was a perfectionist, always finding fault. Most of the team laughed this off, but one member could not cope with criticism and soon was making so many mistakes that he deserved most of it. He lacked the self-confidence of the others, and was an easy victim. He coped with stress in the only way he knew: he ran away. Although jobs were scarce, he handed in his notice and the company lost the skills of a normally satisfactory worker.

WITHSTANDING STRESS

Running away from stress is negative and unproductive. Jane Cranwell-Ward gives the very good advice that you should find your own optimum stress level and by the positive way you handle stress increase your resistance to it, converting it into an ally. Moss Kanter (1989) tells how people on projects entrusted to turn new ideas into products worked long hours to punishing deadlines, yet found their work full of meaning and exhilaration. Extra pressure produced extra performance; it was the spice of life. The secret is to find your own *optimum level* of stress and stick to it. If you are under too much stress and you stretch yourself above this fine dividing line you feel unable to cope, and ill health sets in. Equally, if you are understressed and are working *below* your optimum level you become bored, listless and uncommited. Peter Nixon, consultant cardiologist at the Charing Cross Hospital, draws this 'human function curve' as in the diagram below.

> They were flowing with the pressure.
>
> *Review of 200 managers*

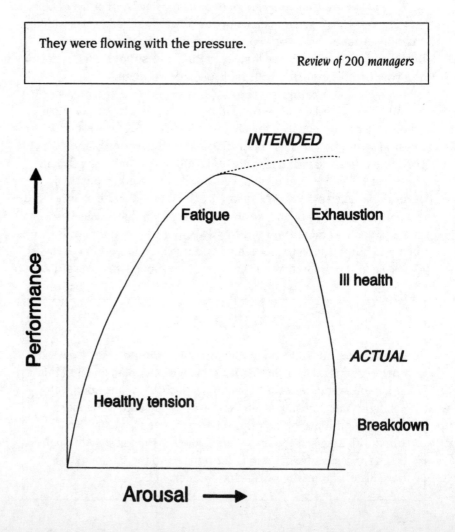

Your reactions and feelings under stress are determined partly by your own temperament and past experiences. Which of the following paired reactions suit you?

Analyse your emotions, temperament and reactions

You feel calm – circumstances do not easily worry you	You soon become anxious, worry about failure and panic in an emergency
You welcome change, like variety, live dangerously at times	You are happiest in an orderly routine, sticking to past values and ways
You are self-confident	You dislike asserting yourself and avoid conflict

If the first column describes you best, your optimum pressure level will be near the top level in the human function curve. If the second column is more like you, you belong lower down the scale.

Work out your optimum stress level

These are just a few examples: you can work out your own. There is no need to cheat – neither reaction is better or worse and each has its downside and its upside. Change for its own sake is unbalanced; anxiety about the future may be very justified; self-confidence can change into arrogance, and so on. Your objective is to discover your own level so that you can handle your own *feelings* towards stress and avoid subterfuge for escaping the truth ('I wasn't quite myself that day', 'My team-mate made a stupid decision' etc.)

Be honest with yourself

> Thriving on stress is difficult to achieve. The skills can be compared with mastering a foreign language: diligent learning and extensive practice.
>
> Jane Cranwell-Ward

The greater the 'dissonance' between the way people see you behaving and your true feelings, the more your stress will rise: for example, if you are, contrary to your feelings, giving orders in a threatening incident, hiding anger, or staying to listen when you are desperate to get to an urgent meeting.

Dissonance increases stress

Equally stressful is the dissonance caused when the job you are doing does not fit your interests, your abilities or your needs – perhaps because circumstances have changed its nature or your needs have changed. If this is short term most of us can cope; but if long-term dissonance becomes too great one day you may blow your top, escape into illness, take flight or begin to underperform.

> Stress becomes distress.
>
> *Jane Cranwell-Ward*

Before this crisis point, watch out for warning signs of too much or too little stress. Slow down or look for more challenges. Change your idea of your own optimum stress level, since although temperament can be modified some of it is innate.

WORKSHOP: FIND YOUR OWN STRESS LEVEL

1. Think back to a critical incident and examine:
   - How did you feel?
   - How did you react and behave?
   - Were there any warning signs of developing stress?
   How much dissonance between your feelings and your behaviour do you now detect?
2. Keep notes for a week or more on:
   - the type and number of occasions when your feelings were negative but you behaved supportively
   - occasions when your negative behaviour echoed your negative feelings
   - warning signs of developing stress
3. Use the evidence you have gathered to plot your own position on the human function curve.
4. Discuss your position on the curve with your work partner, trusted friend or mentor, and perhaps modify your own judgement in the light of theirs.

STRESS IN THE WORK ENVIRONMENT

The cause of much stress lies in the environment and your circumstances. Environmental factors causing stress are legion. Some are one-off, many are chronic: daily hassles building mounting frustration.

Below we list causes which other people have described to us as frustrating:

- *Your workload*: amount, deadlines, variety, resources, unsocial hours, etc. Are you under pressure to do too much to tight deadlines or working with unreliable machinery, for example?
- *Bureaucracy versus autonomy*: A remark of total frustration comes from a French worker: 'You get a form, then the signature of three chaps, you lose hours because of paperwork – it's the century of red tape.'

- *Discrimination* affecting your chances of advancement.
- *Long or irregular hours* interfering with your personal life.
- *An unclear idea of what is expected of you*: no job description, no targets, no obvious career path.
- *As a freelance you are not prospering*: your supply contract has not been renewed and you cannot find new markets, etc.
- *Your financial position*: does your pay reflect your performance? Are you receiving less than a colleague doing a similar job? Is your pension secure and adequate?
- *Your working conditions*: these factors vary greatly. For example, have you a quiet place where you can think and plan? Do you work for a Japanese firm and resent wearing an overall and eating in a common canteen?
- *You are experiencing a period of intense change*, including redundancy or unemployment.
- *You do not get on with your boss* and some colleagues in your teams or across functional lines. A hotel rooms manager once remarked to one of us, 'I'll do anything short of being untruthful to score points over reception.'
- *You feel you are shouldering the responsibilities of the entire work-team*: only you want to get the work done.

WORKSHOP: ENVIRONMENTAL FACTORS CAUSING STRESS

1. Analyse which circumstances cause you stress.
2. Which of these:
   - cause no stress to you but might upset someone else?
   - are conditions like rules which, although irksome, you accept as normal irritants in organisational life?
   - are circumstances which affect you deeply – your work, status, salary, relationships, redundancy, bankruptcy, etc?
3. Compare your list with ours.

You can manage stress more easily if you have thought out your own approach to life – what you expect from yourself and from others, your values and what you believe in. So to keep excessive stress at bay, your mind must stay in charge of your emotions, your body and your mental well-being. When these aspects are in balance, the rewards from controlling yourself at your own optimum stress level will be a deepening of your empowerment skills.

MANAGING YOURSELF AND YOUR CIRCUMSTANCES

> A sense of beliefs – a personal code – is an important part of stress management.
>
> *Eve Warren and Caroline Toll*

Supposing you hear some worrying rumours about a departmental reorganisation which will affect you adversely. First, find out the facts – as much information as possible about the situation. Are the rumours true? Can you confront a colleague in another department and ask for the facts? Does the situation arise out of poor organisation?

Practical methods to control your emotions

It all sounds as if rumours could be true, but with your mind in control from the beginning you can take steps to control your *emotions*. You can:

- recognise the feelings which are causing you stress;
- turn disappointment and anger into positive thoughts (I suppose it could have been worse, I knew something was in the air, I could have been made redundant, etc);
- release your negative feelings by pouring them out truthfully to someone you trust;
- draw on the emotional support of a network of friends;
- call upon the barrier erected between yourself and circumstances (the detachment which all carers such as doctors and nurses require in order to work successfully);
- let go: stop stewing endlessly over a situation you cannot change;
- think of some practical actions which you *can* take.

Support from your body

Your *physical* well-being can now stand you in good stead. Have you developed a healthy lifestyle – eating and drinking sensibly, taking regular physical exercise and recreation? Do you know how to relax your body? (Helpful advice on this practical skill is given by Coleman and by Warren and Toll.) Remember to relax your face, neck, shoulder and back muscles. Do not scowl or clench your teeth in unconscious tension. Can you relax by practising some technique such as yoga or sinking yourself in some totally absorbing pursuit – singing in a choir or learning a new skill?

An inner balance

Your *mental* well-being will flow from consciously building an inner balance between the many factors in your own unique personality and the fast-changing kaleidoscope of your daily life, while staying commited to your priority philosophy and goals. (As a physiotherapist said to one of us, 'It's your space, live in it.')

CASE STUDY: MIND IN CONTROL

James Grantley was a senior in the information technology department of a large conglomerate. Highly qualified technically and with a wide experience of computer facilities, he fully expected to succeed the retiring head of department. Instead, he was told an outside candidate was being sought. The department was being reorganised and its staff dispersed to member companies. A small central coordinating department would be led by someone with wide management experience.

Although bitterly disappointed and feeling let down, James Grantley thought through his position – was his stress arising out of a mismatch between expectations and reality? Did he *really* want to be a manager? He decided finally that information technology was his major interest but that he needed more freedom and power to pursue it. He would temporarily accept work in the devolved reorganisation, but plan to become a self-employed consultant as soon as practicable.

This approach reduced the dissonance within himself, restored his mental well-being and increased his level of resistance to stress. It also increased his ability to control his own circumstances and illustrates one way, among many, of managing your own environment and circumstances which can increase the rewards and minimise the costs of stress.

WORKSHOP: YOUR MIND IN CONTROL

1. Each day try to find time to reflect on any stress you have felt. Analyse its symptoms and its causes. Do these lie within yourself or in your circumstances?
2. If they are within yourself, set a time target for raising your optimum stress level by consciously balancing your emotional, physical and mental well-being.
3. If your environment and circumstances are the cause, decide to take some practical measures to reduce the pressures.
4. Record your successes as you improve your stress management.

Keep a diary of what you do each day for a week or a month.   Work out where you are wasting time needed for more important work, which increases the stress caused by the feeling of always too much work and too little time. How often, for example, could a chat to someone to keep communications open be job oriented rather than gossip?

Develop automatic habits.   Habits reduce stress, because when actions become automatic, thinking and decision making are released for more important or urgent matters. Some executives make a habit of dealing with their incoming post as the first priority of the day; self-managing teams begin with a meeting, and so on. Can you make a *habit* of saving time?

Organise each day.   Look ahead and organise your day as much as possible (but consciously not allowing the unexpected to stress you). Make use of spare half-hours between appointments or jobs. Visit neighbouring suppliers and customers situated close to each other on the same expedition. Set a time limit for meetings, and so on.

Take time off to recharge your batteries.   A natural break occurs when some difficult work is completed. An American survey of hours worked by managers reveals:

- 88 per cent worked 10 or more hours a day
- 94 per cent worked at least one hour per weekend
- 56 per cent spent seven days or more travelling per month

If you are leading an exciting but overloaded life like these people or their staff, take some leave before stress sets in. A young executive caught up in a local government reorganisation spent a year working 12 hours or more each day, not reaching home until 9.30 p.m. and writing reports at weekends. When work became more normal, he took two weeks' leave. The fundraisers in a charity one of us worked with often ran weekend events – they then took time off in lieu.

Confront stressful situations.   Do not run away from stressful situations. Even temperamentally vulnerable people can learn from confronting environments which they find hostile and, through the process of overcoming their stress, build their resistance to it in future.

Put your problems to bed.   Another useful tip given by Paddy O'Brien comes from a manager whose work is very stressful. He told her: when I go to bed I imagine a large box at the bottom of the stairs, and dropping all my problems on pieces of paper into it, then the lid shutting down over them and being clear that I won't open that box until the morning.

Suggestions for executives

Delegate more.   Members of your staff are keen to gain experience. Train them and trust them to take over jobs routine to you but new to them (delegation is discussed in Chapter 6).

Contain your workload.   Do not run too many projects simultaneously – all may run into trouble together. Supervisors of a wordprocessor pool could not give priority to several desperate 'customers'. The customers, equally frustrated, learnt how to use a word processor to type their own correspondence, and all parties suffered stress.

Copy politicians and doctors.   Schedule regular surgery hours when people know they are welcome to drop in. This is much less stressful to you than if they appear at an inappropriate moment and less frustrating to them than if they get short shrift.

Work at home.   You save commuting time, avoid interruptions and reduce needless stress.

Help others to avoid stress.   Observe what causes stress for your staff or colleagues and help them to reduce it, thus removing possible causes of stress from yourself.

As you become proficient in handling stress you gain confidence in the success of the empowering approach. You see others around you maturing and so your job satisfaction increases and your stress diminishes.

WORKSHOP: DEALING WITH STRESS

Think of an occasion when you felt you were literally at breaking point.
1. What was the combination of factors which contributed to stress?
2. Could you have prevented any of these before a crisis arose?
3. How did you deal with the stress?
4. In retrospect, what should you have done?

EMPOWER YOUR FUTURE

The new ways of producing and organising work described in Chapter 1, and some of the awesome possibilities opened up by information technology, outlined in Chapter 4, are making change and discontinuity inevitable. The many radical changes in industrial attitudes, strategies and organisation are unprecedented in their depth and scope, and above all in their revolutionary speed.

Five to ten years ago, automatically controlled tools gave the Germans a competitive edge in the production of specialised one-off goods. Today, Germany is trying to readjust to the speed of newer, high-tech expertise.

Technical changes

Social changes

Over the same time, worldwide changes in social attitudes and the empowerment of more people at work have been leading to the breakdown of traditional attitudes. For example in France, entrenched bureaucratic attitudes once gave to the highly educated cadre élite greater social prestige, especially when working in more highly regarded fields ('selling money rather than socks' as one told Barsoux and Lawrence). Today this attitude is weakening in favour of a new, rapidly developing entrepreneurial class.

Organisational changes

Drastic reorganisations by large corporations and some public bodies over the same period have caused thousands of people to lose their once safe jobs. Banking, traditionally one of the safest fields of employment in Britain, is safe no longer.

Reactions to sudden change

Sudden change is traumatic to the thousands of people involved. A director of a new firm spent some four years getting it on its feet. Without warning the chief executive called him into his office one Friday and said, 'There is no longer a place for you in this company. We will compensate you, of course, but collect your belongings and leave at once.' The director felt shock and disbelief. Consultants Peat Marwick describe this as 'grieving' and 'anger' followed by 'depression'. The director was not prepared for such a disconcerting experience.

> Flow into the tide rather than investing energy in resisting it.
>
> *Bob Garratt*

PREPARE FOR DISCONTINUITY NOW

There are many more avenues open now than even ten years ago. Some people, pioneers of the future, are accepting the inevitability of change by choosing discontinuity now. In the last ten years one woman has changed countries and jobs three times – a television professional in New Zealand, then a teacher of English to foreigners in England, now the administrator of a technical college in Portugal.

Adopt an innovative approach

Tom Peters (1992) advises us all to prepare for change and in order to practise for it, he says, you should ask yourself each week what exactly – however small – have I changed this week? 'The principal enemy is inertia,' he says.

People making plans for this future discontinuity are already deciding where their strengths lie and what they like doing. They list their achievements by examining their past lives, including formative school days, interests inside and outside work, and work knowledge, skills and experience. They ask themselves what have they felt most proud of and enjoyed.

The experience of a physicist brings this exercise to life. His rigorous training in maths and physics gained him a career in secret government work; he seemed silent and introverted. At the age of 60 his lifestyle changed dramatically. He became an acknowledged expert and author on the history of his locality. This work, so different, still used the scientific skills he had learnt, but his relaxed conversation and the sparkle in his eyes showed his enjoyment in it.

Only you can use your initiative, 'think the unlikely' as Handy says in *The Age of Unreason*, and prepare for a future to keep you employable with continuous learning keeping you stretched, fulfilled and empowered.

Keep yourself empowered

WORKSHOP: DISCONTINUITY

1. Try to remember what your work life was like 10 years ago:
   - technologically
   - socially
   - organisationally
2. How have changes, if any, in these aspects already affected your lifestyle?
3. Practise for discontinuity by making regular changes so that innovation becomes a habit.
4. Analyse your own abilities, preferences and experience. What would be the three most preferable options to your current lifestyle and work?

Trends for the future indicate that we have at least 15–20 years of healthy useful life ahead after the age of 65 – some successful Open University students are over 80! Retirement, especially 'early' retirement, is becoming obsolete, so preparing for it involves rethinking your personal profile in the light of new personal specifications. Two crucial aspects are:

- Paid employment as a supplement to your present income (if you have intelligence, skills and motivation a market exists).
- Suitable voluntary work options – think about what you can contribute. One answer is that as an empowered person you have a great deal to offer.

THE 'THIRD AGE'

Endless, mindless leisure has other names, unemployment, imprisonment. Leisure only makes sense when it re-creates for work.
Charles Handy, The Age of Unreason

Help needed

If you have no immediate ideas but would like to give help somewhere, a charity called REACH (Retired Executives' Clearing House) puts volunteers in touch with voluntary jobs which suit their talents and interests. One charity secured a volunteer from REACH for six months or longer, to launch a research fund. If you possess a technical skill, a vast area of need will reveal itself.

Many more opportunities will arise in the future, especially as, with the new emphasis on care in the community, disadvantaged and elderly people in Britain are extremely dependent on any help, however small or unskilled, that volunteers can offer.

WORKSHOP: THIRD AGE

1. Ask yourself whether you want to:
   - pursue your own hobbies and interests
   - earn some money
   - give voluntary help
   - combine all three aspects
2. What plans will you make to keep:
   - 'feeling good' and self-confident
   - your mind in charge of your emotions, your body and your mental well-being
   - empowering yourself through continuous learning
   - empowering others

Part III — Recommended Reading

John Adair (1978) *Training for Leadership*, Gower, Aldershot.
John Adair (1988) *The Action Centred Leader*, Industrial Society, London.
Robert R Blake and Jane S Mouton (1964) *The Managerial Grid*, Gulf Publishing, Houston.
Jan Carlzon (1989) *Moments of Truth*, Harper & Row, New York.
Jane Cranwell-Ward (1990) *Thriving on Stress*, Routledge, London.
Andrew Forrest and Patrick Tolfree (1992) *Leaders: The Learning Curve of Achievement*, Industrial Society, London.
Charles Handy (1985) *Understanding Organizations*, Penguin, Harmondsworth.
Charles Handy (1989) *The Age of Unreason*, Business Books, London.
John Harvey-Jones (1988) *Making it Happen: Reflections on Leadership*, Collins, 1988.
Frederick Herzberg (1966) *Work and the Nature of Man*, World Publishing, New York.
Andrew Kakabadse (1991) *The Wealth Creators: Top People, Top Teams and Executive Best Practice*, Kogan Page, London.
Carol Kennedy (1991) *Guide to the Management Gurus*, Business Books, London.
Charles Margerison and Dick McCann (1990) *Team Management*, Mercury, London.
Douglas McGregor (1966) *Leadership and Motivation*, MIT Press, Cambridge.
Nick Oliver and Barry Wilkinson (1988) *The Japanization of British Industry*, Basil Blackwell, Oxford.
Tom Peters (1992) *Liberation Management*, Macmillan, London.
Donald Petersen and John Hillkirk (1991) *Team Work*, Victor Gollancz, London.
Eve Warren and Caroline Toll (1993) *The Stress Workbook*, Nicholas Brealey, London.
Robert Waterman (1993) *Frontiers of Excellence*, Nicholas Brealey, London.
Mike Woodcock (1989) *Team Development Manual*, Gower, Aldershot.

Part IV
The Skills of
Empowerment

Earlier parts of this book describe the philosophy and practice of empowerment. It stresses that in a liberating organisation the skills of giving and receiving orders, called for in a traditional organisation, are no longer relevant. In order to undertake successfully the many new roles described, both leaders and staff require a wider and more complex range of people skills. Some basic business knowledge and skills and, of course, a high degree of technical excellence in relevant fields, are also vitally important.

The people skills, the most important for empowering leadership, are described in detail in Chapters 10 and 11. It is, however, equally essential to close skills gaps in all other areas as well. Chapter 12 suggests ways in which these can be identified and outlines the many different training programmes which can help you to learn the skills you need. To be truly empowered, *everyone* in an organisation needs to gain some basic business skills which help them to understand how businesses are organised and run, so that customers can be satisfied and productivity increased.

There are some core skills which are common to all encounters between people in empowered organisations, and others which are necessary for special occasions or roles. Leaders need particular skills to create willing consent – staff need to be able to communicate their commitment, intelligence and experience.

Types of people skills

The core skills are:
- listening
- communicating effectively with others
- understanding how to behave supportively in any situation

Other empowering skills

The additional empowering skills required for specific occasions or roles are:
- influencing others and negotiating
- coaching and counselling
- conducting appraisal interviews
- leading discussions and meetings

> Most of our time in business is spent in communication, either in listening or in trying to persuade others.
>
> *John Harvey-Jones (in John Lidstone, 1992)*

Training for these skills

People can be trained to acquire all these skills in the same way as they learn the motor or technical skills of a particular function or trade. Key factors are isolated, then taught and practised with the help of a coach and other learners on the job, or by professional trainers plus a tutor and fellow course members training together.

Training in these skills might have prevented the deterioration of relationships between a supervisor and shop steward, causing the supervisor to say simply to one of us 'I hate him'. Unfortunately, many managers and their staff have the greatest difficulty in changing their attitudes to leadership and the new skills required, typified by one wry comment made by a manager on a training course that 'being a dominant leader wasn't part of it any more'.

The Core *10*

Skills

In this chapter we discuss the main 'people' skills essential for empowerment and empowering leadership. These are core empowering skills because they enable people to understand themselves and others, and help in reaching consensus.

LISTENING

Listening has been called the lost art of our age. It is not a passive activity, but a dynamic responding skill. Few of us really listen; we are too busy making our own points or influencing others to do our will. Many managers feel that effective leadership demands confident orders and brisk decisions: listening indicates weakness. Or our attitudes become barriers and we switch off because we are irritated by the way a person behaves or speaks. Deliberately not hearing others, and defending our own position, can involve misinterpreting someone else. (Car insurance claims abound in this: 'I knocked over a man; he admitted it was his fault as he had been run over before'.) John Lidstone quotes research which helps to explain why we find listening difficult. Our brains process information about four times faster than someone speaks, so we get bored and think of our response, or evaluate and so stop listening.

By contrast, empowering leaders are ready and able to give total attention to each encounter, however brief (that precious minute with a customer, described by Jan Carlzon as 'the moment of truth'), or however long (such as an appraisal interview).

The ability and willingness to listen to others so that you can really

Give your total attention

grasp what they are saying is fundamental to empowerment. When someone sees that you are genuinely concerned to understand their position the joint encounter becomes a liberating experience for both parties.

Stay neutral and objective

True listening like this is founded on our ability to put our own attitudes and beliefs aside so that we stay genuinely neutral and 'unshockable'. Psychoanalyst Jung tells us: 'We get in touch with another with an attitude of unprejudiced objectivity. A kind of deep respect for facts and events and for the person who suffers from them – a respect for the secret of such a life.'

Your rewards

Your rewards for listening in this way are:

- you understand the motivation of other people
- you demonstrate that you care about them as people, not only as 'brains' or 'hands'
- they feel secure enough to express their views, examine their performance, learn new skills and make decisions for themselves
- you excel at influencing people and negotiating, since you can put your case in terms of their needs

Barriers based on powerful attitudes

Yet gaining this unprejudiced objectivity is a listener's greatest challenge. We all possess deep-seated, powerful attitudes from a very early age consisting of needs, expectations, emotions and unconscious material as well as rational thought. Many of these attitudes are accepted uncritically and, although some are likely to be inadequate and flawed, they form the basis from which we judge new experiences, resolve problems and make decisions. We have powerful mechanisms for conserving our attitudes intact which operate in various subtle ways:

Defence mechanisms

- *We ignore or distrust reality.* Impatient with his company's traditional autocratic management style, a team leader, already an enthusiast for management by consent, decided to go it alone, by delegating responsibility for allocating jobs to the team. Soon arguments, clashes of will and feelings of unfair treatment escalated. In order to restore peace and to get the work done, the disillusioned team leader was forced to resume this responsibility. His own strong attitude against authority, based on his treatment by an autocratic father, had led him to ignore the realities which doomed him to failure. He needed some support from top management and his fellow team leaders, all of whom believed in management by control. Without training, his team was not ready for more responsibility, yet there was no company training course for them and he himself had not been trained to train. In his enthusiasm he had ignored the real situation – highlighted by a survey conducted by Wellins, Byham and Wilson showing that 'insufficient training is the leading cause of team failure.'

- We *forget or we rationalise*. Some remarks by a recruitment officer: 'I turned that candidate down because of his weak handshake, I knew that meant he lacked resolution.' From a departmental manager, frightened off maths by an unsympathetic schoolmaster, 'the computer throws useless statistics at me each month.' Or, more simply, 'I wasn't myself that day.'
- We *see what we expect to see (or hear)*. You can probably recall examples of this at countless meetings. Honest chairpersons sum up a discussion by including decisions they favour and ignoring or misrepresenting the rest – not through malice but all filtered through their own attitudes. Hence attitudes influence both the way we receive and deal with communications from others and also their reactions to what we are saying to them. When as listeners or speakers we misuse our reason in these ways, we lose a chance to enlarge our perception of reality.

How to overcome the barriers

In order to avoid these traps you need to make a thorough, objective appraisal of your own attitudes and, above all, retain a *flexible approach* to experience. This would prevent the sort of situation recounted by Zuboff where some managers suppress vital data offered by the computer in order to cling to the power and authority they believe should belong to them. They feel that controlling knowledge is the key to keeping their authority.

This example, among many, challenges you to reexamine your attitudes and modify them if necessary, since they can critically affect your ability and willingness to be objective and to learn new skills and roles.

> We get our parents when they are so old it is hard to change their habits.
>
> *Schoolboy essay*

Modify your attitude to yourself

One powerful attitude which you may need to modify is that towards yourself. To feel empowered or to be able to empower others you must feel good about yourself, yet the picture of ourselves consciously stored in our minds is, in fact, largely a reflection of what we think other people think about us. Powerful statements from authority figures such as parents and teachers, plus other experiences, may have given you a negative image of yourself and your relationships with others. But these self-images are not objectively 'right' (the more negative the self-image, the more likely it is to be wrong). You can therefore:

- change your attitude towards yourself in the light of comments made by contemporaries or offered by experience, and/or
- change your behaviour.

Reducing 'cognitive dissonance'

Cognitive dissonance describes the pain everyone feels when their attitudes and their behaviour conflict. You can reduce the dissonance by changing either one to bring it into line with the other. Thus behaving in a different way will help you to change your attitudes because you will want to harmonise these with your new behaviour.

One of us was involved in a selection process. The senior manager concerned said, 'I can't stand people with brown eyes, I won't interview them.' He could have changed this irrational attitude by changing his interview behaviour and engaging several brown-eyed people, after which he would have discovered that they were good, bad and indifferent, just like the rest of his staff.

Behave trustingly

Again, you may have the feeling that people cannot be trusted but realise that, since trust is vital to empowerment, you will need to modify this attitude. Start *behaving* in a trusting way and, if you are patient and consistent, in time people will respond with trust. A sceptical manager tried this approach. Although he was sometimes let down, he was prepared for this and persevered until, over a time, his staff responded and trusted him in return.

Question your beliefs

Beliefs possess more of a moral flavour. Some things are 'right' and others 'wrong' (stealing from our employers is wrong, but 'winning' a few perks is considered by some to be permissible).

A belief statement is prefaced by 'ought'. People *ought* to be kind, polite, fair, cheerful; they ought *not* to lose their temper, make mistakes, forget to go to a meeting. The philosophy of empowerment is itself a particular system of beliefs – for example in the reasonableness of people and in their willingness to create common goals, etc. (Unlike some belief systems however these are not absolutes. The other belief of empowerment is in the legitimacy of a plurality of views and voices – there is no single right answer).

Modify unrealistic beliefs

Since we all violate our beliefs on occasions, we conclude that some are unrealistic at times, particularly if held in a rigid and uncompromising way. Unfortunately, like attitudes, they colour our vision of the world. So if you believe you have an unfair boss you will interpret his or her criticisms as unfair, instead of examining them dispassionately and learning from them.

> Beliefs are ideas going bald.
>
> *Francis Picablo, surrealist*

Clearly, being objective and behaving objectively is one of the most difficult states to obtain. Yet it is not only critical to beliefs but also to the whole approach to empowerment. To prejudge a statement, an attitude or a person, is inherently oppressive and whenever this occurs it is disempowering.

WORKSHOP: ATTITUDES AND BELIEFS

Analyse your attitudes and beliefs concerning situations, subjects and values you commonly meet at work.

For example:

1. What do you think, feel or believe about the following:
   - Change – Enjoy its challenge? Welcome it? Fear it? or . . .
   - Profit – A measure? Essential? Immoral? or . . .
   - Principles – Concerning what? Essential? Barriers? or . . .
   - Redundancy – A challenge? Necessary? Unfair? Devastating? or . . .
   - Power – What is it? Who for? How used? Inevitable? or . . .
   - Progress – For yourself? Others? Your organisation? or . . .
   - Responsibility – Who for? or . . .
   - Authority – With others? Over you? Giving orders? or . . .
   - Equality – Of abilities? Opportunities? Birth? or . . .
   - Voluntary work – Rewarding? Liberating? Time-wasting? or . . .

2. Make a list of other subjects you feel strongly about. What do these tell you about your attitudes and beliefs?
3. Discuss your analysis with a mentor, work partner or friend. Note his or her comments.

Once you have analysed and modified your underlying attitudes, there are many skilled ways of demonstrating this objectivity:

- Do not pass judgement. One girl remarked, 'Well of course I might not get married.' Her manager replied, 'That's a depressing attitude.' The girl answered indignantly, 'No it isn't.' Further communication between them effectively ceased.
- Do not offer your own views. One person reported what impressed her about her interviewer: 'We were mostly me working on my situation as I found it.'

In contrast we quote a poem written by an old lady and found in her hospital locker shortly after her death (with acknowledgements to Father David Kiely). The first verse reads:

What do you see, Nurses, what do you see?
A crabbit old woman not very wise
Uncertain of habit with faraway eyes

LISTENING SKILLS

Remain neutral and unshockable

A 'whole' person speaks

When you say in a loud voice, 'I do wish you'd try'
I'll tell you who I am as I sit here so still
As I rise to your bidding, as I eat at your will.

The poem concludes:

I'm an old woman now, and nature is cruel;
The body, it crumbles, grace and vigour depart,
There is now a stone where I once had a heart.
But inside this old carcass a young girl still dwells,
So open your eyes, nurse, open and see,
Not a crabbit old woman, look closer – see me.

Perhaps this voice from the dead may help us all to see not 'clients' but customers, not 'brains' but people, and to listen to them understandingly.

HEAR WORDS THAT EXPRESS FEELINGS

The vast majority of information about how someone is feeling comes not from what they say but from how they say it, so hear what lies underneath (the 'latent content') as well as what is said (the 'manifest content').

This involves listening to facts and feelings, and responding to both.

One interviewer heard the sadness underlying a manager's remarks: 'Of course I *am* in charge here, but it's only a small factory. I was in consultancy before.' The interviewer asked two clarifying questions:

Interviewer: Was the consultancy work demanding?
Manager: Yes. I was kept on my toes *all* the time.
Interviewer: Are you as busy now?
Manager: Oh, no. It's mainly routine.

Similarly, a personnel officer heard the bitterness behind a shy woman's comment, 'Always a bridesmaid – that's me.'

Hear what is not said.   Listen for silences and hesitations and *wait*, hear what is *not* being said, but keep contact by showing you are still listening, by a nod or smile.

Watch for non-verbal signals.   We converse with our whole bodies (our true feelings are leaked through our gestures – our hands are particularly expressive). Michael Argyle recommends that you consider the following: How tense do people appear? Do they avoid looking at you? Why do they lean away from you? What is their facial expression?

Hear emotionally loaded words.   Notice *how* things are said, for example: 'Yes, gardening is a *great* hobby'; 'I *bitterly* resented that'.

Hear the tone.   A welcome to a newcomer ('Come in, I *am* glad to see you') spoken in a depressed low voice will be seen as unwelcoming; the seemingly welcoming words ignored.

Ask searching but objective questions to clarify meaning or feelings. Searching questions ensure that you have grasped the facts, but also enable the speaker to clarify or understand the situation for him or herself. The five 'W's – what, why, when, where, who – and how are useful here.

ASK SEARCHING QUESTIONS

For example:
- What is your job?
- Why do you say that?
- When did it happen?
- Where was that?
- How did you cope?
- Who was involved?

Your questions should be open-ended, perhaps starting with a broad comment such as 'tell me more about . . .' This will elicit a more objective reply than a question which is too direct or leading. For example, one interviewer said rather desperately to one of us: 'What I *must* know is are you efficient?' The obvious but probably biased reply might be 'certainly' or 'of course'.

Objective types of questions

'Reflecting' the feelings people express to you shows that:
- you are understanding with the person
- you have become their 'other self' – your own self absorbed completely in the attitudes of another. (This is empathy – feeling *with* someone, not *for* them.)

'REFLECTING'
Understand with a person

Reflecting remarks are a statement rather than a question, and so contain the words 'you' and 'your':
- 'You feel . . .'
- 'You like/dislike . . .'
- 'You are saying that . . .'
- 'Your approach was . . .'

For example:

Useful reflections

Charity commission chairperson:	'I put an enormous effort into the ToyFair. It *should* have been a great financial success.'
Listener (reflecting):	'You feel disappointed', or 'Your hard work was not rewarded.'

These remarks are within the chairperson's own framework. Questions like 'Do you feel disappointed?', or 'How do you feel about it all?' could have been equally useful, but they are not reflections.

Reflections show speakers that they have really been listened to and so encourage them to explore their feelings or problems more

Reflections serve two useful purposes

Make regular summaries

deeply, and enable listeners to check their understanding. If wrong, the speaker may answer, 'Yes, that's half right, but I have to add . . .'

A summary closely resembles a reflection. It not only includes feelings but is a short statement of facts, ideas and decisions which have been discussed and agreed.

It is important to make a summary at regular intervals, and always at the end of a conversation. An interim summary states what both parties have agreed and is a springboard for a change of subject. A final summary outlines all the material agreed. A summary also states differing views ('We are agreed on . . .'; 'We see these aspects differently . . .', 'We have agreed to see each other again to discuss . . .').

CASE STUDY: THE FUNNEL APPROACH

Encounters dealing with feelings and motivation, as well as facts, can contain a useful sequence of questions taking the shape of a 'funnel'. 'Funnels' are useful because they help listeners to systematise their approach. One encounter followed this sequence:

Explanation

Starts with an open-ended question	*Supervisor of fundraisers*: Are there any parts of your job that you dislike?
	Regional fundraiser: Well, running my committees is difficult. I do too much of the work myself, rather than letting them do it.
Asks for more facts and feelings	*Supervisor*: Could you say a bit more about the difficulties?
	RF: It worries me that I may be – you know, telling them what to do – *they* should be deciding.
Reflects	*Supervisor*: You feel uneasy in case you are interfering too much.

---

continued

	RF: Yes, I'd really like them to stand on their own feet.
Asks for motivation	*Supervisor*: Is getting people to be more independent important to you?
	RF: Yes it is, very.
Asks 'why?'	*Supervisor*: Why?
An attitude explained	RF: I believe I should help voluntary workers to become more responsible, and anyway that's how I like to be myself.
Summary	*Supervisor*: So you like being independent and you want your committees to be too.

All these skills involve giving time to others, and that is the greatest listening skill of all.

WORKSHOP: LISTENING

1. A useful way of checking how accurately you listen is to practise with someone you know well and trust. Ask her (or him) to outline a problem or decision which is worrying her. Listen carefully, then tell her what you heard. Did she feel you had missed some important attitudes, feelings or facts? Or misunderstood her dilemma? and so on.
2. Follow the same approach by reversing the roles. Examine, if necessary privately, your own feelings concerning the way she listened to you – Elated or frustrated by the concern and accurate understanding she demonstrated? – More or less empowered to think through your own solutions?
3. When a colleague or friend is facing an important interview – for a job, appraisal, with a customer or supplier, etc. – help him (or her) to plan his approach. Ask searching questions which enable him to clarify his priorities and to work through his possibly worried feelings.

If you used the funnel tool, did you find it helped you both? Ask your partner if she or he had gained more confidence or empowerment as a result of your active listening role.

CASE STUDY: LISTENING

Tom Peters (1992) describes how CRSS, one of the world's premier architectural firms, established and maintained pre-eminence and competitive advantage by taking listening seriously. 'CRSS builds on listening, worries about listening, works ceaselessly at improving its listening skills,' he says. 'Their teams of architects work *with* their clients, taking their drawing tables to that company, eating and sometimes sleeping there, until the project is 'programmed' before it is designed. 'Programming' is problem seeking – listening to the clients so that they receive 'their proper all-too-rare share of patient attention.'

The architects are trained to ask the right questions at the right time until they have separated facts from needs and discovered problems. Detailed devices assist the process. Small analysis cards each focus on one aspect only; work sheets paper the walls grouped under the headings of goals, concepts, needs and problems. The cards test the relationship between goals, facts and concepts. Needs are then uncovered and a resulting statement of the problem emerges. The architects withhold judgement, resist preconceived solutions and refuse to draw sketches or offer designs until they know the client's problems.

This approach illustrates that listening is 'not a passive activity but a dynamic responding skill'. These architects have learnt the skills of funnelling and of asking searching questions about feelings as well as facts until they can accurately summarise the problems as their clients see them.

COMMUNICATING EFFECTIVELY

Another vital empowering skill is that of communicating effectively and clearly to others what you think, feel and want, so that they get your meaning, and strongly enough to indicate your intention to be heard. Although we quite literally do this on our parent's knee, it is still a task which is fraught with errors, even for its most skilled exponents.

The success of managers depends on their ability to communicate to all the people for whom they are responsible.
Alistair Graham (in Garnett, 1989)

Misunderstanding may be caused because the initial thought is unclear, its translation into words inaccurate, or it is just wrongly received and interpreted by the listener. The accompanying non-verbal behaviour ('body language') may not reinforce the sender's intentions. A heartfelt cry from a worker at a workforce session we organised illustrates the result: 'It's so frustrating . . . It's like walking through mud, like we know what we want to do but every time there is always some problem or other.'

Some reasons for misunderstanding

This signals a breakdown in communication which can be seriously disempowering, since we all have a need for continuous reassurance that our subjective perception of the world is the only valid story. So we are constantly trying to impose our definition of reality on those with whom we deal, and they are doing exactly the same.

Disempowering communication

Communicating effectively therefore involves starting from an agreed statement so that all have a clear understanding of the content and a dialogue (a 'negotiated order'), in a way that does not undermine either person's subjective perceptions.

Get an agreed statement of the subject

> The onus is on the communicator to achieve successful communication, and not the receiver.
>
> *John Lidstone*

If your words are to carry weight as well as meaning, you need to learn the skills of assertiveness. The correct use of assertiveness combines good listening with good communicating. Effective assertive people are those who have most empathy for their colleagues.

ASSERTIVENESS

> Assertiveness is when you stand up for your own rights in a way that does not violate another person's rights.
>
> *Peter Honey*

Assertiveness demands steering a delicate line between aggression (which in some way 'violates' the other person) and non-assertion (which means that your interests will be ignored). An all too common pattern of behaviour is to veer between the two, hardly pausing in the more balanced middle ground. Take, for example, the people who allow themselves to be verbally trampled on, are then unable to contain their bottled-up anger and explode in a blaze of temper. Both extremes could cause serious misjudgements or consequences.

Skilled assertiveness

Being assertive may not come naturally, but a few practical tips may help to smooth the way:

- To be assertive you start in a firm steady voice, with a simple, non-antagonistic statement explaining your view of the situation and the way forward. For example, use a core phrase such as 'I would like half a day off next week to go to the dentist. I think I have earned it because I am working late this week.'
- Continue to repeat your core phrase but in a slightly louder voice and give further reasons.
- If confronted by apparently unfair or hostile behaviour, ask why. This encourages a properly assertive reaction: 'I don't quite see why you are refusing me, can you explain?' Conversely, if you are complimented – 'You made a really good job of that' – the assertive reply would *not* be a sarcastic 'So you actually noticed,' but 'Thank you, I was pleased with it too.'

Assertive behaviour does not mean behaving aggressively – threatening, manipulating or forcing someone to do something you want and they don't, being sarcastic or silent, interrupting others or making a personal attack on them: 'You are talking rubbish.' Nor is assertiveness behaving weakly or passively – staying quiet, avoiding an argument, agreeing when the answer should be no, apologising unnecessarily, or not giving a required decision.

Assertiveness is building your own self-respect.

Liz Willis and Jenny Daisley

WORKSHOP: EFFECTIVE COMMUNICATION

1. With a mentor, work partner or friend, and the help of the points we make below, plan how to communicate a problem or idea to a small group of people willing to join you in the exercise. Below are some skills to help you be understood:
   - Obtain an agreed statement of the subject.
   - Make what you are saying interesting to the listener. Never use jargon or technical words familiar to you but not understood by them. Encourage participation and seek responses.
   - Show empathy: indicate you understand their point of view. Listen and use words and images which mean something to your listeners.

continued

- Emphasise a 'you attitude' that positively engages the listener(s). 'Could you produce a plan for speeding up delivery dates?' rather than 'I want a plan for speeding up delivery dates.'
- Respond to your listeners in a way that acknowledges a complementary exchange and gives appropriate 'strokes' ('You have been a great help').
- Be aware that if you damage a listener's self-esteem you put his or her 'ego-defences' on alert and attention is then switched to repairing the damage and away from the message itself. Instead, give a word of encouragement or praise (as we suggested in Chapter 7).
- Be positive: ask for cooperation and give trust. Avoid these six common hidden messages:
  I'm judging you
  I'm in charge
  I can manipulate you
  I don't give a damn about you
  I'm superior to you
  My mind is made up whatever you say

2. Collect your small group, including your mentor, and put your plan into action.
3. Analyse the outcome with your mentor and the group. Did you make yourself understood?
4. Repeat your planned approach in a real situation.

BEHAVING SUPPORTIVELY

Learning and improving the skills of listening and communicating provides a sound basis on which to build the empowering skill of behaving supportively, however difficult it often becomes in practice. This is because, as well as attitudes and beliefs, behaviour is a rich stew of motives, feelings, expectations, abilities and traits.

These ingredients are, however, internal to ourselves: what others *see* is our behaviour. They see what we are doing and hear what we are saying, and this influences their behaviour (we smile, they smile; we get angry, they get angry, etc).

People see our behaviour

Hence, social interaction is more empowering and more effective if we consciously learn to arrange our behaviour so that it is supportive – however you feel, whatever the circumstances and however difficult it may seem. Clearly it takes a lot of self-control to keep so rich a 'stew' from filtering through into our behaviour, often in a most inappropriate, disempowering form.

Classify and control your behaviour

Nevertheless, behaviour can be analysed and skills applied to each situation once you have defined the supportive objectives you wish to achieve.

The first step towards this control is consciously to classify your own and other people's behaviour into types, some useful, some less constructive. Listening, disagreeing constructively, clarifying, summarising, and offering solutions are positive reactions. Talking too much, or too little (silence cannot be interpreted by others), boasting, moaning and interrupting are negative and unproductive.

Analyse your feelings

Next, analyse the *feelings* (especially negative) which underlie these different types of behaviour. Only you know how you are feeling – angry, hurt, worried, bored – yet these feelings inhibit effective action. When angry, we cease to think rationally: we exaggerate and shout. If our feelings are hurt we may sulk rather than argue; if bored, we may offend by yawning, or fall asleep! We can spring blindly to the defence of a deeply held belief, damaging the very cause we want to promote. (One supervisor argued he had the 'right' to be obeyed – his job description said so.)

Control your thoughts

Peter Honey gives advice on the skills of behaving supportively in these and similar circumstances. Unproductive feelings are first heralded, he says, by a thought and we alone are in control of our own thoughts. So you can replace an angry thought such as 'They are incompetent' by another: 'It's not worth getting angry about it', or 'What can I learn from their approach?'. As Paddy O'Brien reports, people who have behaved aggressively often see afterwards that they have made matters worse. As one person put it: 'As I shouted at him I saw his look growing sullen underneath. I felt him getting remote.'

So a busy manager avoided a boring colleague by hiding behind a pillar in the canteen. If behaving supportively, he would have thought first, 'He looks really worried, I'll find out why', and met him with a smile.

Transactional Analysis

Another approach to analysing, categorising and controlling behaviour is supplied by Transactional analysis (TA). According to this theory, we all contain within us three states: the Child state, the Parent state and the Adult state. These are symptoms of feeling, accompanied by a related set of behaviour.

The 'Child' spontaneously shows his or her feelings, but has learnt to adapt behaviour to others; the 'Parent' corrects and criticises, but takes care of people; the 'Adult' processes data, makes decisions based on facts, but has little feeling. Skilled behaviour is facilitated by recognising the state of others and deciding which of our own states to use. We can behave from our adapted child, nurturing parent, or adult states as appropriate, and encourage others to do the same (the 'I'm OK, you're OK' position). These are complementary transactions because they occur between ego states rewarding each other (Harris, 1973).

A crossed transaction would be from the 'child' to a 'parent' which received a reply from the 'adult': 'I have got too much to do' (Child to Parent) – 'So has everyone else' (Adult to Child). A complementary transaction is 'I know how you feel but we're all busy at the moment' (Parent to Child).

Crossed transactions

Making your own transactions from Adult to Adult shows that you respect the dignity and work of the other person and so empowers them.

Adult to adult empowers people

> The more you are in the adult [state] the more you will bring out the adult in your juniors.
>
> *Paddy O'Brien*

To practise supportive behaviour we suggest you observe and analyse the day to day behaviour of yourself and others. Acknowledge that everyone behaves unsupportively and inappropriately in situations when our feelings take over or our expectations are disappointed. Notice when this happens to you and resolve to think before reacting, and then perhaps succeed in producing some empowering behaviour.

11 People Skills for Specific Occasions

In this chapter, we build on the core skills by describing the people skills required by specific circumstances or roles. Everyone should learn them to help optimise their influence as well as to prepare themselves for any occasions when they take a leadership role.

INFLUENCING AND NEGOTIATING

Influencing others and negotiating, like assertiveness, are skills based on good listening and good communicating, since they rely on a feel for the individual or larger audience in order to judge the correct style which will rouse interest. And interest is a precondition for gaining willing consent and building a partnership.

Not threatening or bribing

So the skill of influencing people is to change their attitudes or beliefs with their conscious consent, without recourse to threats or bribery; it is more effective than overt pressure because that only produces a temporary change of behaviour. Furthermore, if the pressure is too intense it produces 'reactance' – people will positively go out of their way to subvert a request.

Similarly, the skill of negotiating with an empowering style rests in treating the situation as a joint problem-solving exercise, not a confrontation.

Some useful influencing skills you can use are:

- Be credible, with a friendly but assertive style, and use a firm steady voice.
- Open with a non-antagonistic statement. For example, show how your proposal will satisfy other people's needs and point out how they and the people they need to influence will benefit. Suggesting to a team leader that he or she should acquire computer skills, you could point out that it would enhance his or her chances of promotion. Make it easy for them to agree by helping them to save face. You really succeed when you convince someone that he or she had the idea first!
- Show that you have taken into account both sides of the argument. Your favoured solution backed up by the facts will be more powerful if contrasted with the admitted strengths of the alternative.
- Outline the disincentive. This does not mean appealing to fear: a friendly hint could have the desired effect. For example to an unpunctual person: 'I know you are keen to join that new quality circle – can you ensure you will arrive at meetings on time?'
- If the desired change in opinion is a large one, consider moving in stages. Start by trying to stimulate feelings of uncertainty or dissonance which can then be replaced by information favourable to your cause. Approaching a large-scale change via a pilot exercise always makes good sense.
- Back up the spoken word with visual aids and written hand-outs, etc. Research emphasises the importance of these visual backups (Lidstone, 1992). People forget very quickly what they learn: 38 per cent in two days becomes 75 per cent in 30 days!
- Choose the correct mixture and style as you go along. Some aspects require a friendly, encouraging approach, others a more rational appeal to logic and facts, or again the issue of a challenge could break a log jam.

> By structuring the presentation around the listeners' point of view the speaker can gain the audience's attention and interest, persuading them of the value of his proposals and drawing them to a conclusion in his or her favour!
>
> *John Lidstone*

When you are successfully influencing others, you are in fact 'persuading' them, but not through coercion or fear.

WORKSHOP: INFLUENCING PEOPLE

- Using the key elements listed above, analyse a situation you have experienced when your manager, team leader or fellow member has tried to influence the team to agree with some action she or he felt strongly about. If the presentation was made by the leader, did you feel that she relied on some disempowering approaches such as her position in the hierarchy to order you to comply? or stated the position in terms of her own needs and not yours?
- Make the case to your own team that everyone could benefit by some practice in how to influence others. Afterwards, ask yourself whether you succeeded.

CASE STUDY: INFLUENCING AN INDIVIDUAL

A team leader of a large charity puts these skills into practice. For some time this team leader had been trying to get the agreement of Norman, one of her fundraisers, to employ a full-time secretary.

After carefully planning her approach she visited Norman one Friday and he still refused her request, saying that he could do the work with volunteers. The team leader realised that his approach to his whole career had been very cautious and his present feeling of uncertainty was based on this lack of confidence. This caused 'dissonance' between the behaviour she sought and his deeply ingrained fear of failing to reach his targets.

The team leader used the correct mixture of our suggested skills to suit her situation as she attempted to get him to change his mind. She explained how some of the fundraisers in other regions had doubled their fundraising income, helped by an efficient secretary. He could gain charity-wide kudos in the same way. However, if he still failed to meet his target, he would be blamed for not having a secretary.

She adopted a low-key and encouraging style, suited to Norman's personality, and stressing she quite understood his fear of overspending. Finally, she suggested he began by appointing part-time help. He was, however, still adamant, and she wondered what she could do next.

continued

> However, on the Monday he rang her to say he agreed to employ a full-time secretary. Her style had been the correct one, but being an overcautious person, he had taken a weekend to decide!

Formally or informally you will spend a lot of time negotiating or bargaining with others. Traditionally, this involves two parties striking a bargain which satisfies neither completely but is the best compromise they can obtain, as each deploys the power they possess based on the resources they can command.

NEGOTIATING SKILLS

This traditional approach, often using the confrontational language of winning, losing, scoring points, striking a hard bargain etc., mixes uneasily with empowerment. A more empowering approach would be to acknowledge that your aim is to reach a solution which satisfied both parties.

A more imaginative negotiating technique called 'principled negotiation' developed by, amongst others, Fisher and Ury aims for more effective results through a process of searching jointly for mutual gain and finding some *independent* measure of a fair result for both parties. Hence, rejecting the traditional 'positional' mode, to get to the root of the issue, the skilful negotiator separates the problem from the person and focuses on interests rather than on arbitrary postures.

Principled negotiation

> We all try to get the facts on the table and let reason speak for itself.
>
> *Matsushita manager* (in *Pascale* and *Athos*, 1982)

The empowering approach goes like this:
1. Empathise with the other person or side and understand what is driving their approach.
2. Describe the situation as a joint problem. Fisher and Ury offer the example of a resident complaining to a building contractor. The resident opens with, 'I understand that a protective fence round this building site will put you behind schedule, but neither of us wants children to be run over by your trucks.' Making the problem a shared one allows you to be hard on the problem ('This is giving me sleepless nights . . .') while being supportive to the person ('You have really been put in a difficult position here').
3. Both of you think of creative solutions to satisfy both sides. Fisher and Ury describe this as 'expanding the pie before dividing it'.

Joint problem solving

Find creative solutions

Separating different components of the problem, using brainstorming and hearing different experts all encourage the invention of new options.

4. Both parties consider the inevitable remaining areas of conflicting interests.

Find objective standards

5. Look for more objective standards by which to measure the wisdom of the solution (e.g. are fences normal around other building sites).

And if all else fails

6. The best defence against an entrenched and more powerful party is consciously to develop your BATNA (Best Alternative To Negotiated Agreement). The other side only remains more powerful while you acknowledge that position. Walking away withdraws this acknowledgement.

WORKSHOP: PRINCIPLED NEGOTIATION

1. Next time you are conducting a negotiation with some other party or you want to strike a bargain with a colleague, ask your partner to sit in as an observer.
2. Suggest that he or she, using our 6-point negotiating plan, should judge which points you used positively and which were not so well received.
3. What did the feedback reveal?
4. If your partner agrees, reverse these roles at an appropriate time.
5. What did you learn when you took the observer's role?

COACHING AND COUNSELLING

Your coaching role, both for individuals and teams, is basic to empowerment because it enhances people's self-motivation and helps them to attain their potential and maximise their own performance. In a nutshell, it encourages people to *want* to learn.

Teaching, telling or instructing cannot produce this result because it supposes that people learn by pouring information into them, whereas coaching helps them to draw inspiration, creativity and enthusiasm out of their own personality. Hence your main tool is to ask searching questions which clarify both the subject and the coachees' attitudes to it.

The coach is then *treating people as whole people*, with respect, and *handing over control* for their own learning – two of the main functions of leadership we described in Chapter 7.

> The full expression of one's potential demands taking full responsibility or ownership . . . if not, it would be partly someone else's.
>
> *John Whitmore*

Many people perform a coaching role. In particular, companies regard it as a priority for department heads and team leaders. So for those used to traditional leadership methods, learning to coach in this way is an empowering experience in itself.

> A number of leading sportsmen, such as David Whitaker, who coached the English Hockey team . . . and Olympic hurdler David Hemery, are setting up consultancies to advise commercial organisations how to apply sporting techniques to business. Their clients range from Barclays Bank, the Woolwich Building Society and ICI's maintenance division to Kent County Constabulary.
>
> *David Oates* (1993)

Comparison between coaching and counselling

This supporting and questioning approach is equally required by a counsellor, described in the next section, and both roles need the support of a continuous learning culture. However, the two roles differ in their purpose. Much of the value of coaching lies in an ongoing discussion on how the person is performing and his or her attitudes, expectations and motivation towards improvement, whereas the main counselling aim is to help people to reach solutions to problems and situations which they feel are too difficult. Again, although some counselling situations also require several sessions, many need only one.

Help people to help themselves

Your major task as a coach is to support and encourage people to become self-motivated. You can best accomplish this by helping them to become more aware of themselves and to decide what they think they need to learn. Below we suggest some aspects you need to explore together

Development needs. Clarify what development needs the people you are coaching think they personally have for themselves, what goals they are aiming for, what is motivating them and how their feelings are helping or hindering their progress. Useful questions to ask:

- Do you want more knowledge or skills or experience? In what area?
- Will you need to plan ahead in order to gain any or all of these?
- Do you think your past experience or training has left you with serious gaps?

● Have you friends or colleagues who are already learning more?

Personal goals.   Set goals for the present and the future. Useful questions to ask:

● What are you aiming for at present?
● Where would you like to be in five years' time?
● Have you an ultimate goal in mind? Do you think it is realistic?
● What will you do? Will this meet your goal?
● When will you do this – have you a time frame?
● What obstacles do you foresee standing in your way?

Motivation.   Explore their own needs and expectations with your support. When people really want to develop further they will find a way of achieving it since, as we saw in Chapter 7, seeking success is based on the needs for self-expression and self-fulfilment – the 'true motivators'. Useful questions to ask:

● Why do you want to achieve these goals?
● Have you always looked for challenges?
● Is doing something you think worthwhile important to you?
● Are there other options you might consider?
● What else gives you satisfaction?

Their feelings.   Explore their feelings about themselves and their work. Useful questions to ask:

● Do you get frustrated sometimes, and at other times feel under stress?
● You sounded very self-confident when you described that incident but anxious about the other occasion – can you disentangle these feelings for yourself?
● Are some of the obstacles you foresee, feelings within you which need to be overcome? What support can I give you?

PUTTING SKILLS INTO PRACTICE

In his book *Coaching for performance*, John Whitmore advises on how to plan each coaching session for best results.

Define the goals of the session.   He recommends that coaching sessions should begin by determining a goal for the session itself. This goal should be spelt out by the coachees concerned – what they want to learn, not what you want them to learn. However, there is much you can do to help them by:

● Posing the question directly: what do you want to get out of the session?
● Defining the perimeters: We have half an hour, where would you like to be by then?
● Calling for the short-term standard of performance they want to reach – within their control and attainable but challenging enough to motivate.
● Asking them to summarise the goals you have *both* agreed.

Be detached and specific.   Ask for specific details including facts and figures, not fuzzy generalisations and judgements. Expect them to make decisions and help with the type of searching questions we itemised in the skills of listening:

- What have you done so far?
- What effects did this have?
- What have you decided to do next?
- How long would it take?
- Who else would be involved?
- Are there likely obstacles in the way?

One coaching circumstance in which the need to be specific becomes paramount is when you coach someone to learn a new practical skill. Here the sequence is:

Coaching for a physical skill

1. Tell and show, emphasising the key actions or stages which are crucial to success.
2. Call for their reactions. What have they grasped or understood? What worries them? What actions are they confident they can copy? What looks difficult and unfamiliar?
3. Listen with all your attention to their replies, looking for the direction of their own thoughts and interests.
4. Building on this lead, tell and show again.
5. Ask them to describe what they intend to do and how and why they have come to these conclusions.
6. Even if it seems misguided, tell them to do it their way and wait until they find out for themselves if this does not work. Encourage them to think through and state the reasons. This makes them more receptive to new approaches.
7. Ask them to try again, coaching them this time to become aware of their senses – the feel of their actions, the sound and the sight. Focusing on this internal awareness releases tension and improves performance skills.

The importance of doing as well as being shown is underlined by an experiment in which three groups of people were taught the same thing in three different ways. The first group was told, the second was told and shown; and the third told, shown and then experienced the task. After three weeks, this third group recalled 85 per cent of the material learnt – more than either of the other two groups. After three months, the gap had widened still further. The third group had 65 per cent recall, the second 32 per cent and the third only 10 per cent (Whitmore, 1992).

Advantages of practising a skill

   This result makes a lot of sense. When told about any skill we can 'know' about it, but to learn to do it we have to practise it. Just as when learning to ride a bike, one day we see we are no longer falling off, so with other skills; in time, we learn to internalise them.

Self-motivation can be greatly enhanced by coaching and then coaching can be used to convert motivation into effective action.

John Whitmore

THE SKILLS OF COUNSELLING

Counselling enables people to confront and deal with problems and talk themselves towards their own solution. By exploring a situation with their counsellor (someone trained to do this work or a trusted colleague, friend, team leader or mentor) they work through their feelings *before* they take action: tension and stress are reduced, they are strengthened to make decisions and feel committed to carry them through willingly. This experience is the very basis of empowerment.

Counsellors, therefore, share with coaches listening and questioning skills, based on trust. But the different objectives of these encounters make two underlying attitudes especially imperative for counsellors:

- to accept the person and situation (however unusual) without judgement
- to use skills which help people to reach their own answers to their own problems instead of imposing a solution upon them

A coach has the same objective of personal responsibility, but to solve difficult personal problems, often very sensitive and deeply entrenched, the extra type of searching but non-judgemental questioning used by counsellors may be needed.

The concept of personal responsibility lies at the heart of the counselling process.

Elizabeth Sydney and Nicola Phillips

CASE STUDY: COUNSELLING

The area supervisor of a cinema chain is worried because he is not visiting his premises often enough and his job, he feels, is suffering. But his overwhelming worry is his health, as he has just returned to work after a heart attack. His manager has been counselling the supervisor for some time, but is feeling frustrated that he has so far failed to help him to come to terms with this situation. The manager has offered his own solutions such as changing to different work, but these have fallen on deaf ears; the

continued

supervisor, although feeling tired, has no wish to change to other fields.

So the manager alters his approach and summarises:

Manager   I understand you are worried about visiting more often and also about your health and feeling tired.

Supervisor   Yes that's true and I don't get out as much as I used to.

Manager   How can you get out more?

Supervisor   Well, would you think it would be all right if I visited more in the evening? Then I could take a rest in the afternoon.

[The manager and supervisor discuss this suggestion for some time and the manager then concludes.]

Manager   Provided you do enough visits, you can arrange your time to suit yourself and your health. Can you think through some targets of numbers of cinemas to be visited and let me know your plans for which districts you will visit, and when – by the end of the week?

Supervisor   Yes, I'll be glad to do that.

By discovering earlier in the interview and responding to the underlying worry, the manager has gained the trust of the supervisor and demonstrated a caring attitude, but he has failed to solve the problem *for* the supervisor. Nevertheless, the supervisor feels understood and offers a solution rather hesitatingly. Later they agree a practical plan for actions which suit the requirements of the job and the needs of the supervisor. Reassured, he 'owns' the plan. The manager then turns it into an action target.

Sidney and Phillips say that a skilled counselling interview needs to go through three stages:
1. exploring the situation
2. helping individuals to understand their situation
3. deciding future action together

Although in reality this plan cannot proceed so tidily, it is useful to hold it in your mind as you plan how you would approach a problem about which a member of staff or a friend has asked you for help. Remember, a counselling session is a meeting between equals; as the counsellor you are not supplying answers, you are prompting decisions.

WORKSHOP: COUNSELLING SKILLS

Stage 1: exploring the situation

Think what type of welcome your person would feel most at home with. You are aiming to settle him or her down, gain trust and agree the purpose of the meeting.

Where will you hold the meeting? The setting should be informal (no desk between the two people, for example) and ensure privacy (no telephone calls or visitors, a separate room, etc.)

Is the situation likely to involve other people? If so, agree who else might need to know the information. This is vital, to encourage free and frank exchanges and to protect the decision about future action, in Stage 3.

Explain the purposes of the interview and its three stages. Then ask an open-ended question, 'Can you tell me what your problems are?', and give reassurance, 'I will do my best to help', which will encourage the conversation to flow. Listen carefully, since people usually say first what they think is worrying them, to get it off their chest. This is the manifest problem but it may not be the only one. By using your skills of listening you will begin to hear the latent content. Here, your main task is to suspend judgement in order to understand what the other person is really thinking and feeling about the situation.

Shoshana Zuboff, researching into the problems managers faced in a fully automated paper mill, described the people she interviewed as being 'on the edge of a historic transformation of immense proportions'. All work processes were controlled by a computer from a central control room. The computer became a person doing all the thinking and referred to as 'Otto'. The departmental managers feared their role was becoming redundant; the computer told their teams what to do.

If you had been part of a counselling scheme at this mill, any one of the managers or supervisors might have presented their problem as 'I am overworked and near to breaking point. There are so many new processes to monitor, I feel if I don't keep in control, the whole thing will fall apart' (words actually spoken to Zuboff).

You would need all the skills of listening (Chapter 10) before you could discover whether underlying causes existed. You could try the funnelling technique.

continued

If, after several funnels, the position of the person you are counselling still seemed confused, a question for further clarification might be needed – 'I'm not sure I understand yet, could you explain that situation again?' We know that the problem presented to Zuboff was not the real one, since we can assess it through her ears. This was described by one of the supervisors as, 'I'm used to having everyone coming to me and asking what to do', and the senior management 'are asking me to build skills in others that I'm not sure I have myself'. The real problem was twofold: that the supervisor felt his traditional role of authority was slipping away and that he had no new authority based on an understanding of the processes to replace it.

Given a trusting relationship the supervisor would certainly have told you what was *really* worrying him (we know this since several of the supervisors made similar remarks to Zuboff when she had established this trusting relationship herself).

Stage 2: help the individual to understand the situation

When you have gained a similar insight the time is ripe to help your interviewee to understand his or her position, too.

Ask searching questions to help him or her to see the position more clearly, and to think more rationally about it. In this case, the supervisor needs to change his perception of his authority and be enabled to learn the new skills which were becoming essential.

Some useful questions to him would be:
- Are your present duties and responsibilities clear?
- How do you think that the computer system changes them?
- How do you feel about this?
- What part of your job do you consider the most important?
- What part of your job do you find easiest/most enjoyable/do particularly well?
- How can you make your new role enjoyable?
- How are you coping with the increasing pressure?
- What are your long-term goals?
- Can I help you? How?
- Do you need more training?

Use similar searching questions to suit the problems of your interviewee and add some further clarifying questions such as:
- Could you tell me more about that?
- What did you do and feel then?

continued

- How do you think that kind of thing could be handled?
- Why do you think that happened?
- If you make that decision what effect will it have?

In your counselling session you may be involved with different subjects, but the searching approach for attitudes, feelings and expectations as well as facts is the same.

The training question is a key to this supervisor's situation, since it implies a need for changed attitudes. It could take more than one interview for the supervisor to acknowledge the training need, but when he or she does, the time to move on to Stage 3 has arrived. Agreeing new duties and skills will help him to own his new role and to become mentally and emotionally adjusted to it. Waiting patiently until this stage has arrived is difficult for all counsellors but essential for you to do.

Stage 3: Deciding future action together

You can hasten the adjustment process by agreeing a concrete plan for action, as did the manager in our earlier case study. Here, you could consider together with the supervisor various ways of gaining new skills being forced upon him by computerisation. We know from Zuboff's research that 'the demands on management had become relentlessly insistent'. Hence the needs of this company were pushing the supervisor to change his behaviour and when he realises this he will devise an action plan.

Further practice

When you have planned your approach to this case, put it into practice in a real life situation. Then review the outcome:

- Did you succeed in helping the other person to solve a problem? resolve a difficulty? make decisions? etc.
- How will you handle a counselling encounter next time?

Check your attitude – do you want to counsel people?

For more detail, there is a complete transcript of an interview in Sidney and Phillips, *One to one management*. Conducted over two sessions, with Cheryl, a supervisor, by her boss Harry, a skilled interviewer discovers that the presented problem is not the real one, and by working through to an understanding of it, they decide on positive actions for the future.

Recognising a counselling moment

Although we have described counselling as following a planned course, the call for counselling skills will often appear suddenly.

Within the hundreds of personal encounters you experience each

week, someone will need your help. A cry for help can be hidden
behind a complaint, poor performance, lateness, an emotionally
loaded outburst, non-verbal signals or silence. Or it can suddenly
erupt when a person asks you to help with a problem.

> Making oneself available, is demanding in terms of time,
> commitment and emotional energy.
>
> *Andrew Kakabadse*

Once you have heard the cry for help – perhaps in a corridor, the   *Respond willingly*
canteen, a pub, a street – recognise it as a counselling situation.
Respond willingly. The people skills and the three-stage structure are
equally valid for informal and unexpected situations. Your reward will
be greater empowerment for another person and for yourself.

CONDUCTING APPRAISAL INTERVIEWS

Regular appraisal interviews are a major tool of empowerment. When
successful, they inspire an individual to want to develop, to improve
his or her performance and to grow. Properly conducted (usually by a
team leader but equally well by a colleague or mentor) they range
widely over all aspects of performance and make plans for future
development.

> Research carried out by Dr Lynda Gratton at London Business
> School reveals that traditional appraisal systems serve only to
> encourage unempowered behaviour, the demanding, aggressive,
> prima donna sort of approach of the traditional boss. Upward
> appraisal systems . . . have been shown to encourage team spirit
> and the sort of supportive behaviour which nurtures
> empowerment.
>
> *Clare Hogg*

Both appraiser and appraisee need training for what is a highly
sophisticated encounter. It should be seen as a joint exercise and
both need time to learn the skills involved – to be skilled at
listening, communicating effectively, behaving supportively and
influencing others. In addition, the appraiser must act as a coach and
counsellor.

If you follow our plan for conducting the interview and allow plenty of time, you will find it can be a satisfying, empowering and exhilarating encounter both as appraiser and appraisee.

> The skills are required of the appraiser and appraisee alike. All too often appraisal has been seen as something a manager does *to* a subordinate, rather than something they do together.
>
> *Roger Holdsworth (in Neale, 1991)*

Prepare in advance.   Both you and your interviewee should prepare in advance. In a formal interview between management and staff, a form can be helpful because it concentrates on the job and sets a pattern for a discussion which, with or without a form, needs to cover the following aspects:

- which key tasks on your job description have received the most/least attention?
- which targets have you been most/least successful in reaching and why?
- what are your personal development plans?

The interview plan.   Both participants should prepare specific incidents known to both, which then form the basis for a joint review of the past. This leads naturally to future development plans and the resources and help you will supply. An appraisal between colleagues or with a mentor will be less formally planned, but should cover the same ground.

A useful plan for the discussion which is helpful to both participants is described by the mnemonic 'WASP':

W = Welcome
A = Acquiring and Agreeing information
S = Supplying information/advice or Selling/Seeking joint solutions
P = Part with a practical plan

Again, this plan can only supply a framework to bear in mind. A free-flowing discussion, especially between colleagues, might bear little resemblance to it, but similar ground will be covered.

Copy the counselling interview

W – Welcome: set the scene.   Welcome follows the pattern of the counselling interview, starting perhaps with some personal circumstances (said one appraisee 'she even knew it was my birthday today').

Remain objective. This was no welcome:

Manager: Please sit down, I'm getting worried about your
              performance.

Job holder: I've got a pretty good record – we're not much down on
                 target . . .

Manager: Let me finish . . . you don't seem to have made any effort to
              make your target at all.

A – Acquiring information.   Using listening, coaching and counselling *Feelings and attitudes as well as facts*
skills, you gather facts, but also attitudes and motivation. Help the
interviewee to express his or her feelings freely. Show empathy rather
than sympathy, the latter illustrated by the following exchange:

Salesman: I do the selling all right and the clients are pleased. Then
               there's no sale, I feel so mad, so frustrated.

Manager: I know the feeling. I used to get depressed just the same,
              but don't get downhearted.

Salesman: I feel mad, not depressed.

Manager: I know how I used to feel droopy but cheer up – I felt so
              heartened when I'd hooked him. So don't you get
              downhearted.

Salesman: [Giving up] I'm not downhearted, I'm mad!

Since this manager did not 'hear' the deep feelings being expressed,
he did not ask searching, non-judgemental questions, starting perhaps
with 'How do you mean, you felt mad?' and going on from there.

One of the points of the interview is to acquire information for your
own development. Ask about your performance – 'Have I helped
enough?' 'What could I do better?' and so on.

S – Supplying information or advice and seeking joint solutions.
When conducting the interview, remember the skills of praising
(Chapter 7) and when giving an assessment of performance:

- Start with strengths. This makes people more receptive and willing   *Strengths first*
  to accept criticism. Research reveals that to mention more than two
  weaknesses in one interview becomes counter-productive.
- Always depersonalise criticism – not 'you are tactless' but 'if you had   *Depersonalise*
  handled that situation differently . . . a more successful conclusion
  could have been reached'. Or better still, 'With hindsight could you
  have got a more successful conclusion there?'
- Turn criticism into praise if possible. Said a professor to a student
  'From anyone else this would be an A paper, I am giving you a C.'
- Always make the discussion point a joint one. Asking for comments   *Find a common approach*
  and explanations is part of the 'supplying information' process and
  should lead both parties to seek and find a common approach.

In fact, a more skilled method is to supply as little as possible yourself
and, by using counselling skills, enable people to recognise their own

weaknesses and solve their own problems. Ask searching questions which stimulate them to continue seeking, leaving as much freedom for as long as possible.

Be economical with your own suggestions

A series of suggestions could begin:
- 'What could you do about this problem?'

After no positive response, continue to supply as little as possible:
- 'In X Department they did so and so. Could that apply to your department?'
- 'I think you could do so and so. How could you implement it – how long would it take?'
- 'You could do it in this way. What would be your first step?'
- 'You could do this. I think it would take so long and it means starting here. What can I do to help?'
- 'When shall we review progress?'

The heart of an appraisal interview

Helping people to solve problems creatively like this empowers people and lies at the heart of an appraisal interview.

P – Part with a practical plan.   Last, agree future plans. Set realistic and agreed work targets (preferably measurable and quantifiable), agree on some aspects to be strengthened and set together some training and development projects.

Appraisee should summarise

Ask the appraisee to say what actions you have both agreed (this commits them). Finally, part on an encouraging note – 'We have made a lot of progress. I'll do my part and follow your suggestions.'

> An appraisal interview is not a substitute for efficient day to day management, but an essential support to it.
>
> *Elizabeth Sidney*

Follow-up

Appraisal systems sometimes fail because they have no procedures for following up the decisions made at the interview. Avoid this pitfall with the following steps:
- Devise your own system for following up decisions.
- Set clear, measurable targets (for each other) so that both parties will see progress.
- Ensure that the appraisee will be able to report some change for the better, however small, in an area you discussed.
- If you are responsible for team leaders who appraise their members, discover how effectively they are performing. Are they keeping to agreed follow-up times and allocating sufficient time for the appraisal interview itself? Are they conscientious in explaining in depth and offering support? How do they evaluate their own performance? What extra help do they feel they need from you?

CASE STUDY: A DEVELOPMENTAL APPRAISAL INTERVIEW

The trustees and director of a small charity decided to increase the numbers of their officers in the provinces. The role included some fundraising (e.g. flag days), but the charity relied heavily on local committees or groups to raise funds, by running a wide variety of projects ranging from a prestigious charity ball through to bring and buy sales, etc.

Hence the local officer's role, although containing some fundraising, mainly required the ability to create and maintain new groups and to gain their commitment to innovative fundraising ventures.

To train the newcomers it was decided that an extra part-time responsibility for this should be added to the job of an existing local officer, supported in turn by her part-time secretary, working additional hours.

Gillian Stokes, the most senior local officer, accepted the job and at her appraisal interview with the director they both concentrated on her development plans.

Gillian was enthusiastic to learn and was confident she could coach the newcomers on a one-to-one basis. However, she voiced worries about other training aspects, for example:

- She led and inspired her own committees, but could she teach others to do this?
- She was not used to group teaching, yet training several newcomers at once would call for this.
- She admired the way the director publicised the charity but she was anxious about doing this herself. She would forget her material and felt she would be far from inspiring.

So together, they devised a systematic weekly development plan backed by reports of progress to the director. A priority was for Gillian to attend two training courses, one teaching the skills of leading group discussions and the other on basic coaching skills.

Gillian's weekly training would then cover these aspects:

Week 1:	review and consider how to teach existing routines
	decide the parts of her present job she could delegate
Weeks 2 & 3:	visit two of her best committees to ask for:

continued

- advice on likely people in new localities who would be interested in joining a supporting group
- opinions about effective group leadership skills (based on their experience with Gillian)

Weeks 4 & 5:   review weekly reports with the director and decide on further action

attend the meetings of two fellow officers (of different sexes) and observe the group leadership skills they used

the director would describe and illustrate the material in her talks – Gillian would prepare and present her own version to the director, who would coach and advise her

When the director and Gillian had run the first course they reviewed it and made plans for Gillian to run the next one on her own. At Gillian's next appraisal, they concluded that the course had been a success, but Gillian confessed she still felt anxious when she gave talks and thought the group became bored. The director realised that attempts to boost Gillian's confidence would be unsuccessful. Instead, she continued to ask searching questions encouraging Gillian to think the problem through and to find some solutions for herself. Finally, Gillian saw the root of the trouble when she said, 'Quite frankly, I keep forgetting what to say next. I feel panicky and my mind goes blank. Could we perhaps buy an overhead projector? Then I could prepare transparencies to prompt me to remember the anecdotes and incidents to make the talks more interesting.'

Gillian acquired her projector and enjoyed making many innovations with it. (For example, she discovered new ways of creating lively and interesting transparencies.) In time, she lost her fear and became an effective presenter.

The director had used two appraisal interviews and an interim performance review to develop the skills of one of her staff. She had:

- become a mentor by encouraging, advising, coaching and counselling
- devised a systematic learning programme with Gillian
- shared her own experience
- monitored progress

continued

- provided the required material resources
- coached an individual to take charge of her own development, to produce solutions to problems and to make these work

---

WORKSHOP: APPRAISAL

1. Conduct an appraisal interview with a member of staff you suspect needs some more training, or join with a trusted colleague or work partner to do the same.
   - Help the staff member decide on some action to improve his or her performance and to set some target dates for this, making sure this would be a training exercise as well.
   - Spend time to discover what future training needs he or she feels exist and decide on a training plan.
   - Ask for an appraisal of your own performance.
   - Outline a follow-up programme.
2. Analyse which interpersonal skills you used. Did these improve your skills for the next appraisal interview you conduct?

LEADING DISCUSSIONS AND MEETINGS

Empowering leaders of any kind, by definition, work with and through their teams, so the effectiveness of the meetings they lead is crucial to their empowerment role and to the morale, commitment and success of their team.

Your leadership task is two-fold. The surface task is to address the *intellectual* agenda, to accomplish the objectives of the meeting, to create, innovate and reach decisions.

Leaders of meetings have two roles

The second task is to take care of the latent *emotional* material (the 'hidden agenda'), the attitudes, feelings, motives and expectations not overtly expressed but always present. Until you satisfy these emotional needs people will not be willing to work on their intellectual tasks. Once these emotions take control the 'surface' task is forgotten; all logical thought stops, some facts are falsified, others disappear. We once witnessed such an incident. A dominating 'madam chairman', abandoning her leadership role, replied to one point from an annoying committee member: 'I don't think that's very important.' He answered, 'I would ask 'madam chairman's' indulgence, if she's got any, she hasn't shown much today.' Someone else said 'I can't hear' and she answered,

'I'm sorry, Mr X is not speaking very clearly today.' The point he had raised was then dropped and never resurfaced.

An even balance between the intellectual and emotional task should be struck and a successful meeting calls for double the number of positive to negative remarks.

Try not to become emotionally involved

For the leader this role of managing both the intellectual and the emotional agenda is daunting. But to join in the discussion, to express an opinion, argue or become emotionally involved as well, makes this task almost impossible. At times this may be inevitable, so ask someone else to step temporarily into the vacancy – perhaps two people, one for the intellectual and the other for the cooperative function. Also appoint a note-taker. This helps you to fulfil your leadership roles.

As we saw in Chapter 8 the *role* of leader still remains in a leaderless meeting. It should move naturally – perhaps from an expert to a creator–innovator and at some time to a concluder–producer, plus always a good team member to maintain harmony. (This natural movement of the leadership role greatly helped the success of the electronic team described in Chapter 8.)

Below we give guidelines for achieving all these objectives.

Plan the opening stage.   On opening the meeting the objective is to gain agreement for the purposes of the meeting and to help people to feel the job is important and that their contributions are essential. Some points to cover are:

- With meetings between people who do not know each other it is important for everyone to introduce themselves, giving their name, role and department and what they hope the meeting will achieve. If people know each other, welcome them individually and mention some past successful event. In this way you are beginning to make people feel they belong.
- Next, state the results you are expecting. Give everyone a chance to argue and disagree. Outline various administrative points – the frequency, length of meeting, finishing time and extra assignments, etc., and remind them of the reasons for the meeting – to advise, initiate, solve problems, decide.
- Finally, ask for comments and encourage participation, since doing this serves both roles by clarifying the task while encouraging negative feelings or opinions to surface. This is the essence of an empowering approach to meetings and could well cover the forming and storming stages described in Chapter 8.
- Beware of non-neutral or critical openings. An office manager's meeting with his staff was doomed to failure by his opening remarks, 'I've called this meeting because I want the practice of leaving file drawers open, to stop.' The staff reacted angrily. They were not to

blame. Instead, the position, size, drawers and even the colour of the cabinets were criticised. The meeting ended with the manager agreeing to order new files!

Manage the intellectual content.   As an empowering meeting leader, your key intellectual task is to seek out and expose different views and disagreements. You must make sure that everyone has a say and that the subject is fully aired. Real consensus does not emerge with a number of members reserving their disagreements to themselves.

Hence the process the members want to follow, as well as the objectives, need agreement. You can, for example, introduce an approach you favour and ask for suggestions.

For instance, an innovative project may require an open, unstructured treatment, perhaps beginning with a brainstorming session followed by a tighter structure for a later evaluation of the ideas produced. Meetings to advise, solve problems and decide require a more systematic approach, since commonly people jump in too soon with ideas, suggestions or solutions. In this case, outline your own plan and ask if people agree or can suggest something else. One useful systematic approach is as follows:

1. Draw out facts and feelings.
2. Analyse the options.
3. Ask for recommendations/solutions/decisions.
4. Weigh their advantages and disadvantages.
5. Make decisions in line with your brief. (We advise . . ., to solve the problem we need to . . ., we have decided to . . ., etc.)

Ask intellectually challenging questions.   As leader, you aim to enable the team to arrive at decisions they own, only supplying your own ideas to further this objective. So your purpose is to ask searching questions which will:

- reveal facts and opinions (Who knows what happened? What did they report? What were their views?)
- Call attention to points, ideas or feelings (What do you think (feel) about . . .?)
- Discover the strength of opinions or feelings (How important is . . .?)
- Introduce a new aspect (What about the implications of . . .?)
- Offer guidance (not I think, but Can we look closely at this aspect?)
- Control the discussion (We've heard one solution, what about others? Is that part of our brief? and so on)
- Make sure everyone contributes (We haven't heard from . . . what do you think?)

Make regular summaries.   Discipline yourself to make regular interim summaries. These check general understanding – Have I got that right? Anything else to add?

- Be scrupulously objective (many leaders or chairpersons tend to extract only material favouring their own views)
- Describe only salient points especially from rambling discussions. But mention irrelevancies (We agreed that was a digression . . .)
- Use summaries to regain control (We're agreed on . . . can we now consider . . .)
- Make a final summary. State the conclusions/decisions already reached and ones still to be resolved (We have agreed on . . . and have scheduled the next meeting to discuss points . . . further)

A final summary saves confusion and shows progress has been made.

Take care of the emotional agenda.   People will cooperate when they feel the job is worthwhile and that they are valued for their contribution. Your leadership role is to encourage this atmosphere of openness and trust.

Skills of encouragement

Many skills of encouragement form the basis for leading this aspect of discussions. Here are some of them:

- Give members your total attention; be a compulsive listener. Show this with both verbal and non-verbal signals (described in Chapter 8)
- Offer reassurance that all contributions are welcome (Can we have some more ideas?)
- Ask non-judgemental questions (not Is that clear? to a muddled statement, but Can we clarify our thoughts on that?)
- 'Reflect' feelings (described in Chapter 10), accepting statements even when negative or disruptive. (In a discussion about ways of improving meetings one man said 'I find meetings a waste of time.' Another chimed in 'Yes I often find myself taking forty winks.' The leader reflected: 'You both feel some meetings are unnecessary')
- Ensure everyone speaks, so call in the shy (ask a question they can answer but say their name first)
- Discourage the talkative without antagonising them (An interesting description, Jim Talkative. What do you think, Carol Expert?)
- Do not criticise (A new approach, clearly and forcefully put)
- Reconcile opposing views (Earlier X said . . . Y is now following that path)
- Protect the minority – they may well be right!

Demonstrate progress.   Avoid feelings of frustration by moving the discussion on (We have twenty minutes left before our hour is up so . . ., or We've considered the options fully, can we now come to a decision?) Frequent interim summaries (essential for the task) also satisfy this need for progress. (So we've settled the three issues of . . . can we now switch to . . .?)

Closing the meeting.   When you close the meeting always finish at the agreed time and include both an intellectual and an emotional statement: We have accomplished . . . We meet again on . . . Thank you all for coming . . . We've made good progress.

If you feel you have done your best to be an empowering meeting leader you may perhaps agree with an ancient Chinese philosopher when he said:

Commitment gained

> Of good leaders when their end is come, their aim fulfilled they will all say we did it ourselves.

WORKSHOP: LEAD YOUR OWN MEETING

1. When you next attend a meeting, analyse how the leader fulfilled his or her role:
   - Accomplished the objective?
   - Kept the balance between the intellectual and emotional content?
   - Summarised regularly?
   (In Chapter 12 we provide an easy-to-use form which you might find helps your analysis.)
2. When you next lead a meeting, or have an informal discussion with friends, use the insights you have gained from this exercise and our advice. Afterwards, analyse your own performance and learn from it.

---

12 *Training for Empowerment*

Continuous learning, built into every operating system, must also be underpinned by the continuous personal development of all staff so that they are equipped with the necessary technical, people and business knowledge, skills and experience to perform work with excellence.

A high degree of individual commitment cannot bring success on its own. It, too, requires the support of an equally high level of individual competence. Thus, as we say in Chapter 5, learning is central to the theme of this book. It is inextricably interlinked with both the empowerment of the organisation and the people within it.

> When [everyone's] intelligence permeates the work system decision making and creative initiatives become decentralised.
>
> *Ken Macher*

Law of ecology

A popular law of ecology goes something like this: 'learning must be equal to or greater than the rate of change of the external environment.' Leaders of large British corporations are realising this truth in various ways. They are starting to use phrases such as: 'our task is people development', 'education drives the business', organisations are 'learning institutions'.

To show what can be done to empower staff though continuous training, we suggest some practical exercises for skills training and outline briefly some of the best of the training policies and procedures some companies are establishing in Britain and elsewhere.

CONTINUOUS TRAINING FOR EVERYONE

Many British companies now possess training policies for the development of their staff. In successful organisations, senior managers support these programmes enthusiastically and are convinced that training makes a vital contribution to their companies, but when times get tough the training budget is still seen as a 'nice to have' and is one of the first costs to be cut.

This is not the case elsewhere. Even in a recession Germany and Japan, two of Britain's most successful competitors, have highly developed systems for continuous technical training and personal development. For example, German industry keeps its competitive edge with a multiskilled, flexible workforce led by 'Meisters' chosen for their technical expertise.

The Japanese system is based on the principle that 'total quality begins and ends with training'. This involves training all workers over a long period, so job rotation through all departments interlinked with training courses is the rule. This increases personal and technical skills and turns employees into generalists rather than specialists.

British technical training

A survey by Stevens and Mackay for the former National Economic Development Office reports that nine out of ten British manufacturing companies want to possess a more flexible workforce. Studies show that the cost of overheads rises with unskilled labour, because of the need for more staff functions (quality controllers, inspectors, maintenance engineers, etc.)

But British managers and workers know they have some catching up to do if they are to match the highly skilled workforces of their competitors. Alhough some British workers have qualifications in various technical skills, many are semi-skilled. In addition, Britain produces fewer graduates and fewer of these enter industry than many of their competitors.

> The level of qualifications present in the work force is lower in Britain than in many other countries.
> *Ron Todd, General Secretary of the TGWU (in Stevens and Mackay, 1991)*

Bridging this gap

Many British companies have realised that a continuous policy of technical training is needed to produce knowledge and skills if the gap is to be bridged. Their staff can then be not only *motivated* to succeed but will possess the *ability* to produce the highest level work – to achieve the '0.01% improvement on excellence' (Peters and Waterman). It is no good waiting for the government to raise education and skills levels, it is for managers to understand what their people need and to ensure this happens.

Many more British organisations in all sectors still need to institute training programmes which guarantee continuous learning in order to empower all their staff.

Identifying skills and knowledge gaps

Their first task is to identify existing technical skills gaps. Skills gaps of every kind are in fact a commonplace of an empowering organisation. By its very nature it will always be asking people and teams to take on challenges for which they are previously unprepared.

Anticipating these gaps is the responsibility of everyone: strategic management, team leaders and individual team members. It is also a two-way process – the people who may be best placed to comment on the performance of managers are those who work under their direction.

For the empowering leader, anticipating skills gaps is a central role, as it is, for example, for the German Meisters. The first priority is to identify the knowledge and skills required to do the jobs successfully and to close any skills gap through training programmes for the people involved.

Skills gaps appear suddenly

Since many companies do not plan their training on a continuous basis, skills gaps can appear quite suddenly – with changes in business strategy, products or technology. When GKN Hardy Spicer reduced their staff, their front-line operators had to learn to keep an automated line in continuous operation. This required new programming and line maintenance skills, previously the job of management, and even the responsibility for housekeeping.

> The worker does not know what he is supposed to do, so he does it wrong because the manager didn't train him properly, but the worker gets the blame.
>
> W Edwards Deming

The sudden appearance of skills gaps is all too familiar in British industry since, once the immediate technical skill gap is closed, many organisations have no policy for developing people through continuous training systems and many British managers will not invest in long-term training to make multiskilling possible. Lane tells how a new production facility was deliberately designed to minimise skill requirements for its maintenance – a return to the disempowering practices of Taylorism.

If British companies are to remain competitive this is an area in which all team leaders and team members need to take action as a matter of the greatest priority, or they will remain disempowered.

Continuous learning must be built-in.

Ken Macher

WORKSHOP: IDENTIFYING AND CLOSING TECHNICAL SKILLS GAPS

1. *Identifying skills gaps.* Ask everyone in your team to analyse their own job skills gaps by:
   - Thinking about their job – what are the key results or outputs they should be producing and acting upon?
   - Itemising in detail the technical skills they require to attain these results. To identify especially the steps involved and the key skills.
   - Making a list of their strong and weak points, when performing the job itself and also when a stressful incident occurred – a machine breakdown? a difficult customer? a near or actual accident? etc.
   - Answering the question, What are my personal skills gaps? by matching their skills against those required for the job.
2. *Close these gaps.*
   - Decide, with the team, who can best teach a skill they possess to others.
   - Ensure they learn the basic coaching skills we described in Chapter 11 – so that they approach their task not by telling and teaching but by encouraging their trainees to *want* to learn and so develop further their own potential and skills.

Nissan's training policy

Nissan Motor Manufacturing UK is an outstanding example of a company with a wide technical training policy. Peter Wickens, director of personnel and information systems, stated, during the crucial start-up period in Britain, that Nissan's training objective was 'to establish continuous development programmes'.

'I felt we were training in what people wanted rather than what the company required its staff to know,' said Wickens. 'These are fundamentally different questions and we found that the only way to determine what people needed to know to do their job was to sit with staff at all levels in each department and put the question to them.' This process took a year and eventually 1200 topics were identified. The elements were listed, described and compared between departments.

The process established that a great deal of commonality existed in many jobs throughout the company, and also that many of the tasks/responsibilities previously regarded as the preserve of people in managerial or supervisory positions were in fact an essential part of the job of many people at the lowest level, right from the time they joined the company.

One of the first changes after the review was to introduce into the induction programme for everyone an appreciation of concepts such as TQM, kaizen, problem solving and JIT. In addition, every employee has an individualised continuous development programme comprising three sections: core skills, professional skills and personal development.

Another 4-year programme, for 16-year-olds, combines academic subjects with practical, multiskilled training. This equips them to handle 'virtually any maintenance task within the company'.

In 1991 Nissan UK spent 4.5 per cent of its payroll on training, and if the salaries of those being trained are included this rose to 14 per cent. On average each employee in Nissan received 8.7 days' off-the-job training (Yeung, 1992).

Quad Graphics

Another example of a company technical training programme, described by Peters (1992), is Quad Graphics, an American firm which is famed for its top drawer quality (describing itself as a knowledge and R & D company). It trains its own staff – 'the average employee,' the company says, 'looks like a loser . . . kids in class that didn't go to college, who didn't make it in school and in many ways had nowhere to go. And what we do is to get them to elevate their sights – to think of themselves as trained technicians who run computers, who run the [printing] press.'

At Quad Graphics all employees are students. During work they run the presses, and those that want to can spend the fifth day – voluntarily and without pay – in the classroom. No one gets promoted until he or she has trained a successor. Learning and teaching, says the chief executive, are the only routes to job security. So everyone has the opportunity to become a classroom teacher and is trained for the job. As a result, there are almost 200 highly motivated and skilled volunteer worker–trainers donating an average of ten hours a week to teaching.

The chief executive teaches his workers and runs classes for customers. Often workers and customers work together on printing improvement projects – line workers being viewed as the sales force.

> Quad/Tech is pure and simple, an unabashed learning machine.
>
> *Tom Peters*, 1992

TRAINING IN BUSINESS SKILLS

Training to do a task empowers, but a still wider general business training is required for your staff to be fully empowered. Four aspects are important.

1. An understanding of how the business runs – how budgets are prepared, the need for added value and total quality, the cost of capital equipment.
2. Developing intellectual skills – how to make continuous improvements, how to control quality, reduce cycle times, run a just-in-time system smoothly.
3. How to solve problems.
4. Learning more sophisticated interpersonal skills – how to handle conflict, make a presentation, negotiate with customers and suppliers, support and influence people in other teams, etc.

Team members, especially people belonging to self-directed teams, need proficiency in all these skills. One *ad hoc* team drawing up job descriptions for their department lacked interpersonal skills, so *told* people what they were doing wrong technically, which was probably good advice – but the people receiving it felt so annoyed they failed to ask how to remedy faults or ignored the advice completely.

Training methods

Training for these skills can take place in specially designed courses at or away from work. Where teams meet regularly, information about the business, its competitiveness, new orders, profits, etc. can form part of the agenda (videos are especially useful to explain company business affairs). Or the CEO can address a meeting of the whole staff at the end of a financial year or at other special times.

> Innovation in training creates a competitive edge.
>
> *Peter Wickens*

Two companies – Lex Service and the sole distributor of office furniture manufactured by a Swedish parent company – link their training programmes specifically to business needs. Staying competitive, they believe, makes a priority of putting the customer first. They train their own staff in a variety of ways, on and away from the job.

Lex Service

Lex Service plc is foremost in the service sector, hiring out commercial vehicles. The high level of service required, according to Jim Burrell, the group training manager (Stevens and Mackay, 1991) can only be attained by devolving authority and responsibility 'to those people actively in contact with the customer', so the company's empowerment training is specifically aimed at the front-line managers and their staff.

Training is linked to the company business plans, and becomes an instrument for change. Managers, called 'facilitators', are seconded to help with the training, where they learn new skills of communicating with customers and suppliers and act as consultants. Thus training in every aspect is related to the real issues facing the company.

The company also pays great attention to 'Lex specific' personal training and development:

- A nine-month course based on distant and residential learning with real-life projects equips supervisors for a National Examination Board Certificate.
- At the second level middle managers can 'pick and mix' between 30 options.
- At the third and fourth level talented people are developed for senior management posts.
- Individual companies are responsible for examining the competences needed and supplying training for the gaps, based on job specifications written by individual workers themselves.

> We now have a structural development ladder based on competencies which have been carefully researched over two years.
>
> Jim Burrell, in Stevens and Mackay (1991)

Distributors of office furniture

The British firm distributing office furniture for its Swedish parent company has an equally pressing need to satisfy the customer, since the efficiency of its installation staff holds the key to company success. The company has therefore instituted a 'customer care' programme, taught off-site in a simulated workshop which at first covered technical installation skills to reduce the amount of errors. This was followed by a second programme entitled 'Front-line customer delight', devised to cover customer service issues – how to deal with complaints, how to dress, when not to smoke on customer premises, arrival, punctuality, etc.

A further programme run by an external trainer reinforced the message, and this was particularly effective since it involved the whole company, including office staff. The company keeps continuous learning alive through follow-up communication meetings and seminars for the fitters.

Results were impressive. Overall customer satisfaction rose to 100 per cent in the Midlands and 90–98 per cent in the south-east of England, with repeat orders continuing to arrive. This emphasises that satisfying a pressing business need – customer care – depends on both technical excellence and interaction skills, and that both can be successfully taught.

In pursuit of the same business aim, Ford of Europe is training its engineers to become 'lateral thinkers' through its Training Quality Improvement Plan (Equip).

SUCCESSFUL TRAINING METHODS

There are so many methods of training for the technical, business and people skills we have described in Chapters 10 and 11 that perhaps 'horses for courses' is the best way of summing them up. For some, skills are best learned on a one to one basis; for others, a training course provides the best option. In some circumstances, people learn best 'on the job'; at other times, the best course is a sheltered environment away from work. A combination of all these methods, perhaps with the addition of distance learning, often proves the most successful approach. We examine below how all these ways are organised in practice.

ON-THE-JOB TRAINING

Wherever possible, and especially for technical skills, on-the-job training is most effective, since people learn best from the experience of being involved in the action. The German apprenticeship system we mentioned earlier is a successful witness to this; trained within this system, Meister and team share the same technical expertise which contributes towards joint production goals.

> Being given real responsibility comes across as more important than formal management training as such.
>
> *Andrew Forrest and Patrick Tolfree*

When you train people on the job, it will usually be on a one-to-one basis, when you will also need training in the skills of coaching (described in Chapter 11).

Training for business skills

On-the-job training is equally successful for learning business skills since it affords real business experience to its participants.

ACTION LEARNING

The method called action learning, first advocated by Revans, is particularly pertinent to business skills. For example *ad hoc* teams meet to discuss and solve problems occurring within their organisation. The team uses all the resources of a real life discipline, work to targets and to a timetable, and produce a well thought-out, documented and practical solution. With the help of a facilitator they are educating each other.

Cummins Engineering

Cummins Engineering Company demonstrated how both business knowledge and intellectual skills can be developed on the job. To support the Just-in-Time (JIT) system, teams of workers, called set up reduction teams, were given ten hours' training on JIT and then became action teams with targets of a 50–70 per cent reduction in set-up time after twelve months. They were trained by a process engineer, a tool room supervisor and a maintenance operator, and video recordings were kept. Ideas for improving set-up times 'flowed like water' and most of the teams reached the 75 per cent target within a few weeks. An interesting aspect of this exercise is that the Cummins workers were initially trained off the job, before being turned into action teams.

TRAINING FOR PEOPLE SKILLS

People skills are nearly always best taught away from the work situation on specially designed courses. There are several advantages of this:
- Each course member gains individual practice, advice and coaching from tutors and fellow participants.
- They learn from observing the practice of others.
- Learning takes place in a sheltered environment. This makes it non-threatening. People at different levels from the same organisation or from other organisations can be mixed and they learn with and from each other, without losing 'face'.
- Although, as we said earlier, skills cannot be learnt simply by 'knowing about', the group needs to learn basic facts about the various skills before they are practised. These can be supplied by a tutor to the group as a whole, and extra information can be gained as the group discusses them and exchanges experiences.

Training programmes

A programme for training the people skills we described in Chapters 10 and 11 can be designed to suit the particular skill or skills being learnt:
1. A short description of the skill involved, highlighting the key aspects and using visual material – transparencies, videos, tape-recordings where appropriate – is given by the tutor to the group as a whole. A period of discussion and questions from the group follows, which

ensures that everyone understands the skill and the reasons underlying its practice.

2. Small subgroups, with a coach, practise the skill. Each person practises individually, after which the coach and the other group members make suggestions and comments for improvement. Working to a form common to everyone encourages maximum effectiveness at this feedback stage:

- It depersonalises the comments.
- It helps the tutor to lead and focus the discussion into positive channels and away from negative criticisms.
- The key aspects of the skill discussed earlier are repeated on the form, and so heighten and strengthen the group's awareness.

3. This process is repeated until everyone has taken on the role of interviewer.

4. Everyone should have a second turn. This is most important. It gives people a chance to improve their skill, taking into account the feedback comments. In our experience quite remarkable progress from the first to the second interview frequently occurs.

5. A report back to a plenary session from each group underlines the lessons learnt, which are often similar and so they are further internalised.

6. At a final session with the whole group, each member is asked to state to everyone at least one practical action he or she will take to consolidate the learning. Research shows that a target stated in front of peers is twice as likely to be acted upon, so this is an important final exercise.

Variations

When time for this training is severely limited or the training group very large, all is not quite lost. The bottom line for practising consists of teams of two taking turns to interview, and to comment on each other's performance. If possible, they then report back to a plenary session on lessons learnt.

Training exercises for different skills

With this general pattern in mind, choose appropriate practice exercises for the skill involved. Below we suggest suitable exercises for some of these skills, particularly the core ones, which will, we hope, spark off ideas of your own.

LISTENING SKILLS

As listening is *the* core skill we begin with that. One useful exercise for helping people to learn to listen goes as follows.

Using a subgroup (four people is an ideal number) ask the members to divide into groups of two. In each group, one will be the interviewer and the other the interviewee, leaving two to observe. In time, people change roles so that everyone performs all the roles before the exercise is finished. The interviewer's task is to explore the interviewee's attitudes to work. Some possible areas to cover could be:

- What do you like/dislike about your present work? Outline some incident which gives you the most satisfaction. Which the least? Why?
- Describe briefly jobs you have done. How congenial were they?
- How important is working in a team to you? Do you sometimes take a leadership role?
- Do you have ideas for your future? Are you confident you could overcome obstacles these ideas might pose?

The coach and the observers concentrate on the *process* of the interview, for example:

- Do you think the interviewer 'heard' both the latent and manifest content of the replies?
- Did he or she explore the individual's needs and feelings?
- What searching questions were asked? Were these neutral and open ended and likely to reveal attitudes, or were they too factually based?
- How many 'funnels' could you count?
- Itemise any 'reflections' or summaries you noticed.

At the end of the interview the observers and the interviewee give their feedback comments and the roles change round.

Such an exercise requires 20–30 minutes per interview and 10–15 minutes for the feedback. People learn a lot from being both an interviewee and an observer. If there is not enough time, try the exercise we suggest in the listening workshop (Chapter 10).

The skills of reflecting

A time-saving and effective approach to the skills of reflecting and summarising (which some people find difficult) is to conduct the exercise with the whole group together, as follows:

- Show a list of statements expressing feelings or attitudes on a transparency.
- Ask for suitable reflecting or summarising responses to each of these.
- Ask the group to decide which were true reflections, echoing or possibly clarifying the inner meaning.
- Finally, ask people to change the non-reflecting responses made into reflections. For example, 'did you feel frustrated?' ranks as a question; 'so you felt frustrated' or 'it seems that caused you some frustration' would be a reflection or a summary.

Listening lies at the heart of communication skills, but practising these skills in a sheltered situation is particularly important to people who wish to increase their self-confidence, improve their powers of assertiveness and learn to communicate clearly but firmly.

The form for communicating and influencing is the same as for listening, only this time each person is asked to make a presentation on a subject of his or her own choosing to a group small enough to make this practicable. The other members of the group listen and give feedback based on the points we make in the workshops on effective communications (in Chapter 10) and the eight key elements when aiming to influence others (in Chapter 11).

The appraisal interview is difficult to simulate since it is too specific to the appraisee. One way, however, is to gain the permission of the appraisee to ask a neutral observer such as a colleague or mentor to listen and observe and give feedback afterwards. When this approach is impractical, the people skills needed by appraisers are best practised on a training course.

TRAINING FOR APPRAISERS AND APPRAISEES

As we saw in Chapter 11, appraisees need to possess all the core people skills and also the particular skills of a coach and counsellor. The best training approach is therefore to design a course which covers separate practices in each of the main people skills and also offers practice in being a coach and a counsellor. Both these roles call for the training we have already described, but both call for added practice in the skills of helping people to solve their own problems, make decisions and if necessary modify their attitudes. As we saw, the ability to do this lies at the heart of an appraisal interview, yet it is one of the most difficult skills to learn. Hence appraisers (as well as coaches and counsellors) need special training and practice in this area.

Design a multi-skilled course

One useful exercise involves each individual in a group of four taking a turn in describing to the others a work problem he or she feels unable to solve. By asking searching questions about the problem and the presenter's attitude to it, the task of the group and their tutor is to continue asking until the presenter solves the problem.

A questioning exercise

The joint pooling of questioning skills has, in our experience, some amazing results. In most cases the presenter sees a solution and announces a decision on how to put it into practice. The other group members learn from this that the approach actually works.

These separate exercises, although taking a great deal of time, combine to prepare an appraiser and appraisee to make a success of an interview in which so many skills are involved. Thus learning becomes an empowering experience in itself and significantly strengthens the continuous learning policy of an empowered organisation.

As we saw in Chapter 11, all the tools of participation – discussion, solving problems, making joint decisions, influencing others, and so on – depend for success on the skill of everyone in leading or participating in meetings. But many meetings are still judged to be unsuccessful, even though these skills are based on the core people skills and are not difficult to learn.

TRAINING LEADERS OF MEETINGS

A training exercise

One exercise to train everyone in their roles is when one member of a group of six leads a discussion on some topic (the more important and controversial the better) familiar to everyone. A second group of six observe the discussion with the help of the simple form below.

The observers are asked to score the remarks of the participants using the relevant symbols and so build a pattern of contributions from each person, concentrating on the leader. The observers soon note a pattern emerging which reveals the roles each is playing, such as intellectual, encouraging, organising, silent, garrulous, deputy, etc. Concentrating on the leader, they ask themselves:

DISCUSSIONS OR MEETINGS

CLASSIFY REMARKS OF PARTICIPANTS:
Helping   =   + sign
Hindering =   – sign

EMOTIONAL AGENDA OF INDIVIDUAL AND GROUP NEEDS		*ACHIEVING THE TASK*	
SYMBOL	*ACTIVITY*	*SYMBOL*	*ACTIVITY*
E –	ENCOURAGE listen use non-verbal signs ask for questions ask non-judgemental questions call in the shy reconcile opposing views protect minority reflect feelings give sense of progress	P –	PLAN state objectives agree a plan of action state purpose collect facts and feelings initiate analysis decide
		Q –	USE QUESTIONS what - when - who - where - why to offer guidance introduce new topics
		S –	SUMMARIES interim and final

PATTERN OF CONTRIBUTIONS

Chairperson or leader 1. _____

_____

2. _____

3. _____

4. _____

5. _____

- Does the leader take sufficient notice of both the intellectual and emotional agenda?
- Does he or she help the group to come to decisions, or is the leader making decisions for the group?
- Is there a plan to keep discussions on line?
- Are some people allowed to ramble while others remain silent?

The observers are asked to note down some of the most significant evidence and, when this is combined with the scoring on the form, an accurate picture emerges. The roles of the two groups are then reversed and a different topic for discussion introduced.

This exercise is a more powerful training tool when everyone has a chance to take the leadership role. This is time consuming, but even allowing only 15 minutes each is long enough for a predominant style – positive or negative – to become apparent. As participants or observers, everyone learns from each other's performance and the feedback on it. They begin to see how to avoid the pitfalls and to cultivate their strengths, and so are able to continue and practise the correct skills in real life.

Many organisations still have to integrate management development into policies designed to develop their own management talents. But some of those who do (including ones we quoted earlier) cover the skills we have been discussing – technical, business and people – and mix a variety of training methods, on and off the job, training courses, experience in practice situations and one-to-one coaching.

Ford, the multinational car company, trains senior managers on a part-time six-week basis interspersed by a project leading to another two-day reporting session. An even more senior executive programme brings chairpersons and senior executives from all around the world to meet and learn together.

TRAINING MANAGERS IN A WIDE RANGE OF SKILLS

> Learning is the new form of labour. Learning is the heart of productive activity.
>
> *Shoshana Zuboff*

Arkin describes the British success story of Oracle, a rapidly growing software company, where sales and technical training had been emphasised – sometimes at the expense of management development. A programme called 'Managing in Oracle' assembled cross-functional groups of about 20 managers to discuss business subjects and internal communications. During 1990, all the company's 100 managers were involved. A second core event on issues that new

Some successful British examples

managers would be expected to resolve at work was designed as a learning experience. A third event was an outward bound course. Participants in all three events were encouraged to identify their own skills and weaknesses. Specific skills training chosen from a 'menu' of skills was then offered.

Another novel approach is taken by British Aerospace which established a programme to identify and encourage high-flyers, open to applications from all comers. People nominated themselves but spaces were limited and a special committee vetted who was to attend.

British Airways mixes distance learning (students working through workbooks at home) combined with six half-day workshops. Course members from all branches, cargo handlers, pilots etc., aim to become supervisors and gain an Oxford Certificate of Management on the successful completion of their one-year course.

Developments in the public and voluntary sectors

Public and voluntary organisations are also beginning to train their own managers. In Milton Keynes, for example, managers from the National Health Service joined staff from local social services plus doctors and nurses on multidisciplinary training programmes. Success led to the 'Optima' programme for managers employed by the Health Service, local government and voluntary agencies. The course covers a wide variety of management subjects, and provides skills training in computing, finance and marketing. There is also an outdoor exercise which tests what participants have learnt about themselves and how they relate to others. This is reported to have improved management–staff relationships significantly.

Charities which have previously relied on buying in people with management skills are beginning to train their own. Large charities in particular, like the Royal National Institute for the Blind, are training their future senior managers, rather than employing outsiders from the commercial sector.

Conclusions

Company-wide training programmes like the ones we have described, which link training to philosophy and business plans, make a great deal of sense to the participants. Britain still needs many more of these integrated programmes by which continuous learning is guaranteed to all staff and everyone gains the opportunity to become empowered. As we saw in Chapter 8, such a training policy is important for teams as well as for individuals.

Business needs people who have learned how to learn because working and learning have become inseparable.

David Kearns, Xerox

Part IV — Recommended Reading

Thomas A Harris (1973) *I'm OK, You're OK*, Pan, London.

Peter Honey (1988) *Improve Your People Skills*, IPM, London.

Lesley Myland (1992) *Managing Performance Appraisal*, Croner Publishing, Kingston upon Thames.

Paddy O'Brien (1992) *Positive Management: Assertiveness for Managers*, Nicholas Brealey, London.

Elizabeth Sidney and Nicola Phillips (1991) *One-to-One Management*, Pitman, London.

Noel Tichy and Stratford Sherman (1993) *Control Your Destiny or Someone Else Will*, Doubleday, New York.

John Whitmore (1992) *Coaching for Performance: A Practical Guide to Growing Your Own Skills*, Nicholas Brealey, London.

Conclusion

A Guide to Enjoying Empowerment   13

Experience of major organisational change programmes suggests that people used to the certainties of bureaucratic life tend to split into three more or less equal groups when confronted by something new and potentially liberating. One-third eagerly embraces the new proposals, one-third is agnostic and the final third can become entrenched in its opposition. This chapter is for all these groups, but especially for the opponents of change.

WHAT IF YOU DON'T WANT TO BE EMPOWERED?

Hostility towards empowerment is entirely understandable. There are many good reasons for doubt, anxiety or downright cynicism, such as:

- If people are thrown in to a level of responsibility which makes them feel out of their depth, the levels of stress can become unsupportable.
- Empowerment means being asked not just to cope with change but to initiate it. Any prospects for the quiet life virtually disappear. Discontinuity and uncertainty replace the ordered reassurance of rules, precedents, a steady 9–5 existence and a cushioned security.
- Empowerment requires a significant leap of faith in the ability of people. It claims that it is possible for each of us to aspire to and

Reasons for hostility to empowerment

reach greater heights as we find success in achieving something much better than we thought possible. By contrast, the eternal sceptic tends to view any scheme for human improvement as futile as the rearrangement of the deckchairs on the *Titanic*.

● Empowerment also has its casualties, especially among those who used to consider themselves at the top of the heap. Those who still have a job find their authority questioned. For some unlucky middle and top managers empowerment can spell redundancy, since when front-line workers take their own decisions these middle roles are greatly reduced.

HOW TO MAKE EMPOWERMENT MORE ENJOYABLE

So one thing we can be certain of is that a programme of empowerment is not likely to be everyone's cup of tea, certainly not at the beginning anyway, and even the most enthusiastic encounter problems on the way. So to all empowerers, but especially to those who are feeling hostile or sceptical, we offer a checklist of steps that can be taken to make empowerment more acceptable, more challenging and, above all, more enjoyable.

Manage your own empowerment

You are empowered to say no.   Being empowered does not mean that you are duty bound to accept every responsibility that is thrown into your lap. Quite the opposite. It actually means that you are the best judge of what level and intensity of load you can carry. You become your own manager.

If you judge that enough is enough then it is your duty to say so. If the organisation cannot cope with that, it is not a liberated organisation. And as a 'learning' and caring organisation, it should provide the support and training which may, in fact, help you to turn your 'no' into 'yes'.

Go at your own chosen speed.   By the same token, we do not all adapt to empowerment with the same facility. People need enough time to come to understand what the new ways of working mean for them. While people must understand that change is inevitable, it is necessary for them to have adequate time for adaptation. Empowerment is an iterative process (one which gets repeated in many different ways). The first faltering steps may feel difficult but after you have chaired three team meetings you will feel differently.

Your personal empowerment

We all have to invent our own version of empowering.   People also need the room to explore for themselves some of the practical consequences of empowerment. Until they have invented and thought through the practicalities of empowerment for themselves (within the broad parameters described in this book), they do not actually believe it and 'own' it. As we saw in Chapter 7, when we make our own decisions we become committed to them and our 'true motivators' are satisfied.

Behave supportively at all times to both yourself and others. We have devoted whole sections of this book to supportive behaviour and the skills it requires, but this can bear endless repetition because it is possibly both the hardest and the most important aspect of empowerment for you as an individual. It is the key test in distinguishing between those who live and breathe empowerment in their daily lives and those who have only accepted it on an intellectual plane. If, for example, you are feeling pressured but can still take time out to discuss what you think is a trivial problem with a troubled colleague and leave him or her feeling good, then you are on the way to your own personal empowerment.

Invest in empathy, understanding and communication. Supportive behaviour comes from empathising with others: relating to them both intellectually and emotionally from the starting point of what *they* are feeling and understanding, not what *you* are feeling and understanding. Systematically practising empathy (based on a deep belief in the power of listening) will pre-empt feelings of alienation before they can emerge.

Empathise

Following closely behind empathy is the positive requirement for communication. If you are good at empathy you will understand the fallibility of human communication and the potential for misunderstanding (about ten times more in any given situation than you would think!) Therefore it is impossible to place too great a priority on effective communication. Nor does it do any harm to repeat messages. In fact, as we saw in Chapter 4, you may have to repeat a communication many times, with intervals in between, before your message gets through to every last person. Until this is achieved you have not communicated effectively.

Communicate

Laugh and cry. As we saw in Chapter 7, a key aspect of empowering is that it accepts whole people – their abilities, their skills, their attitudes, their feelings. So whole people express themselves openly; they laugh, they are sad. Hence, if the workplace is not transformed into a fun place to be, it is not a liberated workplace. A common feature of all the organisations we have visited that are going down this path is the sound of laughter. However well organised, organisations are full of the absurd because they are full of people. They cannot be taken too seriously.

Enjoy the good times

In the same way, by bottling up your anger or your pain you are not just harming yourself but also depriving your colleagues of a slice (and an immensely valuable slice) of reality. Anger has a reason, but neither you nor others can understand the real reason for that anger (and therefore do anything about it) unless you admit that it is there.

Celebrate your successes and the successes of others.   In empowerment you are both the player and the umpire. It is important that you keep the score in a way that properly reflects your achievements. Break down big jobs into smaller sections so that each milestone can be recorded as an achievement. Give yourself a bonus when someone else gets the credit for something that you inspired. Put aside some quality time at the end of each week to mark your successes. Offer the same treatment to others. Remember the power of recognition and praise which we emphasised in Chapter 7.

Pamper yourself (and others).   Empowerment brings greater demands, so it should also bring greater rewards. As we saw in Chapter 9, periods of intense effort should be balanced by periods of relaxation. Commitment, like concentration, can only be sustained if it has breaks. Give yourself (and others) treats every now and again to reassure yourself that you still care. Maintaining hobbies or other interests outside work is vital. Moreover you are not empowered (and in all probability not very effective) if you are not taking your full quota of holidays.

The art of inventing rituals.   Rituals have an especially important role in any social setting as the way the group can join together to share a common emotion or understanding. The liberated organisation is held together by such common understandings and therefore the liberated organisation will need to invent a myriad of its own rituals (like the 'huggy bear' game at the Airspace charity). So tragedy as well as success should be acknowledged. Change should be distinguished by mourning rituals for the past as well as providing the symbolism of rebirth. Everyone taking to themselves the authority to invent and follow the organisation's rituals puts them in charge in a way that a thousand empowering job descriptions cannot replicate.

Keep a sense of perspective.   Empowerment does not get far without a sense of perspective. It gives you the distance to hear the important noises from amid the day-to-day babble. In our dealings with others we are forever playing the odds. We have a hand and all we can do is to play it to the best of our ability – probabilities come in after that. Accept the failures along with the successes for what they are – merely the moment before the next hand reminds you that you are still learning and will continue to do better.

In the long run we are all dead.

Maynard Keynes

ADVICE FOR THE UNCONVINCED

Some people will remain unconvinced by all the arguments: especially the middle managers who have had their whole *raison d'être* questioned. They may even have lost their jobs a number of times as more and more companies go through the painful process of transformation.

In our work circumstances and outside, our many contacts with a wide variety of people leave us in little doubt that this shift in traditional work patterns is already causing changes in society as a whole and may call for more in the future.

Wider changes in society

Within this wider context, however, everyone can consciously take steps to empower ourselves so that we become stronger and fitter to stay in charge of our own destinies. How do you set about this task?

Stay in charge of your destiny

The most succinct advice comes from Bob Garratt and Tom Peters. 'Flow with the tide', Garratt writes, 'rather than investing energy resisting it' – and from Peters, 'The principal enemy is your inertia.'

Accept some changes in your working life as inevitable, but go further than this. Prepare yourself mentally and emotionally for 'discontinuity' – for the fact that your new work may be completely different from the old.

You can put this advice into practice by:

- using the process of leverage we described in Chapter 5 and applying it to your own circumstances;
- adopting the policy of continuous learning already followed by some organisations and by some individuals;

Action

- taking advantage of every opportunity to attend education and training courses relevant to your own development (Part IV should stimulate you to find the exact type of training for you);
- consciously create your own 'discontinuity', changing jobs or direction in your work life in order to enhance your employability (Chapter 9 emphasises that this is *the* crucial employment factor);
- thinking the unthinkable – think laterally. For example, what work would you really like to do? What goals gain your willing commitment? If this work is different from anything you have done what preparations would it incur? How practicable would these be?
- controlling your own stress through the many ways we advise in Chapter 9, and helping other people in similar circumstances to do the same.

Empowerment is a continuous journey with no end. Whether we like it or not we are all on this road. Even the most vulnerable have the power to move and influence others. The decision you must make is whether to pitch tent and settle down where you are, or to press on in search of the exhilaration ahead. We hope this book will encourage you to keep on moving.

In conclusion

References

Argyle, Michael (1983) *The Psychology of Interpersonal Behaviour*, Penguin, Harmondsworth.

Argyris, Chris and Donald Schon (1978) *Organisational Learning: A Theory of Action Perspective*, Addison-Wesley, Reading, MA.

Arkin, Anat (1992) 'Moving Away from Informality', *Personnel Management*.

Baden-Fuller, Charles and John M Stopford (1992) *Rejuvenating the Mature Business: The Competitive Challenge*, Routledge, London.

Barry, David (1991) 'Managing the Bossless Team: Lessons in Distributed Leadership', *Organizational Dynamics*, Summer.

Barsoux, Jean-Louis and Peter Lawrence (1990) *Management in France*, Cassell, London.

Belbin, R Meredith (1984) *Management Teams: Why They Succeed or Fail*, Butterworth Heinemann, Oxford.

Blake, Robert R and Jane S Mouton (1964) *The Managerial Grid*, Gulf Publishing, Houston.

Brown, Wilfred (1960) *Explanations in Management*, Heinemann, Oxford.

Carlzon, Jan (1989) *Moments of Truth*, Harper & Row, New York.

Clarke, Deborah (1989) *Stress Management*, National Extension College Trust, Cambridge.

Coleman, Vernon (1988) *Overcoming Stress*, McDonalds, London.

Covey, Stephen R (1992) *The Seven Habits of Highly Successful People*, Simon & Schuster, London.

Cranwell-Ward, Jane (1990) *Thriving on Stress*, Routledge, London.

Crawley, John (1992) *Constructive Conflict Management*, Nicholas Brealey, London.

Donkin, Richard (1994) 'Rover's Cultural Revolution', *Financial Times*, 9 May.

Drucker, Peter (1961) *The Practice of Management*, Heinemann, Oxford.

Fisher, R and W Ury (1991) *Getting to Yes*, Business Books, London.

Forrest, Andrew (1989) *Delegation*, The Industrial Society, London.

Forrest, Andrew and Patrick Tolfree (1992) *Leaders: The Learning Curve of Achievement*, The Industrial Society, London.

Garnett, John (1989) *The Manager's Responsibility for Communication*, The Industrial Society, London.

Garratt, Bob (1987) *The Learning Organization*, Fontana, London.
Hammer, Michael (1990) 'Reengineering work: don't automate, obliterate', *Harvard Business Review*, July–August, 104–112.
Hammer, Michael and James Champy (1993) *Reengineering the Corporation: A Manifesto for Business Revolution*, Nicholas Brealey, London.
Handy, Charles (1985) *Understanding Organizations*, Penguin, Harmondsworth.
Handy, Charles (1987) *The Making of Managers*, NEDO, London.
Handy, Charles (1990) *The Age of Unreason*, Arrow Books, London.
Harris, Thomas A (1973) *I'm OK, You're OK*, Pan, London.
Harvey-Jones, John (1988) *Making it Happen: Reflections on Leadership*, Collins, London.
Hennig, Margaret and Ann Jardim (1978) *The Management Woman*, Marion Boyars Books, London.
Herzberg, Frederick (1966) *Work and the Nature of Man*, World Publishing, Cleveland and New York.
Hogg, Clare (1993) 'Empowerment', *Human Resources*, 71, Winter.
Honey, Peter (1988) *Improve Your People Skills*, IPM, London.
IBS (1990) 'United Biscuits Stress Programme and Counselling', IBS *Top Pay Unit Review*, No 115, September.
IR-RR (1985) 'Employee Communication at Rowntree Mackintosh', IR-RR, August.
Jaap, Tom (1989) *Enabling Leadership: Achieving Results with People*, Gower, Aldershot.
Jackson, Sara (1991) 'Empowerment to the people?', *Director*, April.
Kakabadse, Andrew (1991) *The Wealth Creators: Top People, Tom Teams and Executive Best Practice*, Kogan Page, London.
Kennedy, Carol (1991) *Guide to the Management Gurus*, Random Century, London.
Lane, Christel (1989) *Management and Labour in Europe*, Edward Elgar, Aldershot.
Lewin, Kurt (1935) *A Dynamic Theory of Personality*, McGraw, New York.
Lidstone, John (1992) *Face the Press*, Nicholas Brealey, London.
Likert, Rensis (1961) *New Patterns of Management*, McGraw-Hill, New York.
Machiavelli, Niccolò (1979) *The Prince*, trans. Peter Bondanella and Mark Musa, Penguin, Harmondsworth.
Manz, Charles C (1992) 'Employee Self Management without Formally Designated Teams', *Organizational Dynamics*, Vol 20 No 3, Winter.
Margerison, Charles and Dick McCann (1990) *Team Management*, Mercury, London.
Maslow, Abraham (1943) 'A theory of human motivation', *Psychological Review*, 50.
Mayo, Elton (1945) *The Social Problems of an Industrial Civilization*, Harvard University Press, Boston, MA.
McClelland, D (1961) *The Achieving Society*, Van Nostrand Reinhold, New Jersey.
McGregor, Douglas (1966) *Leadership and Motivation*, MIT Press, Cambridge MA.
Mintzberg, Henry (1979) *The Structuring of Organizations*, Prentice-Hall, New York.
Moss Kanter, Rosabeth (1989) *When Giants Learn to Dance*, Simon & Schuster, London.
Neale, Frances (1991) *The Handbook of Performance Management*, IPM, London.
Oates, David (1992) 'Power to the People Who Want It', *Accountancy*, December.
Oates, David (1993) 'Buzz words: Learning the Language of Business', *Accountancy*, August.
O'Brien, Paddy (1992) *Positive Management: Assertiveness for Managers*, Nicholas Brealey, London.
Parkyn, Amanda (1991) 'Operating Equal Opportunities', *Personnel Management*, August.
Pascale, Richard Tanner (1991) *Managing on the Edge*, Penguin, Harmondsworth.
Pascale, R T and Athos, A G (1982) *The Art of Japanese Management*, Penguin, Harmondsworth.
Pegg, Mike (1989) *Positive Leadership: How to Build a Winning Team*, Lifeskills Publishing, Leeds.

Peters, Tom (1988) *Thriving on Chaos*, Pan/Macmillan, London.

Peters, Tom (1992) *Liberation Management*, Macmillan, London.

Peters, Thomas and Robert Waterman (1982) *In Search of Excellence*, Harper & Row, New York.

Petersen, Donald and John Hillkirk (1991) *Team Work*, Victor Gollancz, London.

Pickard, Jane (1993) 'The Real Meaning of Empowerment', *Personnel Management*, November.

Revans, R W (1982) *The Origins and Growth of Action Learning*, Chartwell Bratt, Bromley and Lund.

Sargent, Andrew (1990) *Turning People On – The Motivational Challenge*. IPM, London.

Schein, Edgar (1980) *Organizational Psychology*, Prentice Hall, Englewood Cliffs, NJ.

Scott Morton, Michael S (1991) *The Corporation of the 1990s*, Oxford University Press, New York.

Semler, Ricardo (1993) *Maverick! The Success Story Behind the World's Most Unusual Workplace*, Random Century, London.

Senge, Peter M (1990) *The Fifth Discipline*, Doubleday, New York.

Sidney, Elizabeth and Nicola Phillips (1991) *One to One Management*, Pitman, London.

Smith, Adam (1976) *An Inquiry into the Nature and Causes of the Wealth of Nations*, R H Campbell, A S Skinner and W B Todd (eds.), 2 vols, Oxford University Press.

Sorge, Arndt and Malcolm Warner (1986) *Factory Organization: An Anglo-German Comparison of Manufacturing Management and Manpower*, Gower, Aldershot.

Stevens, John and Robert Mackay (1991) *Training and Competitiveness*, National Economic Development Office Policy Issue Series, Kogan Page, London.

Stewart, Alex (1989) *Team Entrepreneurship*, Sage, London.

Taylor, Frederick (1929) *The Principles of Scientific Management*, Harper, New York and London.

Tichy, Noel and Stratford Sherman (1993) *Control Your Destiny or Someone Else Will*, Doubleday, New York.

Trevor, Malcolm (1988) *Toshiba's New British Company*, Policy Studies Institute, London.

Trist, E L and K W Bamforth (1951) 'Some social and psychological consequences of the longwall method of coal getting', *Human Relations*, vol 4 no 1 pp 3–38.

Warren, Eve and Caroline Toll (1993) *The Stress Workbook*, Nicholas Brealey, London.

Waterman, Robert (1993) *The Frontiers of Excellence*, Nicholas Brealey, London.

Weber, Max (1947) *The Theory of Social and Economic Organization*, trans. Ann Henderson and Talcott Parsons, Oxford University Press, New York.

Wellins, Richard S, William C Byham and Jeanne H Wilson (1991) *Empowered Teams*, Jossey-Bass, San Francisco.

White, Michael and Malcolm Trevor (1983) *Under Japanese Management*, Heinemann, Oxford.

Whitmore, John (1992) *Coaching for Performance: A Practical Guide to Growing Your Own Skills*, Nicholas Brealey, London.

Wickens, Peter (1985) *Management Philosophy Nissan Style*, Nottingham Trent Polytechnic.

Willis, Liz and Jenny Daisley (1990) *Springboard Women's Development Workbook*, Hawthorn Press, London.

Woodcock, Mike (1989) *Team Development Manual*, Gower, Aldershot.

Yate, Martin John (1991) *Keeping the Best*, Kogan Page, London.

Yeung, Sally (ed.) (1992) *Development as a Strategic Activity*, AMED, London.

Zuboff, Shoshana (1989) *In the Age of the Smart Machine: The Future of Work and Power*, Heinemann, Oxford.